DATE			

THE
CONTEMPORARY
THEATRE

*The Significant
Playwrights of
Our Time*

BOOKS BY ALLAN LEWIS

American Plays and Playwrights of the
Contemporary Theatre

The Contemporary Theatre

THE CONTEMPORARY THEATRE

The Significant Playwrights of Our Time

ALLAN LEWIS

with a foreword by John Gassner

REVISED EDITION

CROWN PUBLISHERS, INC. NEW YORK

To Brooke

© 1971 BY ALLAN LEWIS
LIBRARY OF CONGRESS CATALOG CARD NUMBER: 74–147317

PRINTED IN THE U.S.A.
PUBLISHED SIMULTANEOUSLY IN CANADA BY
GENERAL PUBLISHING COMPANY LIMITED
Second Printing, February, 1975

CONTENTS

FOREWORD
by John Gassner

The modern drama is undoubtedly remarkable in many ways, but it is especially remarkable for its ability to arouse serious critical comment. This is partly the result of our living in the so-called age of criticism, but it is also a consequence of the richness and scope of the modern theatre. And, I should add, its tenacity, for ours is surely one of the longest periods of continuous activity in theatrical history.

The volume it is my pleasure to introduce in these pages is one of several useful essays on this subject, and my interest in it is by no means exhausted by the fact that it is the most recent study to come to my attention. I find this book particularly commendable as an introduction aimed at the general reader, who has every right to be bewildered when he tries to bring order into his conception of a span of theatre that spreads across a century or so and includes a very considerable variety of content and style as well as of aim and achievement. For the specialist other volumes, monographs, and articles are already abundant. But it would be a marvel if much agreement could be found among them and if, reflecting as they are likely to do, a specialized bias, they could illuminate the total field without obfuscating some large area.

Things were simpler once. They were simple three-quarters of a century ago—say, around 1881 when Ibsen's *Ghosts* was published—for modernity then meant realism or naturalism to the progressive playwrights and playgoers. Things were still simple even several decades later after realism had been challenged but not actually invalidated by resurgent romanticism and emergent symbolism. Realism, besides, remained progressive, at least in content, because of intensified social conflict and psychological interest. As a matter of fact, the two pilots Marx and Freud still keep a large portion of the theatre afloat, although the voyage tends to be risky when Marx grounds us on the shoals of humdrum economics and Freud entangles us in the Sargasso Sea of "depth psychology."

The pursuit of realism is no longer as simple an enterprise in social and psychological, "critical" and "analytical," drama as it once seemed. Realistic content and form have become complex; and in retrospect, in viewing the old social and psychological dramas with twentieth-century eyes, we are forced to doubt that these works were ever anything but complex. Neither Ibsen's *Ghosts* nor Strindberg's *The Father*, for example (not to mention works like the former's *Master Builder* and the latter's *Miss Julie*), lives for us as exemplary modern art without an intriguing doubleness, a yea- and nay-ness, which criticism currently places under such formal headings as ambivalence, ambiguity, and irony. Where admirers of the modernism

vii

of the 1880's, led by a Georg Brandes, a William Archer, or a Bernard Shaw, saw light, we see chiaroscuro; where they confidently saw the face of Truth, our eyes trace the silhouette of Uncertainty. It is as if Haydn's symphonies were to reach our astonished ears as dissonant *Enigma Variations.* There is apparently only one alternative to preserving the classics of modernism by finding complication in them, and that is to dismiss them on the grounds of primitive simplemindedness—in short, as not being exemplary of modernism at all.

As if this were not enough of a bother to the expounder of modern drama, there is the entire dizzying post-1880 sequence, overlap and near-cycle—*vortex,* if you will—of symbolism, expressionism, theatricalism, futurism, dadaism, surrealism, Pirandellism, constructivism, epic theatricalism, existentialism, and theatre-of-the-absurd nihilism to be accounted for. It has to be described (a formidable task), explained (an even more formidable one), and evaluated (a well-nigh impossible one!), although here, too, alternatives are no doubt available.

There is the possibility of dismissing the realism-antirealism argument as a damnable nuisance and its representative plays, whether engendered by social conscience or esthetic purpose, as deplorably barbaric. We have, indeed, the loftily academic, if fundamentally futile, alternative of regarding the entire modern drama as the degenerate product of a long-deteriorating world, alien alike to the cool clear altitudes of "high comedy" and the purgatorial fires of "high tragedy." In fact, this judgment has been entertained from time to time, and ably advanced. But the reverse attitude appears to be even more seductive at present. It is the ultramodernist view that assumes a play cannot be salubrious, affirmative, congenial, or direct without being hopelessly behind the times—the "times" meaning, of course, the decade or the portion of a decade during which a coterie advances a presumably new program for the arts.

Whoever listens to this Lorelei of the complex too long is likely to be lost—although, I believe, rather interestingly lost. And the temptation to assume the risk is understandable. For a mid-century critic, now that all the proper obvious things have been said about the modern drama, it is more tempting to undertake bizarre explorations than to allow himself to become bored with the subject and start boring others. The truth is that, in bulk, the modern drama can become a rather tiresome subject when viewed apart from the frequent transformations plays undergo when staged. At least this is true of drama that can be discussed in normal terms of characterization, plot, and "spire of meaning"—as that most "normal" of twentieth-century playwrights John Galsworthy optimistically put it. It would seem that a fresh view of the subject can be obtained only by means of some breakthrough effected by an erratic temperament or acutely opinionated mind, which is likely to be one-sided whether young and radical or middle-aged and conservative. A balanced evaluation is the least likely one to eventuate; I last encountered it, and only within stringent limitations of space, in the early 1950's when Joseph Wood Krutch, as civilized a critic as any we have had in America—and we have not had a great many!—published his Cornell University lectures, *"Modernism" in Modern Drama.*

Still, it seems to me incontrovertible that more than ever before, general readers and unspecialized students stand in need of lucid and many-sided exposition such as they will find in the present book. They need a guide who is not blinkered on one side so that half the field is overlooked while the other half acquires exaggerated importance. They need a guide who is not oblivious to the old in welcoming the new and who does not assign extravagant significance to either the "Realism" that was once considered paramount in the theatre or the revived surrealism and inverted romanticism currently regarded as the last word in progress. They need someone who can reconcile the Apollonian and Dionysian polarities of the modern drama, or someone who is willing at least to grant them equal recognition. And this is where Allan Lewis comes in, for he is that person; he has the tact and taste of an eclectic and the philosophical temperament of a mediator. For providing guidance through the *whole* field rather than through merely those pieces of the property that appeal to private need and evoke partisan fervor, he has the proper disposition as well as ambition. He is judicious and seemingly unperturbed—he is certainly extremely patient—among those who offer us the grand tour through modern drama, although it cannot be said, of course, that we can be with him at every turn of the itinerary without demurring somewhat.

In the long run, indeed, the possibility of disagreement is reassuring in the case of a commentator who might seem, from my description of him, colorlessly impartial and therefore a nullity. To assume that this is so would be more unfair than to take issue with him at one point or another. Nevertheless, granted the possibility of some disagreement, it must be apparent to the reader that this tour, though fairly rapid, is comprehensive (not, of course, exhaustive) and is anything but erratic. Allan Lewis is experienced and well-informed and sure of the way; he is not easily halted by roadblocks of theory with which existentialist, epic theatre, and surrealistic theatre sometimes impede the traveler, and he is not trapped or even sidetracked by any particular vogue in drama and criticism. He certainly does not plan an itinerary on the assumption that the least traveled ways are the best and the unvisited sites the most rewarding. The perceptive tourist has need of this genial guide and can rely on him.

March 1962

1. The Theatre and Society

"The purpose of playing, whose end both at first and now, was and is . . . to show . . . the very age and body of the time his form and pressure."

Hamlet

The Theatre as Necessity

THE TRIBAL ORGANIZATION is the origin of society. The articulation of its needs is the origin of theatre. Song and music and dance in which purpose and poetry were one and in which the entire community participated were devised as school and language and the source of common strength. The subsequent history of the theatre is an effort to recapture this initial unity at a complex level of civilization. In this sense, the history of the theatre is the history of man, for the stage deals with man's conflict with himself and the external world, with the general sweep of history as it comes into the personal life of Dicaeopolis, M. Jourdain, Hedda Gabler, Mme Raynevsky, or Mother Courage.

The nineteenth century with its leisured middle class emphasized, largely through the works of Scribe and Sardou, the idea of the theatre as idle entertainment. An audience beleagured by everyday problems was presumed to prefer avoidance of life. Bernard Shaw dismissed this notion with the epithet "Sardoodledom," but it persists today, encouraged by a people anxious to defer responsibility for a world of their own making. The theatre should be as large as life, and those who seek a pleasurable image in the escape from meaning have a right to regard it as a place for diversion.

1

But so long as there are others who seek a fuller recognition of truth, the theatre as a meeting place for the common awareness of man will remain a necessity. And whether buffoonery or ballet, musical comedy or drama, it preserves the myths of an established order, seminates new myths for generations to come, offers a glimpse through fancy or fact into the seeming chaos of a world in transition, and is always the "form and pressure" of an age.

Criticism has too often, in the words of Gilbert Murray, concentrated on "the external and the accidental, on the mannerism not the meaning" of an age, and failed to see the poet against his background as "a daring pioneer in the advance of the human spirit." To know the theatre, it is fruitful to know the age that spawned it, for as T. S. Eliot has said, "The great poet in writing himself writes his times." Thus, *Peer Gynt* is a weird fantasy on a high level of abstraction, but it is also an imitation, a re-creation, of the spirit of bourgeois compromise in the nineteenth century that deprived life of moral vigor. And *The Divine Comedy* of Dante in the fourteenth century refashioned Christian mythology to defend the Church against dissent and dissolution. The worlds of history and art are endlessly interconnected.

The poet voices what has been sensed by others and permits a re-examination of what has been lived. He imprisons in permanence what is forever in flux. It is the same process as that of the scientist who, isolating elements of a complex, holding them in stasis, concentrates on what for the moment is essential.

What the poet as playwright offers may appear more real than reality. Don Quixote, watching the puppet show of Maese Pedro, draws his sword to protect Melisendra and Don Gaiferos from the pursuing Moors, and smashes the marionettes to bits, exclaiming, "In truth and earnest, I assure you gentlemen who now hear me that to me everything that has taken place here seemed to take place liter-

ally." Hamlet knows that an actor, ". . . his whole function
suiting with forms to his conceit," can "make mad the guilty
and appal the free." This magic of the stage gave Pirandello
an opportunity to dramatize the relativity of truth, and the
play within a play became a device for seeing man in interacting levels of reality.

The Problem of Good and Evil

Social changes effected by man in turn affect him. They
influence all his relationships—man and his friends, man
and his family, man and his work, man and God, man and
the state, man and himself. The drama is concerned with
recording these relationships at the moment of crisis. Decisions have to be made, decisions that are functions of man's
conscious will. The playwright, through his characters, even
though they be fully alive and self-motivated, indicates his
own preferences. He is therefore a moralist, dealing with
what is right or wrong, with the question of good and evil,
and all plays in the final analysis are problem plays. Shakespeare, too often absolved of philosophic comment, repeats
the theme of the power of evil to corrupt the individual
and society. Hamlet sought not only revenge but the murder
of the King in such a way that evil would be uprooted.

Even the most hilarious comedy skit is based on an
axiomatic acceptance of what ought to be. Molière ridiculed
the pretensions of the bourgeoisie against a background of
courtly taste. Charlie Chaplin mocked a mechanized world
where man is in danger of losing his individuality. Social
customs alter humor. Harrigan and Hoyt, popular vaude-
villians at the turn of the century, would have a most un-
appreciative audience in New York today, for they based
their humor on racial intolerance, their butts being the
Irish drunk or the Negro clown.

The choice of action—to resist, to resign, or to rebel;
for good or for evil—manifest in the smallest group relationship extends implicitly to the entire social fabric. Moral

decisions may have political overtones. Should a man refuse to go to war (*The Acharnians*), should he fight for higher wages (*Waiting for Lefty*), should he defy the ruling gods (*Prometheus Bound*), should he seek new gods (*Dynamo*), should he submit to tyranny (*Goetz von Berlichingen*), should he deny the truth in the face of torture (*Galileo* by Brecht), and should a woman who operates a house of prostitution be socially acceptable even to her own daughter (*Mrs. Warren's Profession*)—these are questions faced by individuals, but they have wider repercussions. In fact, an interesting history could be written about the interrelationship of the theatre and politics.

Hans Sachs and Thomas Kirchmeyer, in the service of the Reformation, poured out anticlerical satires, and when England needed support in her break with the Papacy, the Protestant bishop, John Bale, a playwright himself, translated their work from the German and had it produced by Thomas Cromwell. The plays were a great success until a king recanted. Then Bale was blacklisted and Cromwell beheaded. With Shakespeare's own theatre, the Essex conspirators encouraged a performance of *Richard II* on the eve of their uprising in 1601, to evoke popular approval for deposing a monarch. And George Bernard Shaw, who had written *Heartbreak House* during the war, withheld it from the footlights until peace had been declared, for he did not want to ridicule a civilization while it was fighting for existence.

Individuals, like society, have their moral crises, their spiritual revolutions, and the theatre is the partisan instrument for "imitating" them. The playwright and performer not only mirror the times but, consciously or not, speak actively in the competition for truth.

The Theatre as Art

Like all art, a play is a union of form and content, and as H. D. F. Kitto has said, in "a first-rate work, structure and style are identical with meaning." Overemphasis of either element can dislocate the balance. Too great concentration on theme results in an overt "message" and belongs more properly to social documentation or moral essay; overdependence on form can result in preciosity or cultism. Theme and form are both related to the contemporary culture, the moment of living from which no poet can escape and which imposes its measure on all art.

Even the past is continually transmuted in the light of the present. No writer can fully recapture the life of Athens of the fifth century before Christ, any more than a production of *Oedipus Rex* can repeat the performance at the Festival of Dionysus. Though much of the outward physical production has been lost—the music, the movement and sound of the chorus, the nature of the voices—the more important loss, that which can never be repeated, is the spirit of an age, lived but once in time.

Some epochs are more conducive to creative energy than others. Such was the time of the modern theatre, which began with the Renaissance, when long-established feudal ways succumbed to trade and commerce, to new concepts of time and space, to the process of becoming, and to the uncertain adventure of change. But the Renaissance came at different times to different countries; first to Italy, then to Spain, Holland, England, and France; to Germany and Russia only after the French Revolution. But wherever and whenever the modern world came into being, the theatre rose to welcome it in magnificent splendor. Ariosto, Aretino, and Machiavelli led the way in Italy; Lope de Vega, Calderón, and Alarcón in Spain; Marlowe, Jonson, and Shakespeare in England; Corneille, Racine, and Molière in France; Lessing, Goethe, and Schiller in Germany; Pushkin, Gogol, and Ostrovsky in Russia. That same civilization conceived in the Renaissance, having encircled the globe by the late nineteenth century, then turned upon itself for re-examination. This was the time of Ibsen, Strind-

berg, Chekhov, and Shaw. More recently, the growth of
science and technology, the breakdown of faith and of man's
relation to God and nature, the imminence of possible
annihilation, the failure of reason to achieve a rational
world, and the quest for alternatives have led to the theatre
of Pirandello, Brecht, Sartre, and Ionesco.

It has been said that our age has no "form and pressure," that it is wild, unfathomable, and formless. But this
is the very pressure of our time, and the role of the artist
is to create form as distinct as the age itself. Thus, Ionesco,
Beckett, and Genet are related to the absence of communication between men in an epoch of perfected communication
techniques, to the destruction of self in an age of advanced
means for exploring the nature of self, to the alienation of
man in a world of intimacy with the universe. Our theatre
is characterized by diversity of form and multiplicity of
meaning. To bring order to this chaos is a task so weighty
and frightening that the poet becomes conscious of his
loneliness, the most recurrent theme in the theatre of
today. Even the audience is physically removed, sitting in
the dark while glaring lights are focused on the performers.
On the world-wide scale, however, that audience is growing
in numbers and in willingness to accept any playwright who
has something to say. Commercial houses on Broadway may
be fewer, but theatres are mushrooming throughout the
country and everywhere in Europe. And the new nations of
Asia and Africa are also seeking to express themselves.

In spite of the violence and despair of our age, it has
the same fever that inspired the Renaissance. Nietzsche once
said that convictions are prisons, for they exclude from life
the joy of doubt. This idea may have had a particular ap-
plicability to a people emerging from the Middle Ages, but
today the reverse is true in the theatre. Too much doubt
does not make good drama, and it excludes the joy of conviction. The function of the theatre as a necessity of man

is to bridge the loneliness and to offer the communion that art makes possible. It is an adventure in the search for freedom. For T. S. Eliot, freedom for the few to insure the freedom of the many and to return to the grace of God; for Sean O'Casey, freedom for the many to insure the freedom of the few; for Sartre, the freedom to live without God and stand responsible for one's actions; for Strindberg, freedom of the imagination to explore the impossible; for Shaw, freedom from poverty and outworn convention; for Brecht and Miller, freedom to place blame; for Ionesco, freedom from the overburdened symbols of logic.

The playwright may work in isolation, but his work is not, as Cyril Connolly has said of the poet, "made by the alone for the alone." The director orchestrates his own insight with the individual contribution of each actor. Stage designer, costumer, musician, and technician alter the mood, the effect, the totality. The final product—and it never really is final—is a distinct art form, a synthesis molded by the experience of many. But all this is the dress rehearsal. The house is still empty, the words echo unfulfilled. Despite the levels the play reaches in pre-production, it has significance only when an audience reacts. The first night has gone far beyond its purposeful function, yet it is the moment when the work, long in gestation, is finally born —the moment when it becomes part of society.

This is the living theatre. Once it has welcomed an audience, it has power to influence men's minds, hopes, and actions.

2. *The Middle-Class Drama—Ibsen*

GHOSTS

The Paradox of Ibsen

Shakespeare stood at the threshold of a world in promise. Ibsen, three hundred years later, was the dramatist of that world in crisis. Shakespeare was the poetry of the exaltation of birth. Ibsen, when the bourgeois world had reached the peak of its achievement, was the search for moral vigor to offset the complacency of victory.

The last words of *When We Dead Awaken,* produced in the closing hours of the century, are the song of Maya, "I am free as a bird! I am free!"—as though Ibsen, then past seventy, wished to hammer home a final exclamation point before the curtain came down on an era. For the old Viking wrote no more. A few months later, the first of a series of paralytic strokes left him crippled and he had time only for the clipping of coupons from jealously guarded investments, until in 1906 he was laid to rest with official pomp by king and court and hailed as the glory of Norwegian literature. At the end, he embraced the values he had condemned all his life. He had traveled full circle in the unresolved paradox of the quest for certainty.

Chained by illness, the senile Ibsen was singing bravely of freedom, as he had all his literary life, but Maya had nowhere to fly. Hers is a wild hope in the wilderness. She sings of abstract freedom, but she is the pleasure-seeking, earthbound spirit. Rubek, the artist, heaven-storming, in search of attainable freedoms, is buried in the mountains under an avalanche of ice and snow.

8

The sixteenth century had been a struggle for free-dom from feudal restrictions. Shakespeare embraced the freedoms thrust upon him, sensing tragedy in the failure to achieve the possible. But the nineteenth century des-iccated an inherited morality. Ibsen was compelled to seek new freedoms, creating his own mythology to impose upon a shriveled sense of the tragic. Shakespeare never wrote a play about Christ. Ibsen, in a far more material world, re-turned to the Christ theme repeatedly.

The bitter paradox of his life was evident in the formal premiere of Ibsen's final play. The once poverty-stricken rebel, a voluntary exile from his native land for most of his creative life, attended in full dress and high hat, resplendent in his medals and orders of the cross, which he coveted so passionately. The former clerk in an apothecary shop was now a pompous, rather prim and stodgy old capitalist. He who had been termed an enemy of the Church, a subversive influence on enduring middle-class values (it was said that his plays, "lewd, immoral, consistently dirty, and deplorably dull . . . pervert life . . . and augment ignorance and mislead weak minds")[1], was honored by the very elements he had assailed. He who had condemned the curse of bondage to material greed was still making strenuous efforts to have his annual government subsidy increased even though he was now financially well off.

Yet in the fifty years of his productivity, Ibsen trans-formed the material of the poet's vision, mastered conflict-ing forms in his restless and unsuccessful spiritual emancipa-tion, and hammered out the revolution that was the con-temporary theatre.

The Romantic Missionary

The first phase of Ibsen's work ended with 1867, when the dramatist was almost forty years of age. He had written ten plays, been granted a minor government stipend, and

gained practical theatre experience in Bergen and Chris-
tiania, but the two major works that crystallize this formative
period, *Brand* and *Peer Gynt,* were written abroad after
Ibsen had absorbed the ripened romantic movement of
Germany and Italy.

Drastic changes were occurring both in his native
country and in the rest of the world. In the United States,
a Civil War had unfettered the march to monopoly. The
productive capacity of a technical age was soaring to such
vast proportions that it was qualitatively altering human
relations as well as social institutions. The civilization
ushered in by the Renaissance was plunging headlong to its
logical fulfillment.

In Europe, close at hand, Denmark had been gobbled
up by Prussia, and a humiliating treaty had deprived her of
Schleswig-Holstein. Norway had promised aid to her Scandinavian brothers, but when the chips were down used every
pretext to avoid involvement. Ibsen was shocked by the
cowardice of his country. Norway had separated from Denmark in 1814, and achieved semi-independence, but her
economic development was most peculiar in that it preserved small-scale enterprise, thereby arresting growth and
delaying national aggressiveness. Marcus Thrane, whom
Ibsen knew, had effected an active alliance of workingmen's
clubs, which in the 1850 elections were strong enough to
win a substantial minority in Parliament. The workers' representatives, however, proved easily pliable and offered little
protest. The government jailed the opposition leaders, including Thrane and his lieutenant Abdilgaard, with whom
Ibsen had roomed. On their account, Ibsen took part in
the only political meeting he is known to have attended
and even signed a petition for their release.

But politics was not his concern. He was most disturbed by the dishonesty of bourgeois life, which he termed
the Social Lie, capitalizing it even in his prose plays. The
Lie was the profession of beliefs that were violated in prac-

tice, the promise of greatness and the persistence of greed, the smug dedication to pettiness and gain that sacrificed Christian ethics on the altar of business. Ibsen had witnessed the betrayal both of liberal and conservative leadership. In *Brand,* he shouted for a re-creation of the spirit of man. In the tradition of Hugo and Shelley, of Goethe and Schiller, he pitted his romantic hero against the world.

Brand and Man's Will

Brand is a poetic drama set in a small village in the mountains of the north. Brand, the minister, brings to the community the fearful will to be unafraid. He acts, no matter what the odds. He will not compromise. He chops off all human sentiment, all physical weakness, and pursues his call with the frenzy of a man who knows that a morally weak world can be regenerated by the undeterred will. Society—the mayor, the schoolmaster, the dean—is corrupt, rendered impotent by endless self-seeking. Brand defies them all, and like John Brown of the Curry portrait, reaches in mad splendor for the rugged mountaintop. He braves the angry flood to succor a dying man, though none will accompany him; he persuades his wife Agnes to remain in their sun-bereft cabin, though it means the eventual death of their only child. He throws to the winds his mother's money, which she had guarded all her life for a moment of security. He wins a following by the intensity of his unswerving single-mindedness, but is deserted by all when immediate financial awards and the lying promise of work turn the unemployed multitude against him. Alone, bleeding and broken, stoned by those he had led, he climbs still higher into the snowcapped mountains until he hears the Invisible Choir, and cries aloud, "Shall they wholly miss Thy light?" only to have the Voice reply, "He is the God of Love."

Brand is a Sermon on the Mount without the tender-

ness of Christ. Nor need Brand be a priest. He is a man
dedicated to a cause. In a letter to Georg Brandes, Ibsen
wrote:[2]

> I could have supplied the whole syllogism just as
> well to a sculptor, or a politician, as to a priest. I could
> quite as well have worked out the impulse which drove me
> to write by taking Galileo, for instance, as my hero—as-
> suming, of course, that Galileo should stand firm and
> never concede the fixity of the earth.

Brand is the moral force of individual regeneration, the
answer to the Social Lie. He spurns convention:

> Faint heart, who marches slack and slow
> Because old Wont would have it so.

Nor will he tolerate appeasement:

> Of all men, God makes one demand,
> No coward compromise.

Passionately unequivocal, he repeats:[3]

> Know that I am stern to crave,
> All or Nothing I will have.

He would transcend the divorce between the ideal and
the real with the wholeness of personality, the absence of
inner conflict:

> . . . from these scraps and from these shreds,
> These headless hands and handless heads,
> These torso-stumps of soul and thought,
> A Man complete and whole shall grow.

Ibsen would restore the original glory of the Renaissance, equating the middle class to Man. Brand can steel
himself to endure all. There is no middle road, but an
equally steeled community will crush him without remorse
when it is dedicated to material gain. Gerd, the wild
mountain sprite, the only companion left to Brand, shoots
the black hawk, which turns white as it falls dead at her
feet, and the blast loosens the avalanche that buries Brand

beneath it. The myth of the absolutely free individual has no roots in reality, and a merciful God will not tolerate a disciple more holy than Himself.

Peer Gynt—the Core of the Onion

Peer Gynt is the companion dramatic poem of this early period, the reverse side of the coin. Peer is all compromise. Brand is the redeemer; Peer, the man to be redeemed. *Brand* is the stark gloom of the mountain crags; *Peer*, the exotic frolic of Anitra's dance. Brand holds to his vision, rejecting the material claims of this world; Peer, vacillating, unstable, takes all the world has to give. Brand is what man ought to be:

> Whence rose that laughter in my mind?
> Ah, from the gulf, dimly divined,
> Between the living world we see,
> And the world as it ought to be.

Peer is what man is, the slow unpeeling of an onion with no substantial core. Over the house of Gynt is the motto, "To thine own self, be enough"; over the hut of Brand, the words, "To thine own self, be true." Both are in a sense caricatures, exaggerations to drive home the ethical extremes of the modern world. Peer is the self-made man who amasses wealth, tours the world, engages in any nefarious enterprise, shipping idols to China in the spring and missionaries in the autumn, and finally exclaims, "I have done everything, seen everything. I have achieved my destiny. I am myself "—only to discover that he has been least himself. Like all men, Brand and Peer seek fulfillment: the one, devout and principled; the other, cynically unprincipled. Both end in defeat, one crushed by society, the other by himself. Brand is released by a God more relenting than he. Peer cradles his head in a woman's lap, the return to the *ewig-weibliche* that alone can recreate another if not a better man. Peer is the embodiment of the

Social Lie; Brand is the self-appointed incarnation of Creative Truth. Brand moves to his death under ice and snow;
Peer awaits the day when he will be melted down in the
ladle of the Button Moulder.

Though Ibsen exhausted the romantic form in these
two masterpieces of poetic fantasy and universal concepts,
it remains a powerful resurgent force in the theatre of
today.

Descent into the Real World

With the military achievements of Von Moltke, Ibsen
came down from the mountaintop. Even conquest had lost
its adventure, for the Prussian army moved with mechanical precision worked out on a timetable. Abstraction was
too remote from reality. Brand and Peer put on their
civilian clothes, and the Troll King's cavern gave way to
the living room of the conventional home. The next two
decades were Ibsen's richest creative moments.

This middle period begins with the "political" or social problem plays, *The League of Youth*, *The Pillars of
Society*, and *An Enemy of the People*, written five years
later in 1882 but grouped with the other two for con-
venience. After the Paris Commune, Ibsen wrote:[4]

> Up till now, we have been living on nothing but the
> crumbs from the revolutionary table of the last century, a
> food out of which all nutriment has long been chewed.
> The old terms require to have a new meaning infused into
> them.

Such a statement would seem to indicate Ibsen's deep interest in revolutionary movements, but he was not referring
to political or social reorganization, for he added:

> What is all-important is the revolution of the spirit
> of man.

This explains the seeming inconsistency of these three plays.
In *The League of Youth*, the liberal Stensgaard is an op-

portunistic demagogue; in *Pillars of Society,* the wealthy Consul Bernick is dishonest and inhuman; in *An Enemy of the People,* Stockman finds all society arrayed against him—the businessmen prefer to save their investment, and the "compact majority" prefer to save their jobs—but Stockman himself is a quite pompous buffoon.

Ibsen's society was now concerned with class politics, public housing, economic security, and psychological insight into subconscious motivation. He used their own interests to expose the moral pollution, the immediate and personal manifestations of the Social Lie. As in *Brand,* he carried aloft the banner of Truth and Freedom. Consul Bernick is most explicit. In his redemption, he shouts triumphantly:

> Let everyone examine himself, and let us all realize the prediction, that from this opening we begin a new era. The old, with its tinsel, its hypocrisy, its hollowness, its lying propriety, and its pitiful cowardice, shall lie behind us like a museum . . .

And a few minutes later, to the assembled throng:

> My fellow citizens, I will come out of the Lie . . .

But to be certain there is no mistake, Lona, the first of Ibsen's free women, rings down the curtain with:

> No, no. The spirits of Truth and Freedom . . . these are the Pillars of Society.

Today a more cynical world regards such utterances as naïvely evangelistic, but Ibsen was equally scornful of social reform and political maneuvering. The characters like Stensgaard are ludicrous and patently unheroic. Arthur Miller, in rewriting *An Enemy of the People,* made Stockman a grand, lonely figure, but to Ibsen even the title was ironic.

The supreme achievement of the middle period was

the plays that are closer to the family, *A Doll's House,
Ghosts, Hedda Gabler, The Wild Duck.*

GHOSTS

The Theme

Ghosts opens at a crisis in social relationships when
accepted values are re-examined by compulsion. Oswald's
inherited tragedy is the dramatic representation of the con-
cealed inner rottenness that has infected the home, property relations, and the outwardly respectable family. Ibsen
fearlessly introduced congenital syphilis and hereditary influences as factors in human drama. To Victorian audiences in a day of accentuated sex taboos, the shock was
sufficient to cause riots in the theatre and invoke police
interference. This, however, was the incidental fury of the
passing moment. The play is the companion piece to *A
Doll's House,* much as *Peer Gynt* is to *Brand.*

Ibsen had been blasted by his critics for undermining
the home, the bulwark of a stable society. Nora, leaving
husband and children, was a work of "a disordered mind,"
filled with "disgust and gloom" that perverted life and
destroyed the sanctity of marriage. No woman of the nineteenth century had the right to desert her family. Ibsen's
answer, two years later in 1881, was *Ghosts,* written at
white heat, one of the most magnificently constructed works
for the theatre. It is the story of a Nora who did not leave,
who remained with her husband, who sacrificed for the
sake of preserving the outward form of respectability. It
is a trenchant and thoroughgoing indictment of the lethal
vapors that mount from a scrupulously observed Christian
marriage, from domestic piety, and from charitable enter-
prises aimed at publicly purging a life of sin. Branded as
smutty and immoral, it is in fact the reverse, an effort to
purify what is basically wrong, a power-laden charge against

the febrile immorality that rises out of the Social Lie. The home of the Alvings is a microcosm of the bourgeois world at large.

The play has one set, the living room of Mrs. Alving's country home, near a large fiord in western Norway. Though not in this case, as in so many of Ibsen's other plays, "the tasteless parlor," it is still the pallid, overstuffed garden room into which Ibsen invites his audience. Here is where the middle class lives, the colorless refuge of a dull society.

ACT ONE—*The Opening Scene*

Regina, the maid, is preventing her father, Engstrand, from entering the room. There is no love lost between them. Engstrand, crippled, blasphemous, a drunkard constantly mouthing moralisms, plans to open a sailors' hostel and has come to take Regina with him. He is the only working-class character in all of Ibsen and a most unsavory one. His snobbery is revealed when he says his place is not to be "a mere pigsty for common sailors, but for captains and mates . . . and all those swells."[5] There is no doubt as to the nature of the hostel and the role he expects his pretty daughter to play in attracting the clientele. Regina, young, pretentious, vibrantly sensual, resents having her father near her, and is openly insolent. "You've often said I was no child of yours" is a seemingly ill considered angry retort, but it prepares the ground for later disclosures, for every line in Ibsen's rigid architecture builds character or buttresses the plot. Even the apparently casual comment about the rain unfolds the misty background against which human warmth must contend, and foreshadows a climate hostile to Oswald, who needs love and growth. Regina ushers her father out of the house when she sees Pastor Manders coming down the walk.

This initial, brief encounter announces the opening

moral degeneracy, a family relationship freighted with deceit and self-interest, the counterpart of Mrs. Alving and her son.

Regina admits the Pastor. Engstrand has already requested of him the blessings of the church for the sailors' inn, on the ground that it will be dedicated to saving men's souls. The Pastor, an easy prey for Engstrand's duplicity, urges Regina to go with her father as is "a daughter's duty." Regina bluntly replies that she has no objection to the services she will be required to render, but she would rather perform them for a single gentleman, provided it were in an outwardly conventional home. She too would like the Pastor's help and asks him to recommend her. Completely fuddled, he asks her to call her mistress.

In his first appearance, Manders has unwittingly advised prostitution, so long as it is submerged in a father's protection, but when the idea is directly expressed by Regina, he recoils in horror. Self-willed deception by the guardian of decency.

The Conflict of Ideas

Mrs. Alving enters. The core of the play is the four scenes between these two. Mrs. Alving, the central character, has with diligence and patience struggled to control her environment, to reach "emancipation." Hers is the immorality of intelligent morality. Pastor Manders represents the code that society demands, its dead past still alive. The clash between these two is a complicated series of triumphs and defeats in ascending crises, out of which comes the clearest portrayal of Ibsen's recurrent theme. The critic Francis Fergusson terms it the "agon" of Greek drama, and in a strained effort at literary comparisons it is, but Ibsen's magnificent construction differs from its classical prototype in its endlessly varying interplay. It is the action as well as the debate of the drama, and the three remaining characters, each with his own individual problem, weave in and out of the major conflict until the final departure of Manders, when Mrs. Alving is left alone with her son.

Manders is the puritan, the bigot, the denier of life, the enemy of love. He is all that is false in society, not like Captain Alving or the crippled Engstrand, but as the reasoned representative of an ethical tradition that has failed, that no longer beats with human needs. In the extreme sense he is death, for he has squeezed all creative impulse from his self, stifled and denied the rhythm of existence. All the animal is gone from him, or is hidden and suppressed. He is dehydrated platitudes, what society terms a good, upright man, the standard-bearer of what it would preserve. That is why wherever he goes preaching what he is himself, to men who must be *themselves,* he encounters cynicism, trickery, and fraud, and he is too ill-equipped to know them. At best, he encourages dishonesty. The surface response, the conformity, contents him. What lies beneath, he prefers to be guileless enough to avoid. Yet he is no caricature. He is handsome, well-intentioned, and helpless. Mrs. Alving had once been in love with him!

As before with Regina, Pastor Manders is now again confronted with honesty and directness, but whereas Regina's honesty was of the flesh, Mrs. Alving's is derived from inner strength. She need not resort to Engstrand's hypocrisy. Her weakness is that in long association with Manders and his pattern of living in a sunless land, she has absorbed much of Manders. But she has the will to be free.

The Pastor observes the books on the table, the rational scientific works of the nineteenth century, and rebukes Mrs. Alving for having them in her home. Her answer is calm, assured:

> I seem to find explanation and confirmation of all sorts of things I myself have been thinking. For that's the wonderful part of it, Pastor Manders; there's really nothing

new in these books, nothing but what most people think and believe. Only most people either don't formulate it to themselves, or else keep quiet about it.

When she asks what he finds objectionable in these books, he replies that he has not read them. Bernard Shaw, a few years later, has a similar scene in *Man and Superman,* when Ramsden condemns Tanner's *The Revolutionist's Handbook,* with:

> I have in my hand a copy of the most infamous, the most scandalous, the most mischievous, the most black-guardly book that ever escaped burning at the hands of the common hangman. I have not read it: I would not soil my mind with such filth; but I have read what the papers say of it. The title is quite enough for me.

Manders, without the comic spirit of Shaw, concludes the first skirmish with a pronouncement that would destroy individual inventiveness in thinking:

> My dear Mrs. Alving, there are many occasions in life when one must rely on others. Things are so ordered in this world; and it's well that they are. How would society get on otherwise?

The immediate business at hand is the orphanage to be dedicated to the memory of the late Captain Alving. The ceremonies are to take place the next day and Manders is to deliver the dedicatory address. He likewise has scrupulously taken care of the business details that Mrs. Alving left to him. Her attitude is removed, disinterested, and somewhat disturbing to Manders. When he mentions insurance for the orphanage, Mrs. Alving replies it is quite the customary thing to do, but Manders proposes that a building devoted to higher purposes should be entrusted to the hand of God. Though he has no objection to insurance, what would the "really responsible people think"? "What do you mean by the really responsible people?" asks Mrs. Alving, to which Manders replies most meaningfully, "I mean people in such independent and influential position that one cannot help allowing some weight to their opinions." He is the defender of established order, on the highest spiritual grounds. "They might interpret our action," he says, "as a lack of faith in a Higher Providence." The building will not be insured, to insure the good name and social standing of the Pastor.

Mrs. Alving gives in. Manders has his way. He then mentions Regina and the advisability of her going with her "reformed" father. To his surprise, Mrs. Alving says with sudden abruptness and finality, "I have taken Regina into my house and there she shall stay . . . Don't say any more about it."

Oswald, Mrs. Alving's son, enters. He has just returned from Paris, where he has established a considerable reputation as an artist. Pastor Manders stares at him as though a ghost had appeared, for Oswald is smoking his father's pipe, and, for a moment, the pastor sees the father returned.

The conflict of ideas shifts to the Pastor and Oswald. Both have a high regard for the deceased Alving, for Oswald has been nurtured on the reputed greatness of his father. They therefore begin with a common agreement, even though later this proves to have been on a false basis, but when Oswald defends the homes of the artists in Paris, homes in which mother and father have sometimes never been wed, but in which there are deep love and tenderness, the Pastor is aghast, decrying such "open immorality" where it even has a "sort of prestige." Oswald defies the Pastor, condemning the so-called "responsible" people who seek out Paris for their debauchery and gloat in places that the "immoral" artists have never even known about. Overexcited, and apparently easily uncontrolled, Oswald leaves, crying out, "Oh, that that great, free, glorious life out there should be defiled in such a way!"

Mrs. Alving has found an ally in her son.

The Second Round

Oswald is the catalyst that forces the Pastor to dig more deeply into a defense of his own way of life. Both mother and son, each in his own way, is supporting a morality that denies the Pastor. He therefore lays aside all details of the Memorial and speaks to Mrs. Alving as her conscience, her guide. He reminds her of her past life, and with Ibsen, this becomes in itself a series of dramatic climaxes.

It is now ten years since Alving's death. In the first year of her marriage Mrs. Alving had fled from her husband, and she now replies that the Pastor has probably forgotten how utterly miserable she was. He pounds home, his heaviest artillery brought to bear:

> It is only the spirit of rebellion that craves for happiness in this life. What right have we human beings to happiness? No, we have to do our duty! And your duty was to hold firmly to the man you had once chosen and to whom you were bound by a holy tie.

Mrs. Alving reminds him of the abusive and disgusting life the Captain had been leading, to which Manders answers:

> A wife is not to be her husband's judge.

She should have borne her cross with humility. Her reputation and that of others are important. When she ran away from her husband, she had gone to the Pastor. How strong he was to have sent her back! And he had been right. She had "resumed the yoke of obedience" and her life had prospered. And Alving had turned out for the better—he had been named a chamberlain to the king, the sign of a respectable household. Manders is proud of his achievement, of his carrying out of God's will, for he had been in love with Mrs. Alving himself, and she had come to him. But he had rejected all earthly passion and denied his own happiness. It was his greatest victory. All that, however, is of the past. Now he must speak of her second error.

Mrs. Alving had once been headstrong enough to "disown a wife's duty"; she would now disown a mother's. She had sent her child away among strangers, to foreign and evil influences, and she had been dominated by a spirit of self-will:

> All your efforts have been toward emancipation and lawlessness. There is still time to save him. For, Mrs. Alving, you are a guilt-laden mother!—This I have thought it my duty to say to you.

There is silence. Then Mrs. Alving answers, without any rancor: All that the Pastor says is based on local gossip. He himself has not visited her in all these years. Just as he will not read the books he condemns, but bases his objections on hearsay, so too he judges her life. He speaks without knowing the facts. Alving had lived all those years in corrupt dissolution, a bedridden syphilitic. She bore her yoke, sitting with her husband at night, listening to his ribald tales, drinking with him to keep him quiet, so that none would know the truth. She followed the Pastor's advice. She preserved the outward reputation. But when Alving had an affair with the maid in her house and a child was born out of wedlock, she sent Oswald, then seven years old, away from the home environment. She took over the business, built the family fortune, established the good name, and now that her husband no longer lives, the Foundation will deaden all rumors and set all doubts at rest. She will buy the demanded respectability. The money for the orphanage is her purchase price, the money Alving had when she married him. But everything about him is to be purged from the house; not a shred of him will remain. No, she has preserved her son, not neglected him. Now the two of them will build a free life. Beginning with tomorrow, once Alving is enshrined in the orphanage, all of him will be gone, cleansed from her life.

Mrs. Alving is triumphant. She has demolished Mander's morality with her calm recital. Oswald enters. The rain is miserable. He excuses himself to help Regina with the wine. As Mrs. Alving and Manders rise to go to the dining room, cries are heard, and Mrs. Alving, standing in the doorway, is transfixed with horror when she hears Regina scream, "Oswald, are you mad? Let me go!"—the same words she heard years ago when Chamberlain Alving was alive. The world she has so valiantly planned, the assurance with which she has been able to meet Manders, now collapse around her. All she can say is "Ghosts!"—one of the most terrifying speeches in the entire history of the drama. With supreme control, Mrs. Alving takes the Pastor's arm and enters the dining room.

At the moment of her victory, the past has returned. She has subdued the Pastor. Her setback comes from within, from her own family, from her champion. Nineteen years of patient endurance, of slow liberation, crumble as the spirit of the father is renewed in the son.

ACT TWO—*The Next Generation*

The action resumes a few minutes after dinner. Mrs. Alving must act differently now. The Pastor remains grooved in his formulas. He offers consolation with, "At least your marriage was in accordance with law and order." Shaken to the roots, Mrs. Alving brushes his maxim aside with the cry of all who have had to conform to the demands of a lifeless, entrenched society:

Oh, that perpetual law and order! I often think that's what does all the mischief here in the world.

Then, more to herself:

I must work my way out to freedom.

Manders is horrified. Oswald has always honored and respected his father. That illusion at least should be preserved:

Is there no voice in your mother's heart that forbids you to destroy your son's ideals?

But Mrs. Alving will endure cowardice and deceit no longer. Her son's actions have forced the truth, and she is prepared to face it. In a few powerful lines, she sums up the full intent of Ibsen:

> I almost think we're all of us ghosts, Pastor Manders. It's not only what we have inherited from our father and mother that "walks in us." It's all sorts of dead ideas, and lifeless old beliefs. They have no vitality, but they cling to us all the same, and we can't get rid of them. Whenever I take up a newspaper, I seem to see ghosts gliding between the lines. There must be ghosts all the country over, as thick as the sand of the sea. And then we are, one and all, so pitifully afraid of the light.

This belief is the result of reading those "revolutionary free-thinking books," retorts the Pastor, but Mrs. Alving replies that he is mistaken. It is the result of his own teaching, for when he sent her back to her husband, when he praised as "right and proper" what her "whole soul rebelled against as something loathsome," she began to look into the seams of his morality:

> I wanted only to pick at a single knot; but when I had got that undone, the whole thing raveled out. And then I understood that it was all machine-sewn.

This is dangerous doctrine. The Pastor's greatest victory has been converted into his greatest defeat. Engstrand interrupts the impasse between the two.

Mrs. Alving has disclosed that Regina is the Chamberlain's illegitimate child, Oswald's half-sister. Needing a victim for his embarrassment, the irate Pastor turns on Engstrand for never having told him that Regina is not his daughter. Manders now clamors for the truth, but Engstrand, the wily hypocrite, justifies his silence by using Mander's own phrases. Did he not help a fallen woman by marrying her? And is he not planning to open a sailors'

home that will be an orphanage for wayward men? When
Engstrand leaves, Manders is joyous that he has misjudged
a human being. Then follows the one tender moment of
the play. Mrs. Alving, smiling, places her hands on his
shoulders, calls him a "great baby," and adds:

> I've half a mind to put my arms around your neck and
> kiss you.

The blushing Pastor leaps back in horror, victim of a lifetime of suppressed emotions. Even now he is afraid to kiss
the woman he has loved for twenty years! In fact, he will
not trust himself to spend a single night under her roof,
but has taken lodgings at the local inn.

The Pastor leaves for the orphanage as Oswald enters.
Mrs. Alving must immediately exercise her decision to tell
him the truth about his father. But she has not counted
on Oswald himself. He speaks first, and tells her he is seriously ill with the disease that comes from sexual dissipation. His own life has been above suspicion, and since he
knows from his mother's letters that his father was the
model of decency, it must be an accident, a fateful mis-
fortune. His mind too has been affected. It may give way
at any moment, and therefore he wants to marry Regina—
in view of his expected death, she is the one hold he can
have on life. What a staggering blow to his mother! Not
to her, but to the maid, he turns for hope. He is planning
to leave too, for he has always painted "the joy of living"[6]
and he fears that with his mother his instincts will be
"warped into ugliness."

Regina joins them. A bottle of champagne is opened,
contrary to the custom of the house, and all three drink
together. Mrs. Alving will now tell them both. The Pastor breaks in. He has been holding a prayer meeting with
Engstrand at the orphanage, burning candles. He is full
of enthusiasm. Engstrand's sailors' home is a wonderful
idea, and Regina should not hesitate to go with her father.

To his amazement, Oswald replies that Regina is going with him as his wife. The Pastor stares at the champagne, at the servant drinking with her mistress. Mrs. Alving begins to speak just as cries are heard outside. The orphanage that is to be dedicated tomorrow is in flames! The curtain comes down with the Pastor declaiming that judgment has fallen on this abode of sin, and then he adds, "And uninsured, too."

ACT THREE—*The Price of Decency*

The monument to the memory of Captain Alving, his monument to respectability, has burned to the ground— the symbol of purification by fire. Pastor Manders is most disturbed, not about the moral issues at stake, but about his own reputation, for he had refused to insure the buildings and he was seen with a candle during his private services with Engstrand. He will indeed be marked as the one whom the hand of God has singled out for punishment. But the unctuous Engstrand comes to his rescue. He will assume the blame for the accident. The price is support for his sailors' home. Manders is delighted and blesses Engstrand. They leave together, but not before the Pastor gives his departing benediction, "May the spirit of Law and Order descend upon this house!" Engstrand, as he helps Manders on with his coat, contributes the most ironic words of the play. His brothel will be called "Captain Alving's Home" and it will be worthy of the Chamberlain's memory.

There is no further need for Manders; the rest of the final act goes on without him. He has been living proof of the emptiness of his own morality. His integrity is self-preservation. His ideals too are uninsured. Mrs. Alving must now face Oswald and Regina alone. And when she does speak of Captain Alving, she does not say what she originally intended, not what she had told the Pastor, for the occurrences of the past few hours have caused a qualitative change. The previous interruptions have been intentional.

Herein lies one of the most far-reaching of Ibsen's contributions to the modern drama. Characters influence events,
but events also alter character. A hitherto unexplored dimension in human tragedy is released, the interpenetrabil-
ity of cause and effect, of man and the complex forces of
which he is both agent and result. Mrs. Alving understands her husband for the first time, and realizes why he
had refused to live with her. Oswald's honest but brutal
words that he would disintegrate in this environment have
forced a re-evaluation. Mrs. Alving had judged her husband with abstract criteria, with what she had inherited
from all those like Manders. She had not seen him as a
product of his social restrictions. She speaks now with sympathy and compassion: How could Alving have survived in
this smug, ingrown community? He had no outlet for his
"joy of living." He was driven to dissipation, and she, his
own wife, was in part responsible, for, as she says:

> They had taught me a lot about duties . . . which I
> had taken to be true. Everything was marked out into
> duties, and—I'm afraid I made home intolerable for your
> poor father.

This is a tremendous admission. She too is to blame.
Her will has at last fought through to self-awareness and
self-criticism, but she has not counted on a changed response likewise in her auditors. Regina refuses to remain.
She will not be sacrificed to an invalid, nor can she easily
forgive the fact that she was not brought up as a lady. Mrs.
Alving repeats that if Regina ever needs a home, she will
always be welcome, but there is too much of the Dionysian
in Regina to be restrained any longer. She can always have
a place to stay in "Captain Alving's Home for Wayward
Sailors."

Mrs. Alving is finally left alone with her son, but he
is no longer the Oswald of her dreams. He has no love for
his mother. He has never known her; the separation of

many years has made them strangers. Mrs. Alving is willing to start anew, to build from the ruins, to earn his love, but Oswald replies that he needs Regina, not his mother. His disease is more serious than he has indicated. At any moment he may become a babbling idiot. Regina, least affected by Manders' preaching, would not have hesitated to feed him the poison pills that he always carries with him. If his mother would earn his love, she must promise to take Regina's place. Mrs. Alving agrees, discounting his words as the fantasy of an overwrought mind. They will live together. There will be truth between them. She pulls the curtains open, and sunshine, warm and full, floods the room. The rain is over, the mist gone, but Oswald is slumped in his chair, muttering, "The sun, the sun." He has had his stroke. He sits there—blind and helpless. Mrs. Alving is panic-stricken. She reaches for the pills and holds them hesitantly in her hand. The play ends as Oswald repeats, "The sun. The sun."

Freedom and Truth

Ghosts is not a play about venereal disease, nor the sins of the fathers, nor fate. It is a scathing indictment of the bourgeois world in which there is no livable Truth and Freedom, the same theme as *Brand*. The form is different. The diffuse fable of *Peer Gynt* has given way to the intense personal drama of Mrs. Alving, and she comes as close to tragic proportions as modern drama permits.

Hedda Gabler is the situation in reverse. Born an aristocrat, Hedda is compelled to accept the safe Tesman when society offers no more attractive outlets for the unmarried woman. But she hates the "mean and the ludicrous," a synonym for middle-class values, and is restless in a marriage that is the epitome of conventional boredom. She lacks the self-sacrifice of Mrs. Elvsted, who creates through others. Hedda, loathing life, turns to death. Though she is

in love with Lovborg, she burns his manuscript, his brain
child, in a ritual of ecstasy, and kills her own child by killing herself. She can only destroy. Her encouragement of
Lovborg to kill himself beautifully symbolizes the horrible
idea that within the social necessity, suicide is the only positive act.

Ibsen could not go on forever repeating his theme.
The Wild Duck betrays his awareness of his own paralyzing
contradiction. Truth too may cause destruction when people
prefer their illusions. On the mountaintop, Brand could
demand undivided spiritual discipline, but in the world
below, man's will thrown against an unyielding environment buckles into a distortion of itself. The herald of Truth
becomes an evil that brings ruin to others. Ibsen had
turned on himself. Death was becoming too welcome a
solution. In *Rosmersholm,* Rebecca West goes to her doom
joyously, taking with her down the mill race an equally
inspired Rosmer. Ibsen had no choice but to return to the
mountains.

The Master Builder, first in a series of symbolic plays,
climbs as high as a church steeple, but Rubek and Irene,
in *When We Dead Awaken,* end up in the ice and snow.
The same avalanche that engulfed Brand buries them. The
circle was closed, and Ibsen died soon after, turning his
back on the twentieth century.

His literary life began with the publication of Dar-
win's *Origin of Species* in 1859, and closed with Einstein's
first paper on relativity in 1905. Mastery over nature called
for comparable majesty of the human spirit. The middle
class preferred the preservation of old myths and the apolo-
getics of control, bolstering them by repeating them more
loudly. The result was an intolerable mismarriage, and the
dislocation of the poet. Ibsen pioneered in the quest for
new and more relevant myths, a consuming passion for the
regeneration of man. He dismissed all political solutions.

When Björnson appealed to him to join a mild, peasant reform group, Ibsen wrote:

> I am more and more confirmed in my belief that there is something demoralizing in politics and parties . . .

He added:[7]

> I myself am responsible for what I write, I and no one else. I cannot possibly bring trouble on any party, for I do not belong to any. I stand like a solitary franc-tireur at the outposts and act on my own responsibility.

He despised the peasantry, and once said that he looked forward with eager anticipation to a revolution in Norway, for it would give him the pleasure of shooting at them from the barricades. Toward the working class he was more tolerant, yet in addressing a workingman's group in Trondheim in 1885, he repeated his insistent theme of the aristocracy of the will:[8]

> An aristocratic element must come into our political life, into our parliament, and into our press. I am, of course, not thinking of aristocracy of birth, emphatically not that of money, not of the aristocracy of knowledge, not even that of ability and talent. But I have in mind an aristocracy of character and mind and will. It is that alone can make us free.

If social and economic improvement interested him little, it follows that the burning issue of the 1880's— woman's emancipation—was not, as is commonly believed, a battle slogan for the author of *A Doll's House*. Whereas the women of the world hailed him as their champion, Ibsen began to mock even their efforts for legislative reform. Georg Brandes, his admirer and teacher, had translated Mill's *Subjection of Women* in 1869, and he and Ibsen had discussed the problem often. In Norway, women were admitted to the University in 1882 for the first time, and in 1884 a bill was introduced giving women legal rights to property as well as to their own earnings. It had as its supporters Björnson, of course, and strangely enough, Ibsen, but in a speech made in 1898 at a banquet of the Norwegian Society for the Woman's Cause he said, to the consternation of his audience:[9]

> I thank you for drinking my health, but I must reject the honor of having consciously worked for the woman's cause. I am not even clear what the woman's cause really is. For me, it has been an affair of humanity . . . I have always looked on it as a mission to elevate the nation and give the people a higher status . . . to rouse a conscious sense of Culture and Discipline. These must be created in human beings before the people can be raised higher. It is the women who will solve the problem of humanity. *As mothers they are to do it. And only so can they do it.* [Italics are mine.]

What Ibsen did believe in was the spiritual regeneration of man. This was the consuming passion in everything he wrote. But he was essentially the artist, and the struggle for freedom became the metaphor of his vision.

He wanted men completely free. He had been disturbed by Brandes and his translation of Taine, in which milieu, race, and moment contribute to define literature. In Act Three of *Emperor and Galilean,* one of his most ambitious undertakings, he had Julian shout:

> I defy necessity! I will not serve it! I am free, free, free!

Almost the same as the last words he wrote, the song of Maya, and re-echoed in Camus' *Caligula,* written fifty years later.

Peer thinks that doing as he pleases makes him free, but he has no moral integrity. He vacillates with every situation and winds up conforming to the traditional. Brand is free because he follows his call to Truth with unwavering virulence, but he is deserted by society and a repentant God chides him. Nora must be free of a conventional husband if she is to know the Truth, even though an American version had her come back before the final curtain.

Much of this sounds like the Kierkegaard slogans that Ibsen found current in intellectual circles—"Do the impossible once again," "Truth is in the minority," and "A single individual is the highest power"—a refurbished Protestantism asserting the rights of the individual will against all intermediary institutions, long in advance of the existentialism of Sartre.

Ibsen's Truth and Freedom are necessarily vague and abstract. His is a general call for men of moral greatness, but specifically how they should achieve moral greatness, he ignored. He was caught by the social necessity from which he fought to free himself. He never understood the freedom that lies within the consciousness of that necessity. His characters change, and change one another, but they never alter the social institutions that distort the human will. The Lie is concrete and social; Ibsen's logic is abstract and personal. He exposed his middle-class characters to a withering analysis. He stripped them spiritually naked before the footlights, then pulled down the curtain with a call for Truth and Freedom. Not knowing where to go from there, he must either leave them naked or have them commit suicide. The latter was morally preferable. Death was not tragic but a welcome release. He was therefore bound to repeat himself until, divorced from social nourishment, he became the poet who alone bore the Truth, a bit pompous and self-righteous.

Yet in seeking Truth, Ibsen recognized the falsity of contemporary society. This was what hurt, and his early plays were a shock to middle-class audiences. He was assailed as anti-Christ. Arnold Daly's efforts to introduce him in New York landed Daly in jail. Special theatre clubs were organized to circumvent police laws. It took William Archer and Bernard Shaw to get him a London showing. Riots greeted the opening nights in France and Germany. The lonely poet had become a political issue.

The Form—Romanticism and Realism

Out of Ibsen's moral intensity is constituted the form of his dramas. He utilized all available dramatic techniques, perfecting each in turn, and summing up the varying literary currents in a half-century of work.

When Ibsen was born, romanticism was at its feverish height. Goethe was still ensconced at Weimar. Schiller was the popular god of the theatre, with his rebellious and sentimental heroes. In France, Victor Hugo was pouring out manifestoes announcing the triumph of the new art, to be followed by Byron and Shelley in England, the Duke of Rivas in Spain, Pushkin and Lermontov in Russia. The classical mold of the eighteenth century—reason and restriction, the world within authority—could not contain the whirlpool of the French Revolution. Everywhere the poet was dreaming of liberty, equality, fraternity, singing the triumph of man as if, long held in subjection by rulers and rules, the milennium was, though not here, at least on its way. The dream rose to universality, its excesses tempered only by the fact that the immediate environment was not always the theatre of application. Every play ended with a cry for Liberty and Freedom. Even when Goetz von Berlichingen, a knight of the Middle Ages, dies in a rather muddled local feud, Goethe had him call for "Freedom! Freedom!"—although the later and more conservative Goethe changed the final words to "lawful freedom."

Romanticism, like the French Revolution itself, blasted authority, challenged every entrenched dogma, and championed the endless perfectability of man. But since it was highly generalized, the newly enthroned middle class, after a moment of interest, went to the theatre to see Scribe rather than Hugo.

Eugene Scribe and Victorien Sardou were the prolific masters of "idle entertainment." Their manufactured plays were constantly in demand everywhere for more than sixty years. Their trick was the *pièce-bien-faite*, the well-made play. Superb craftsmen, they could turn out adroit manipulations of any plot well-calculated to stimulate for the moment. The stage became the forum for intrigue and incident, exercises in the dexterity of the writer. Scribe was the spirit of monopoly in the theatre. He became a big business, paying royalties for other men's ideas, hiring a stable of underlings, and turning out over five hundred box-office successes, a first-rate example of efficiency, organization, and uncreativeness. He and the pedestrian Sardou wrote to order, robbing the theatre of its poetry until, with one puff of "Sardoodledom," Shaw blew them into the discard. But they did perfect a form of construction that is our inheritance today. Ibsen took the form and gave it content, transforming a mechanical device into a work of art.

Ibsen's middle period, from *Peer Gynt* to *The Master Builder,* was that of the realistic, well-made play. *Ghosts* from the point of view of sheer structure has taught every playwright since. The writer's technical dexterity is subservient to emotional and intellectual participation in the problems that confront Mrs. Alving. The central theme is amplified by every move, word, and character so that the entire work composes as a variation, with a terrific climactic crescendo in the finale.

The play has a single set and only five characters, and the action takes place within the space of a few hours. The taut construction restored the unities to the theatre. Not that this in itself is any particular virtue, save to those who worship presumed classical form, but with *Ghosts* the constriction of time, place, and action intensified the final dramatic explosion. The set is one room in the home of the family, like all the rooms of all the Alvings of the world. The compression of space packs more tightly the strangling mores of a little cosmos. Mrs. Alving has no area in which to move.

There are no superfluous characters. In the Scribe

formula the butler, carrying the tray, informs the maid, pinning the antimacassars, that his lordship, returning after five years in the colonies, will be surprised to find out that his beloved brother has squandered the family fortune and that the expected marriage with the lovely Lady Witherspoon may never take place. All the butler and the maid do for the rest of the play is serve tea and answer doorbells. In *Ghosts* all characters are central. The interaction of people determines the social milieu. Today, with the high cost of Broadway production, a producer's eyes gleam when he finds a one-set, few-characters play, and writers execute deft handsprings to cut down the cast. Ibsen faced no such problem. His economy of characters was designed to enable the playwright to probe more deeply. The outspread canvas of the romantics, with its army of characters, its prodigality, hindered psychological introspection. Ibsen explored his five characters in *Ghosts* so intensively, with so many contributing strains, that in the short space of an evening they became full-bodied, multidimensional, and provocatively human. Mrs. Alving is as completely known as any character in our drama.

The method of advancing the plot in *Ghosts* was that of the suspense melodrama. Scribe, however, used the first act for exposition, carefully laying the groundwork for the involved complications to be unraveled later. Crises came at fixed intervals, a periodic arrangement of tensions. Ibsen opened *Ghosts* abruptly at a major crisis and closed each act with a suspense-packed curtain line, but the interest was always in the moral caliber of the characters at a moment of decision. There was no preliminary build-up to move into entanglements. Characters were caught in their dilemmas when the play opened, for such was the historical moment of the society they reflected. Development lay in *how* and *why* they responded; rather than in action for its own sake.

Ibsen also employed the technique of the classical drama

—opening at high tension, and revealing the past in inter-spersed fragments. Each revelation is so well integrated that it is as dramatic as the action in the present. In the crucial scene when Mrs. Alving tells Oswald the truth about his father, the past merges with the present. Thus, the restricted space became an arena for the dynamic interweaving of time.

Ghosts indicates the nature of realism—specific indi-viduals in conflict with the conditioning environment. The particular becomes the type. Mrs. Alving, unique person-ality, is all middle-class women who seek to be free of "law and order." And the language is prose—the restricted sym-bol of everyday living.

Peer Gynt indicates the nature of romanticism—man in conflict with nature, with the universe. The general re-flects the particular. Peer is the embodiment of the self-centered ego, of perpetual compromise. And the language is poetry—the far-flung metaphor of fantasy.

The two forms are rarely complete in themselves. By the very nature of their content and the complexity of hu-man existence, elements of each merge into the other, since the poet articulates his world differently at varying stages of his own growth, and fuses techniques within the confines of a single work. He seldom sees his environment whole. It is pertinent that neither form arose as a distinct literary vehicle until the nineteenth century. Classical literature had leaned toward the realistic in comedy and the picaresque, whose content arose from the people; tragedy had more of the romantic, for it was of the gods, both human and Olympian. After the French Revolution, the two forms grew wider apart. Romanticism was the dream; realism, the fact. Ibsen always combined the two.

Characters Worthy of Tragedy

In the plays of his dominantly realistic period, Ibsen became the first great playwright to bring the middle class on stage and make them worthy of tragedy. Convention, mostly Aristotelian, well-preserved by a jealous aristocracy, had required at least a king or a nobleman to fall, before tragic values came into play. Occasional comedies, such as Dekker's *Shoemakers' Holiday* in 1600, had dared to give the artisan increased dignity, but it was not until more than a hundred years after Shakespeare that a merchant could be a tragic protagonist. George Barnwell, in Lillo's *London Merchant*, dies heartbroken because he betrayed the glory of the virtuous business man. The play was a popular success wherever the middle class rose to power, and much praised by Diderot and Lessing. Diderot, playwright as well as Encyclopedist, had called for *le genre dramatique sérieux*, or Serious Drama, by which he meant drama of society as it existed. Beaumarchais, his successor, abler dramatist and lampoonist of the aristocracy as well, had written, "The nearer the suffering is to my station in life, the greater the claim upon my sympathies." Both advocated the middle-class family, the core of the social system, as subject matter for meaningful drama. Lessing went further, demanding emotional truth, awareness of social relationships, and above all, the *bourgeoisie* as heroic figures.

These efforts were sporadic and quite fruitless. Ibsen, in the last half of the nineteenth century, made the middle class the full substance of his dramas. A salesman could now die with honor.

There have been consistent realists in the theatre—Chekhov, Gorky, and in our time, such Ibsenites as Lillian Hellman and Clifford Odets. Zola was perhaps the most extreme of realists, employing what he himself called naturalism. Ibsen saw the difference between the two. He said:[10]

Zola descends into the sewer to take a bath. I do in order to scour it.

But the sewer was physical. Ibsen's scouring was spiritual. Realism is a preferable mold for a thoroughgoing materialist. Ibsen mastered the technique but the message was the same. His content writhed to escape, until finally the imbalance between method and conclusion was resolved in favor of the spirit. The plays of the final period, especially *Rosmersholm* and *When We Dead Awaken,* achieved mastery of a distinct form, the limitations of realism being broken to encompass an abstract unity in which the symbol dominates the entire work and a figurative language restores a poetry of meaning beyond the particular. But Ibsen's personal disillusionment resulted in a terrifying mysticism.

These later symbolic plays are forerunners of much that is current in the theatre, for the obscure is honored when confusion replaces conviction. Innumerable plays owing much to the later Ibsen are devoted to similar themes: love sublimations as psychopathic problems, gifted and unique individuals torn loose from their promise, and above all, suicide to gain one's freedom. The pursuing contradiction became enshrouded in the Norwegian mist.

The Revolution in the Theatre

The blast at Victorianism in the realistic plays fostered an adventure in exploring honesty in human relationships. New and vital theatres defying convention in staging and acting, in design and production, sprang up everywhere: the Théâtre Libre of Antoine in Paris; the Freie Bühne of Otto Brahm in Berlin, which opened its first season with *Ghosts;* the Independent Theatre of Grein in London, whose single performance of *Ghosts* in 1891 split England wide open in a heated literary controversy over the merits of realism; the Irish Literary Theatre of Yeats in Dublin, and later the Abbey Theatre, and most enduring of all, the Moscow Art Theatre of Stanislavsky. Playwrights, as well as designers, technicians, and directors, responded to the challenge. The novel, most apt medium for delineating the modern world, had charted the way with Dickens, Balzac, Flaubert, De Goncourt, and Tolstoy. The transition to the theatre, pioneered by Ibsen, was strengthened by Hauptmann, Strindberg, Chekhov, and Bernard Shaw, making the 1890's one of the most illustrious decades in the history of the theatre.

Realism in content demanded realism in acting. The old declamatory system with the performer winding up for his big scene was ill-suited to psychological interaction, consciousness of group relations, and projection of inner struggle. The voice and body virtuoso could not portray the meaning of Ibsen, for there were no grand-action heroics, no poetic asides, no inflated oratory "to split the ears of the groundlings." The speech was natural dialogue. Antoine and Brahm worked for months to retrain their groups in the new method of acting, and Danchenko and Stanislavsky took their actors to a country barn in Pushkino, laboring diligently until a cohesive unity could be achieved. Nor did they hesitate to rehearse a play for a year if necessary. The actor began to study psychology, history, and the play itself, seeking to submerge himself in the role and discover "inner justification." When the Moscow Art Theatre was preparing *The Lower Depths,* Gorky suggested to Olga Chekhova that she have a prostitute live with her if she would know "the empty soul of Nastya." In line with Ibsen's recurring theme, it is interesting to note that Stanislavsky said of his role in Gorky's play that its real meaning to him was: "Freedom at any cost! That freedom for which men descend into the depths of life and become slaves. But they become slaves of their own free will."

Whereas the change in acting techniques was a major contribution to the theatre, that in realistic stage design was of less enduring value, even though today most plays—and certainly the cinema—maintain a meticulous regard for actual detail. In Ibsen's day, it was a needed revolution against the faded, flowery drapes, the stale floats, and the baroque perspective drawings of the romantics. With a thoroughgoing realist like David Belasco, it meant that the theatre was life itself, the curtain the fourth wall, so that to his uninspired imagination a Childs Restaurant scene should have the white tile, the chrome railings, and the odor of fresh coffee and hot cakes! The emphasis was on environment as material fact, as theatrical effect, rather than on meaning, and such men as Gordon Craig and Meyerhold soon tired of its restrictions. Today, abstractions, unit sets, light rather than objects, mood rather than detail, theatres in the round rather than in the picture-frame model, are all expansions into the possible.

The modern theatre, born in the Renaissance, reached a climactic impasse in the work of Ibsen. Complex and contradictory as the last half of the nineteenth century was, it is embodied in the totality of his work. Every playwright since, whether he acknowledges it or not—and most do not—has sat at his feet. The direct progeny of his middle period, the social realists, have altered locale and situation, but they echo the disintegration of middle-class values. Sixty years have passed, and there is a monotony in repetition. The continuing theatre of the present day is the effort to go beyond Ibsen.

3. Realism and Beyond—Strindberg

THE GHOST SONATA

The Turbulent Years—"Cast out this Bondwoman and her son . . ."

The revolution that surrounds the name of Ibsen was carried to further heights by his contemporary, August Strindberg. In the work of these two dramatists is encompassed the poet's exploration of every aspect of the present-day theatre. Few have gone beyond them.

Sweden had contributed little to the international theatre before Strindberg, and after his death, none of equal stature rose to complete the promise. The same is true of Norway and Ibsen. Perhaps the vastness of the shadow they cast obscured the work of other men, or perhaps the greatness of their art and the thoroughness with which they laid bare an age in transition left little to say until the changed conditions of a postwar world required new voices. However, though restrained in Scandinavia, the new movement spread throughout Europe, and its impact on playwrights is the continuing history of the theatre.

Alike as Ibsen and Strindberg are in their early work, their personalities were in sharp contrast. Ibsen kept quietly in the background, rarely known except through his plays. Strindberg threw his personal life into the headlines of every newspaper. His was a wild, seething, tortured, and oversensitive spirit that, crashing against the rigid conventions of his age, shattered into fragments of disillusionment and suicidal intent that provoked repeated scandals, lawsuits, confinement in a mental institution, and a terrifying despair that sought first in the mystical revelations of Swedenborg, and later in the subconscious depths of his dream world, to find some personal solace and consolation. Much of his life was spent in enforced isolation and self-imposed asceticism, but his contact with the real world was a series of disasters. He was one of eleven children who lived in abject poverty. His mother was a barmaid, whom his father married just before August was born. Strindberg hated his mother for his low birth and his narrow escape from illegitimacy. In the final part of his play *To Damascus,* with its autobiographical references, The Stranger says, "I am the Bondwoman's son, of whom it was writ—Cast out this bondwoman and her son: for the son of the bondwoman shall not be heir with the free woman's son." But he defended her when, shortly after her death, his father married a former housekeeper. At the University of Uppsala, he lived miserably, joined the bohemian and radical groups of the time, and studied medicine and journalism. He failed in his first job as an actor and tried to commit suicide by taking an overdose of opium. In the delirium of its aftereffects he wrote his first play, no copy of which has survived. His three attempts at marriage ended in the divorce courts. His first wife, Siri von Essen, left her aristocratic husband to marry Strindberg, and though they managed to stay together for thirteen years, their life was a succession of mutual recriminations and violent quarrels. The young Austrian journalist, Frida Uhl, he deserted on their honeymoon. When past fifty, he tried again with the pretty actress Harriet Bosse, but they separated three years later. His savage indictment of marriage in his books of intimate confessions resulted in a lawsuit for blasphemy and libel, which left him penniless and almost sent him to jail. He spent years in laboratories attempting to reformulate the science of chemistry, and later experimented like a medieval alchemist to transmute the baser elements into gold. In pur-

suit of peace, he studied the religions of the East, and he
probed deeply into the subconscious for an answer to the
unhappiness of man. Yet this lonely, suffering, restless soul
is the greatest name in Swedish literature. His *History of the
Swedish People* is read second only to the Bible. His essays
and novels are accepted classics and his plays are the basis
of all repertory theatres, but beyond his own country he
gave to the theatre a vastness of concept and a boldness of
imagination that deterred a return to complacency.

The Battle of the Sexes

Strindberg's early plays reflect the influence of Ibsen.
The two most important are *Lucky Per,* a lesser *Peer Gynt,*
and *Master Olaf,* based on Swedish history at the time of the
Reformation and comparable to *Brand.* Both are in the
tradition of romanticism, with the many characters, short
scenes, wide canvas, political implications, and abstract
generalities. Strindberg never deserted his interest in historical themes, and despite radical changes in technique
returned frequently to write of the Scandinavian past. None
of these plays would have earned Strindberg more than
local recognition. The transition to the powerful works of
the realistic period occurred after his first marriage and the
publication of *The Red Room,* a novel which bitterly
satirized existing society and made him a controversial figure
in literary circles.

Two volumes of short stories followed under the general title *Married;* these contain a violent attack on all
women, and reveal his hypersensitivity and a frenzied self-
destructiveness bordering on the psychotic. To escape a
breakdown, he voluntarily entered a mental institution.
The plays which were written after his release brought
Strindberg international recognition and marked an insight
into psychological drama that has not been equaled. The
most important are *The Father, Miss Julie, Comrades,* and
The Creditors.

The Father is a tightly constructed, mounting conflict between husband and wife in which the woman finally drives the man insane in a battle of wills that is remorseless and uncompromising. The marriage of Laura and the Captain, full of a hatred which binds them together, has been a drawn-out fight for domination. They are on the edge of financial ruin because of Laura's interference with his investments. She undermines his scientific research by withholding his correspondence, but the immediate crisis is over the daughter. The Captain would send her to boarding school to escape the confining religious hypocrisy Laura and her mother impose on the child. With satanic skill, Laura turns the daughter, the old nurse, and the doctor, his only friend, against him, and by planting the suggestion that he may not be the real father, breaks his last hold on sanity. In the final scene, it is the trusted old nurse who puts him in the strait jacket.

The form is the well-made play: the single living-room set, a few characters intensely developed in psychological detail, the unities of time and action carefully observed. Ibsen had achieved this before. What distinguishes the play is its content. Much like D. H. Lawrence, drawing from his own experiences, combining bits of Nietzsche and Schopenhauer and more of Herbert Spencer, Strindberg conceived of life as a battle for survival between irreconcilable forces. All change results from opposites in conflict. Man and woman are in a savage sex struggle for supremacy, a brutal, animal war of annihilation in which one must destroy the other, an inexorable war of wills in which the stronger triumphs. Woman is more subtle, more insidious, and has the sharper weapons, for they are fashioned from instinct and passion and possessiveness. Man is more rational, but equally unscrupulous. The outcome is never certain. The man may triumph as he does in *Miss Julie,* or both may be condemned to eternal hate and guilt as in *The Dance of*

Death, which ends with the Captain and Alice too weary to fight any more, destroying each other with silent contempt.

Strindberg was never modest. In a note about *The Father,* he declared that it was the fulfillment of the modern drama, for "the struggle takes place between wills. It is a battle of brains, not a dagger fight or poisoning with raspberry juice as in *Die Rauber.* The French of today are still seeking the formula, but I have found it."[1]

Zola was so impressed with *The Father* that he recommended it for production at Antoine's Théâtre Libre, and wrote to Strindberg requesting another play. The answer was *Miss Julie,* but neither play can be directly attributed to Zola's influence. Unfortunately, the word "naturalism" has been used to describe Strindberg's work. Zola, better at writing polemics than dramas, had, particularly in the preface to the stage version of *Thérèse Raquin,* called for the presentation of a "slice of life" in which scientific knowledge and social research would contribute to the theatre the unfolding of the laws of nature. Zola was protesting against the melodramas of contrived situation, the "poisonings with raspberry juice," but what resulted was slavishness to observable objectivity, and photographic reportage of the sordid, the ugly, and the lives of the underprivileged. A long succession of such plays has contributed little to the theatre, and for the proper distinction should be called naturalistic. Such plays are foreign to Strindberg. He was never interested in the accumulation of documentary evidence. Ferdinand Brunetière, the most penetrating critic of his time and a devout Catholic, correctly assailed Zola with the thesis that essences and not appearances were the concern of art and that drama did not exist without the conscious human will struggling against the forces that surround it. Realism is an art form in which the playwright exercises selection, emphasis, distortion, and the imposition of a point of view. Zola was most probably delighted with

The Father as an indication to Brunetière that reality could likewise include the powerful drive of the human will.

Strindberg was far removed from Zola's manifestoes. He was closer to Shakespeare and the Greek theatre. *Confessions of a Fool,* a book of personal revelations published soon after *The Father,* includes an account of the play's genesis. The Captain was intended as a combination of Agamemnon and Lear. The Greek hero was brought to disaster by three women, Iphigenia, Clytemnestra, and Cassandra, and Lear was driven mad by the cruelty of two daughters.

Strindberg is more explicit as to the meaning for society. Aeschylus indicates that violation of established mores may bring an entire civilization to ruin. Clytemnestra murders her husband and cannot go unpunished. Laura, far more subtle, operates within the law. She goads the Captain to self-destruction through doubt, domesticity, and debt. Orestes, after a long ordeal, finally attains forgiveness through the mercy of the gods, and justice is restored to the state. With Strindberg there can be no harmony, for marriage is a writhing whirlpool of destructive opposites that undermines the rotting foundation of an anarchic social structure.

Watching the painful conflict of human monsters seeking to devour each other can become repetitious and lacking in tragic dimension. None of Strindberg's characters achieves the stature of Ibsen's Mrs. Alving. She consciously challenges the evil that surrounds her, and fails because unseen forces far too powerful for a single individual's rebellion overwhelm her, but Mrs. Alving continues to resist, no matter what the failure. Strindberg comes closer to case studies in psychiatry. The outcome is preordained, and our morbid curiosity is fascinated by the dissolution of human will. Yet in *Miss Julie* Strindberg fashioned a masterpiece of realism, form and meaning being united in a gripping, powerful drama.

The play is the clearest example of the sex struggle. Jean and Julie, man and woman, are opposites on all levels save in their animal passion and the drive to dominate. Drawn instinctively to each other, needing each other, they battle to destroy each other. The third character is the cook, who eases the tension and proffers moral censure. To Julie, her pietism and practicality represent an alternative worse than death; to Jean, her dullness and insensitivity are the fate that normally would be his.

The place is the kitchen of the manor house, the time Midsummer Eve. There is no division into acts, and so the flow of action is continuous. The only interruption is the erotic dance of the peasants at the moment of Julie's seduction. She is the aristocrat, caught in a vacuum that offers no release for her vitality. Jean, the lackey, is culturally pretentious, socially ambitious, and basically cruel, caught in a world where the ringing of the master's bell is the symbol of servility. In the first part, the tide of battle rises and falls in favor of one or the other, with Julie in control, but the soft night air, the music of the dance, the aphrodisiac perfume of the flowers, and the closeness of Jean become irresistible, and she yields to him. The physical union reverses the roles. His triumph brings out his uglier nature, his arrogance, his contempt for her now that he has possessed her. His dream is to have an inn of his own with Julie as landlady. She has no choice but suicide.

In the preface to the published version of the play, Strindberg offers radical suggestions for staging, which include elimination of footlights and a minimum of makeup, and explains the motives of his characters. He calls Julie "a half-woman, the man-hater" who openly sells herself for power, but to whom degenerate men are attracted, "and so they multiply and bring into the world progeny of indeterminate sex to whom life becomes a torture."

The Road Beyond Realism

Though Strindberg wrote realistic dramas in his later years and returned to the war of the sexes repeatedly, the first decade of the new century marked a decisive change in his work. His second marriage had ended again in divorce. Repeated attempts at reconciliation with Frida Uhl failed, and particularly painful was the loss of the children. His literary activities ceased and he buried himself in the study of theosophy and philology. He felt himself the persecuted victim of unseen foes, and became involved in devising a system of black magic to offset their determination to destroy him. His absorption with his next book, *The Inferno,* an account of his own travail and disillusionment, probably saved him from a mental breakdown. From then on, he wrote less of the relation between man and woman, and more of the relation between man and God. He had reached the point where concern with immediate issues uncovered no satisfactory answers and only unraveled the skein leading to the forces that lay beyond, in the realm of the mysterious. He found some consolation in the eighteenth-century mystic Swedenborg, and when he returned to the theatre with *To Damascus,* he gave expression to his travels in *The Inferno.*

The play is rarely done. It is too long and diffuse, but it marks the beginning of his efforts to go beyond realism. The central characters are The Unknown One, The Woman, and The Unseen One. No longer are they specific individuals, but abstractions of human experience. The Unseen One is God, who does not appear on stage, but as in the prologue to *Faust* is the invisible voice. The Unknown One is man, Strindberg himself, who is in rebellion against God and curses the evil that permeates the earth. The Woman is the prototype of the *ewig weibliche,* the eternal feminine. The actress who played the role in its first production became, years later, Strindberg's third wife. The

unfolding of the relationships is in moody, terrifying sequences in which man questions the nature of the universe
and his destiny on earth, a bizarre odyssey of him who is
nameless and all-suffering in direct confrontation with the
Almighty, who remains unseen. The form is exploratory.
There is no plot in the usual sense, no connected series of
episodes. Strindberg, in his own analysis of the play, preceded the efforts of a half-century later. He wrote:[2]

> The author has tried to imitate the . . . seemingly
> logical form of the dream. Anything may happen; every-
> thing is possible and probable. Time and space do not
> exist. On a minimum background of reality, imagination
> designs and embroiders novel patterns; a medley of mem-
> ories, experiences, free fancies, absurdities, improvisations.

The change in theme and form accompanied a change
in Strindberg's outlook. The conflict is no longer sharp and
destructive, as in the earlier plays. The protagonist seeks
peace and order and redemption as he senses, somewhat
reluctantly, the deeper meaning of God's enduring grace.
The mystery of life on earth is paralleled by the mystery
of God's way with man. It is not the God of institutionalized
religion. The dogma of all faiths, dutifully interpreted, is
of no avail. Strindberg tried to hammer out a personal religion, as O'Neill much later, under the influence of Strindberg, attempted to do in *Dynamo*. The concept is Pro-
methean; the realization, a combination of Dürer and
Kandinsky.

Strindberg did not pursue the exciting challenge of this
technique with the dedication of the artist who discards
old forms as he encounters new ones. His manic-depressive
nature was too volatile to hold to a single concept, and the
tension of wrestling with God was too exhausting. Moreover, his sensitivity was so acute that he rarely groped his
way to slow assurance. He rushed into dangerous areas heed-
lessly and achieved mastery with lightning perception. The
prolific output that followed *To Damascus* included a re-

turn to historic dramas, among them the heroically pro-
portioned *Gustav Vasa,* which he wrote to recapture the
symphonic structure of Shakespeare, whose plays he now
reread with intense enthusiasm. The brash musical dis-
sonances and the interweaving of minor themes in the
chronicle plays were his model for the tales of Swedish
Kings. These dramas of war and statehood were interspersed
with the gentle calm of *Easter,* a religious play in which
the hardships of a family are reversed when Lindquist, who
can bring them to complete ruin, offers help instead. It is one
of the few joyous plays of Strindberg, with the lovely character Eleonora, the wood nymph, who talks to the leaves
and the birds, affecting all with the vision of Good Friday.
The next play was a complete contrast, a return to the
diabolic brutality of conjugal warfare in *The Dance of
Death,* in which the pattern of the parents' hate is repeated
in the lives of the children. He also wrote a series of short
stories, including "At the Edge of the Sea," which exposes
the absurdity of the dreams of the superman who stands
apart from humanity, a theme repeated later by Camus in
Caligula. But the plays that carried further the ideas inherent in *To Damascus* have had the most enduring influence.

Of *The Bridal Wreath, A Dream Play,* and *The Ghost
Sonata,* the first is comparable to *Easter,* for it treats of redemption for sins on earth; even the child-murderer may
find forgiveness. The other two are Strindberg's final testa-
ment, man's pitiful state of unrelieved evil. In *A Dream
Play,* the daughter of Indra comes to earth to investigate
the plight of man. What follows is a multiplicity of fantastic scenes in which all aspects of hell on earth are not
only observed but experienced by Indra's daughter, since
she becomes both the messenger of the gods and an earth
woman in many guises, witnessing political debauchery,
social injustice, the poet's torment, the self-seeking avarice
of rich and poor alike. Grotesque figures appear out of
nowhere, wear masks, vanish mysteriously; the same char-

acters are many different people, and physical objects grow and change in a moment's time. The scenes are held together by the central figure who, at the end of each episode, sings the refrain, "Man is to be pitied." At the end, the Castle rises out of the surrounding manure, and the bird at the summit, the symbol of faith, bursts into a chrysanthemum. Strindberg commented that in the play "characters split, double, multiply, solidify, blur," a concept later incorporated into Dadaism, adopted by the surrealists, distorted by Artaud in his theatre of cruelty, and developed for varying purposes by Pirandello, O'Neill, and Claudel. Motion pictures have used the technique extensively. Even Bertolt Brecht, in such early work as *In the Jungle of Cities,* plays with the indeterminate nature of character and the fusion of many into one.

The most misunderstood of Strindberg's plays, for it is the most extreme in dream techniques, is *The Ghost Sonata.*

THE GHOST SONATA

SCENE ONE—*"What is the meaning of all this?"*

The setting, a street scene, is described in detail. Though the play deals with a world of unreality, the physical objects are real but symbolic. On the ground floor of the corner house is visible a Round Room with a white marble statue surrounded by palms, the residence of The Colonel, the enclosed, circumscribed, and elegant façade for a seemingly rounded life with its underlying dishonesty. The statue is the youth of his wife.

As the curtain rises, church bells are heard, the presence of God enveloping the evil that is equally universal. The crippled old man, Hummel, is in an invalid's chair reading a newspaper. The Milkmaid enters and washes at the fountain. To Hummel she is invisible, for he, the observer who knows all about everyone, cannot see those whom he has injured. The Student, unshaved and disheveled, asks her to bathe his face, for a house collapsed last night and he has been rescuing the trapped and aiding the injured. She hesitates, then complies, and leaves without saying a word. Hummel offers The Student riches if he will follow his advice and marry The Young Girl, The Colonel's daughter. Hummel touches The Student's hand and it is a touch of ice, a warning that the offer of help will lead to death. During their conversation, other figures pass by in an ominous pantomime. The Dead Man on the second floor appears as a Ghost and walks off to see that the flag of the consulate where he worked is at half-mast. The Janitress sprinkles sprigs of hemlock on the sidewalk, the ritual that precedes a funeral. Hummel is wheeled off to make his rounds of stealing people and holding them in his power.

This first scene of apparently disconnected references and events is comparable to fragments of dreams that hold the possible revelation of buried possibilities. The Milkmaid cannot speak. The Dark Lady cannot move. Their names, like those of other characters, are abstractions, whereas Hummel and his servant Johansson are individualized. Objects and people shift from the specific to the general. Fantasy and realism are combined to heighten the fantasy but maintain the relevance to life. Different conversations go on simultaneously, a device ingeniously used by Ionesco in *Rhinoceros*. The Student, the adventurer on earth who risked his life to save others, is opposed by the ghouls who surround him, and he asks of Johansson, "What is the meaning of all this?"[3]

SCENE TWO—*"Happy indeed is the guiltless man."*

The second scene takes place in the Round Room. The physical objects are again placed as if in a surrealistic canvas, particularly the clock on the mantelpiece and the view of the adjoining Hyacinth Room, in which The Young Lady is seated reading a book. Hummel enters mysteriously, and The Mummy, who gurgles like a parrot, comes out of the closet to speak to him. She is The Colonel's wife, once Hummel's fiancée, and The Statue is her frozen youth. She threatens Hummel with death if he interferes with the life of The Young Lady, who is in reality their child. The people who appeared in Scene One are now the guests at The Colonel's party. All prove to be interrelated, adulterous and guilt-laden, their marriages a continuing burden of endured hatred. Hummel knows the source of their crimes and holds them in his power. He strips away their outward respectability and leaves them naked without their falsehood. Strindberg is always intense about the deceit that underlies the pretense to culture. With The Colonel, Hummel is ruthless. He exposes him as not a nobleman but a former servant masquerading under a stolen title, not even a real colonel but merely the possessor of an honorary rank that has long since been abolished. Nor is The Colonel even physically what he seems. He has a wig and false teeth and is held together with iron stays. Hummel is about to remove them all to make a cleaner life possible for the beautiful Young Lady and The Student of noble deeds, when The Mummy stops him. She exposes Hummel as also a fraud, guilty like the rest of them, and says, no longer chattering like a parrot but in a dignified tone, "I can wipe out the past and undo what is done." She holds back time by stopping the clock. All are miserable human creatures, she adds. All have sinned and are not what they seem. "We are better than ourselves, for at bottom we disapprove of our own misdeeds." The recognition of sin may, through suffering and penance, lead to redemption. Hummel is beyond salvation, his crime being the most heinous and unforgivable. He would exercise control over other humans and sit in judgment on them. The Mummy changes Hummel into her own former self, making him cluck like a parrot, and confines him in the closet to hang himself by his own hand. As she finishes, The Student joins The Young Lady in the Hyacinth Room, and to the accompaniment of her harp sings an Eddic hymn ending with, "Happy indeed is the guiltless man."

SCENE THREE—*"Saviour of the World, save us, for we perish."*

The final scene is the reverse shot of the previous one. It takes place in the Hyacinth Room, and through the door The Colonel and The Mummy can be seen seated at a table. They do not move or say a word. They are the background against which innocent youth must strive. The Student and The Young Lady talk of love and death and flowers in a nostalgic mood of haunting, lyrical beauty. The hyacinth is the earth. The bulb rests on water or is buried in the soil, and from the stem, straight as the axis of the globe, rises the six-pointed starlike flower, the symbol of the earth that may eventually be heaven. The Student would prepare their wedding, but The Young Lady asks him to await the ordeal. The menacing figure of The Cook enters with a Japanese soy bottle. She is the vampire symbol. The Young Lady lists the little chores of daily living that must be done first. The Student cries for music, but she replies, "Wait! Work comes first, the work of keeping life's filth at a distance." Strindberg had such an aversion to domesticity that he made servants the instrument of human torture, and household tasks the suffocating ordeal. The Student must speak out, but The Young Lady tries to hold him back because the truth will mean her death. Beauty created out of falsehood will vanish if honesty prevails. It is Strindberg's final agony, his own compulsion to speak out or die, even if speaking means the loss of what he loves. The world is an asylum and the words of madmen come closer to the truth. The Student reveals his knowledge of what has happened in these past hours: All is decayed and diseased, but keeping silent would only rot the truth. With her, he had entered what seemed to be Paradise. He wants a life of song and music and poetry with her, but The Cook has sucked all life out of her, and The Young Lady, the most beautiful

of flowers, is also poisoned and has poisoned him. The fra-
grance of the room is deadly. There is a curse on all creation. He cries aloud Strindberg's defense of his own life,
"I have been born with a different poison. I cannot call
the ugly, beautiful, nor evil, good." The Student prays,
"Woe is us. O Saviour of the World, save us, for we perish!"

The Young Lady dies and is placed behind the death
screen. The final song of The Student is one of sadness and
hope. He calls for sleep to bring her ultimate happiness, a
sleep without dreams, and prays she will awaken in a world
where love is without flaw, where the sun does not burn,
and where the house has no dust, for she is the innocent
victim of a world of eternal change, of illusion, guilt, suffering, and disappointment. As his prayer ends, the scene
disappears, and in its place rises the painting by Arnold
Böcklin of "The Isle of the Dead."

The Form and Meaning—Expressionism

Hummel is the central symbol. Possessiveness creates a
nightmare of personal hate. And he can never achieve complete power over others, since the past clings to all things
and comes back to torment the living. Not even young love
can rebuild the world. Böcklin's dark and brooding scene
replaces the statue of Buddha, who sits and waits for heaven
to spring from earth like the hyacinth.

In presenting visually the nebulous world of dreams,
Strindberg mastered a distinct dramatic form. Few playwrights have dared to attempt it. For Sophocles, Racine,
Ibsen, the form was established. Strindberg fathered, out of
necessity, what is now called expressionism, to reveal the
illogic of dreams and the disconnectedness of the subconscious. Instead of repeating old themes, he sought, as the
playwright should, new meanings out of new experiences,
and gave dramatic shape to what had been formless. Time,
space, and action have no significance in the world of fantasy. Characters cease to be specific and dissolve into the

corporeal form of ideas, concepts, suggestions, feelings. Moments of recognizable objectivity vanish, converge, disappear, as they do in dreams. Scenes are short, rapidly shifting, with little regard for fixed positions. Intensity is not on psychological depth but on images in motion.

The criticism has been made that whereas art should, above all, have clarity, Strindberg's expressionistic plays are vague. With modern painting, sculpture, and music leading the way beyond abstractionism to nonobjectivity, a reaction toward identifiable meaning is understandable. On the other hand, there unquestionably are those who exploit meaninglessness and make a fetish of the absence of sense, riding the wave of noncommunication and clamoring that if meaning is obvious, art has vanished. These arguments have little to do with Strindberg, and critics who belabor his obscurity are transposing the confusions of today with their often glib negativism to the painful, difficult journey of Strindberg. If his meaning is vague, so is the world he explores, a world that defies clarity. Ordinary terms are useless where the customary logical relationships no longer prevail. The mystic cannot reach identity with God by precise mathematical means, nor can Strindberg be expected to reveal the world of dreams in the language of everyday common sense. Like all seminal minds, he coins a new set of symbols, a new language, with sufficient relevance to bridge the gap.

One need not be under the influence of drugs or mentally disturbed to accept another logic, one that expresses the relationship of the imagined, the inconceivable, the impossible. The role of the artist is to bring order to chaos. Strindberg was faced with the more extreme chaos of the irrational. The theories of science today are no more clear to the layman than Strindberg's dream play, but science produces observable results and is accepted on faith. In dramatic art, the observable result is the play, and it can be accepted only if one suspends prejudice and is venturesome enough to try the unknown.

Strindberg's world is not a pleasant one, but his despair at the triumph of evil does not result in his rejection of man, but in a deep compassion for man, a need to recognize pain and sorrow as the road to salvation. He is never certain as to how that road must be traveled, but he never ceased in his search to know where it led. His recently published letters to Harriet Bosse show him with a great capacity for love, and a demonic demand for perfection that rendered love impossible to find. He must have been a difficult man to live with. Despite everything he said about women, he adored them. He loved all humanity, too insistently, and could get along with no one, not even himself. In his last play, *The Great Highway,* the Hermit asks, "Do you love your fellow men?" and the Hunter (Strindberg) answers, "Yes, far too much, and fear them for that reason too."

In art, as in love, he demanded no compromise. Both are irrational forces capable of conquering human decay, but they have been distorted by moral cowardice. He spent a lifetime to discover their inherent power for beauty, and the literary expression that resulted is an extraordinary adventure in man's creative possibility. His works include the gay satire of a folk comedy like *Lucky Per,* the massive, heroic, historic drama like *Gustav Vasa,* and grim psychological studies of domestic infelicity in which he, as though by means of a microscope, unpeeled the layers of human motives to observe the residue of hate. These are the more sensational plays like *Miss Julie,* which established his reputation as a morbid misogynist, but he was far more complex an artist than this restricted definition indicates. He turned to moments of anguished hope and religious faith in the delicate tenderness of *Easter.* In creating the magic of theatre he avoided the compliant repetition of the accepted. His greatest achievement lies, however, in his expressionistic plays, for here he widened the limits of the stage and exerted the most lasting influence on the playwrights who followed. After Strindberg, the theatre could not remain the same. He tried to encompass all of life, and in doing so, left a heritage that others have continued to enrich.

An extreme experimentalist like Arthur Adamov says that he began to write after reading Strindberg, because he then was able to see new symbolism in everyday events. Eugene O'Neill, deeply indebted to Strindberg, which he openly acknowledged, called him "the precursor of all modernity in our present theatre . . . the greatest interpreter of spiritual conflicts which constitute the drama—the blood —of our lives today." Sean O'Casey and Friedrich Duerrenmatt, among a host of others, paid tribute to Strindberg. Old George Bernard Shaw, who in his youth had said, "The giants of the theatre of our time are Ibsen and Strindberg," donated his Nobel Prize money for better translations of "the only genuine Shakespearean modern dramatist"—August Strindberg. His plays are produced today more than ever before. If time is the test, Strindberg has stood it well. Above all, he was a dramatist's dramatist.

4. The Comedy of Frustration—Chekhov

THE CHERRY ORCHARD

THE REALISTIC FORM developed by Ibsen and Strindberg was brought to its logical perfection by Chekhov. Moreover, he gave it a content of comedy not usually associated with the serious character of realism. The result was a disturb-

ing synthesis and a unique theatre experience which, even
in the Moscow Art Theatre, caused widely differing interpretations. Few deny the greatness of Chekhov as a dramatist, yet few agree on the nature of his artistry. The word
"Chekhovian" has been applied to plays that are formless
and undramatic, yet half of Chekhov's life was an uncompromising pursuit of mastery of form, from the action-
packed suspense drama *Platonov* to the carefully balanced
architecture of nonviolence in *The Cherry Orchard*. Some
have called him the playwright of despair, of Slavic gloom,
whereas Soviet critics have hailed him for his dreams of
revolution and a better life for man. Such diversity of opinion can be resolved only by approaching Chekhov without
critical preconceptions and by returning to the plays themselves, believing, as H.D.F. Kitto has said of Shakespeare,
that "the dramatist said exactly what he meant through the
medium of his art and means therefore exactly what he
said."

Even though his early reputation was based on his
short stories, Anton Pavlovitch Chekhov, like most Russian
writers, was interested in writing plays. The Russians have
always been emotional about the theatre. The critic Belinski
summed up their attitude with the cry, "Let us live in the
theatre. Let us die in the theatre." Tolstoy and Turgenev
and other leading novelists, with the exception of Dostoievsky, also wrote plays, and so many of Dostoievsky's works
were dramatized that he too belongs to the stage. The young
Russian theatre was predominantly realistic, influenced by
the novel and the general concern with social problems.
The four most popular comedies were Fonvizin's *The
Minor,* written at the time of Catherine the Great, Griboye-
dov's *Woe from Wit,* Gogol's *The Inspector General,* and
Ostrovsky's *The Bankrupt,* written at the time Chekhov was
born. All four are warmly human satires on corruption and
pretense. Chekhov followed in the national tradition.

Banality's Most Tired Foe

Anton Pavlovitch Chekhov came from peasant stock and knew the life of the country folk which formed the basis of all his plays. In fact, his own grandfather had been a serf and had purchased freedom from serfdom. Though the family remained poor, Chekhov was able to study medicine at the University of Moscow, supplementing his income by writing for the popular magazines. He became a dedicated rural doctor, but his own illness forced him to devote more time to writing. His poor health barred him from active participation in the great political movements that were sweeping the country, though he did defend Zola in the Dreyfus case when it was dangerous to do so, and he resigned from the Royal Academy when Gorky was denied admission on order of the Czar. His greatest happiness came in the few years granted him after his marriage to Olga Knipper, a leading actress with the Moscow Art Theatre. Persistent tuberculosis ended Chekhov's life at the age of forty-four, at the peak of his creative productivity. He had gone to the Black Forest region of Germany to recuperate, and it was there that he died. His body was shipped back in a refrigerator car marked "For Oysters." It was life's final irony, and Gorky remarked that it was "the triumphant laugh of banality over its most tired foe."

Although Chekhov was immediately successful with his short stories, his early association with the theatre was a series of failures. His full-length works are mere formative explorations. He wrote in all eighteen plays, but most of them are one-act sketches and exercises for actors. *Ivanov,* his first serious play, about the emptiness of a tired liberal at thirty-five, was greeted with whistling and catcalls; *The Wood Demon,* the early version of *Uncle Vanya,* after few rehearsals and bad acting, failed to please anyone; and *The Sea Gull,* first of the four major plays, opening in St. Petersburg with the famous Vera Kommissarzhevskaya in the title

role, was so misunderstood that the audience laughed in all
the wrong places. Chekhov was known as a humorist, and the
public was unprepared for his newly developed, more subtle
comedy of pathos. In disgust, he said, "The theatre is
where one is decapitated," and declared he "would never
write for it again."

Fortunately, Nemirovitch Danchenko persuaded him
to permit the Moscow Art Theatre to revive *The Sea Gull,*
and the result was theatre history. The young acting company, after meager success with its first two efforts, *The
Merchant of Venice* and *Tsar Fyodor,* was rescued from
oblivion, and Chekov went on to write the three later plays,
each of which is a continuing search for a meaningful and
poetic realism. The Moscow Art Theatre became known as
the House of Chekhov; the posters, the building, the lapels
of the ushers, to this day proudly wear the emblem of the
sea gull. Chekov wrote only two plays with this group ex-
pressly in mind, but they were essential to its repertory, and
prove again that the happiest circumstance in the theatre
arises when an important playwright is associated with an
enterprising group. Not only Shakespeare and the Globe,
and Molière and his own company, but repeated examples
in contemporary life—O'Neill and the Provincetown Players, Odets and the Group Theatre, Giraudoux and Jouvet,
Camus and Barrault—attest to the enrichment of the theatre
when the playwright is not subject to the demands of commercial producers.

The Dilemma of Realism

New times cry for new expression, and old forms grow
weary with overwork. Today, the realism which a century
ago had militant vigor and refreshing content has become
exhausted and repetitious. Its early success was based on
concern with psychological insight and social problems. The
universal hero of romanticism, which realism mocked, was
now confined to the living room, and audiences were able to

identify with characters on stage. The most mediocre member of society became the social archetype—Willy Loman, ordinary salesman, burdened with refrigerators and monthly down payments, was designed to encompass the universality of a Werther. Few critics raised the question of the aesthetic validity of realism. The subject matter was obvious; as an art form, it remained elusive.

The theory of realism may be reduced to a logical absurdity. It insists on "truthfulness to life" without defining what kind of truthfulness. Every artist is concerned with the search for truth, and the history of art could well be described as artists' differing responses to that search. For its innovators, "truthfulness to life" meant lifting the curtain on "a slice of life," a photographic reproduction that belongs more to social research than to the theatre. Moreover, the term itself is a contradiction, for art is a reordering of life. The artist imposes form through selection, arrangement, emphasis, a point of view. As a matter of fact, the mechanics of art become more apparent the closer one approaches reportage. In "The Living Newspaper," one of the major American contributions to dramatic form, effectiveness was achieved by careful editing, intentional accentuation, and full use of technical devices, giving conscious order to assembled evidence. The artist gives form to action that to casual observation may seem meaningless.

Lifting the curtain on "life as it is" is an impossibility. The basic problem of realism is to what extent and to what end "life as is" should be ordered. To Chekhov, the problem became "life as it is" against "life as it should be." But "life as it should be" can arise only out of a social, moral, or poetic concept and the distinctive quality of the artist. And whatever the concept, its imposition on nature supplies form. Realism meant a minimum reordering and a maximum fidelity to actuality. However, no observer can encompass the totality of life, and the presentation of "a slice" may eliminate factors that are decisive. Actuality presumes objectivity, the absence of "a point of view." But realism, even while presenting life "as it is," was injecting open advocacy of social justice. Partisanship was nothing new with playwrights, nor was it the decisive element that distinguished realism from romanticism. Hugo and Schiller cried aloud for Liberty and Human Rights, as did Ibsen, who had Lona lay her hand on Consul Bernick's shoulder and end the play with, "Truth and Freedom! These are the Pillars of Society." The point of view of the rival camps remained the same. Realism differed in bringing the protagonist down to earth where that freedom was to be obtained. Situations and setting were closer to the daily life of the audience. But whereas romanticism had borrowed the open, episodic Shakespearean structure, realism appropriated the tight Scribe suspense techniques. Neither created a form of its own.

Chekhov, artist and scientist, was uncomfortable with the artifices of realism and became the first to master a logical solution, but his long and painful effort proved to be a dead end.

When Chekhov first turned to the theatre, Ibsen was the admired hero. In a letter to Vishnevski, an actor of the Moscow Art Theatre, he wrote:[1]

> Since I am coming to Moscow soon, please set aside one seat for me for *Pillars of Society*. I want to have a look at this amazing Norwegian play and will even pay for the privilege. Ibsen is my favorite author, you know.

In the decade of the 1880's, the Ibsen-influenced period, he wrote five full-length plays, of which three have been preserved—*Platonov, Ivanov,* and *The Wood Demon*—in addition to eleven sketches and one-act pieces. All are in the conventional form. Chekhov knew that the handling of characters and situation was contrived. About *Ivanov*, he wrote:[2]

> Our modern playwrights stuff their plays exclusively with angels, villains, and buffoons—go and find these elements in the whole of Russia! . . . I wanted to be origi-

nal: there is not a single angel or villain in my play (though I could not resist the temptation of putting in a few buffoons).

And later, fearful of misinterpretation by actors, even the actors of the Moscow Art Theatre, he insisted that Lopakhin in *The Cherry Orchard* not be the stereotyped merchant, nor Vanya the conventional landlord. Of the stock types so prevalent in the nineteenth-century stage, he wrote:[3]

Retired captains with red noses, bibulous reporters, starving writers, consumptive hard-working wives, honorable young men without a single blemish, exalted maidens, kindhearted nurses—all these have been described and must be avoided like the pit.

When Chekhov returned to the theatre and began working on *The Sea Gull,* he was prepared to vary the form to create dramatic effectiveness with "life as it is." In one of his most quoted remarks, we find the following:[4]

The demand is made that the hero and the heroine should be dramatically effective. But in real life, people do not shoot themselves, or hang themselves, or make confessions of love every minute. Nor do they go around all the time making clever remarks. They spend most of their time eating, drinking, flirting, or talking stupidities—and these are the things that should be shown on the stage. A play should be written in which the people come and go, eat, talk of the weather, or play cards, not because the author wants it but because this is what happens in real life. Life on the stage should be as it really is and the people, too, should be as they are, and not stilted.

And he added significantly:

People eat their dinner, just eat their dinner, and all the time their happiness is being established or their lives are broken up.

The problem was clear. Avoid the devices used in the well-made play, create people as full as they are in life, and underscore the drama that is ever present. Since people do not "shoot themselves, or hang themselves," but spend most of their time "eating, drinking, flirting, or talking stupidities," the use of violence should be avoided. This would leave most playwrights helpless, but Chekhov progressively worked out a solution. In *Platonov,* Sasha takes poison, Platonov attempts suicide, and is finally shot by Sonya in a burst of gunplay; in *Ivanov,* Ivanov shoots himself on his wedding night; in *The Wood Demon,* George shoots himself, and the three couples are happily reunited in a contrived resolution; in *The Sea Gull,* there is a suicide off stage at the end of the play; in the final *Uncle Vanya,* there are two pistol shots but Vanya does not kill himself and also misses when he fires at the professor; in *The Three Sisters,* there is a duel but it takes place in the garden and not on stage; and finally, in *The Cherry Orchard,* there is no violence whatsoever, only the breaking of a harp string and the chopping down of the trees, sounds heard in the distance.

The Cherry Orchard, rushed to completion before his untimely death, attains that delicate artistry of seemingly no artistry, a mastery of form that conceals the mechanics. The "point of view" had been added, but gently, hidden within lines and actions. In a remark to Suvorin, Chekhov stated:[5]

> The best of them [writers of the day] are realists and depict life as it is, but because every line they write is permeated, as with a juice, by a consciousness of an aim, you feel, in addition to life as it is, also life as it should be, and it is that which delights you . . . But he who wants nothing, hopes for nothing and fears nothing, cannot be an artist.

THE CHERRY ORCHARD

The Form

The title itself is an extension of the use of symbol. *The Sea Gull* had metaphoric meaning only to Treplev and

Nina, the poet and actress. *The Cherry Orchard* is an image for every character in the play; to each it has different meaning, and each responds in terms of his own self. It is not superimposed, but rises out of the core of the action. It is the home become symbol, and in doing so explores more deeply the unsaid, reaches from the surface reality into the texture of poetry, yet always is the orchard itself, the place around which the characters move. To Mme Raynevsky, it is her youth, her memories; to Lopakhin, it is waste and unproductiveness; to all, it is a way of life. The varying levels of the symbol transform "life as it is" into dramatic poetry.

But the orchard is not the only symbol. Time itself, slow, fluid, unhurried, is encompassed between an arrival and a departure. As in other plays, an estate is sold, but now the composition is more compact, with severe economy, the four acts in symphonic arrangement: the first act—arrival, nostalgia for the past, the nursery with memories of childhood, then quiet and slumber. The second movement is reflective, in the twilight of the autumnal cold—thoughts of the future, the sounds of the broken harpstring in the distance, the strong silences, the nearby playing of a guitar. The third movement is a scherzo—the dance at the house, the dismal party a sad replica of the fashionable gaiety of former days; the announcement of the sale of the estate. The final movement is the departure—the closing of the house and the sound of the axes cutting down the cherry trees. And always weaving in and out is the minor theme with its interlocking images of sleep, cold, peace, and work as the balm of tired souls.

The final factor in the structural innovations is the abandonment of linear development of plot. So long as this borrowed formula of Scribe and Ibsen was used, then the inner logic demanded a succession of emotional crises, the rise to physical violence, and the inevitable peripeteia, or reversal of fortune. The development in *The Cherry Or-*

chard is like a series of inscribed circles in constant motion, tangential to one another at varying and differing points, a spatial arrangement in time, with the counterpoint the intricate revelation of character as each acts, talks about himself and is talked about by others, and responds to the central symbol. In the traditional realistic play of a craftsman like Lillian Hellman, the explosion comes as the tensions below the surface are revealed, and the entire play is the accumulation of pressures prior to the climactic outburst. The Aristotelian principle requires a tragic flaw in character, which precipitates the downfall, accompanied by the recognition that in Butcher's translation of the *Poetics* is "a change from ignorance to knowledge producing love or hate between the persons destined by the poet for good or bad fortune." Chekhov is the very opposite.

The "recognition" is now the deeper awareness of what was already known, as it is "in life." The inability of Mme Raynevsky and her brother Gaev to face reality leads us to suspect that they will not be saved from financial ruin and that the cherry orchard will be sold, and so it is; and we suspect that Varya, too concerned with her keys and domesticity, will not marry Lopakhin, and she does not, and he remains even more inarticulate in her presence. Even for Lopakhin there is no "reversal of fortune"; he is already a successful merchant, and with the acquisition of the orchard becomes still more wealthy. The change is in the effect the symbol—the cherry orchard and its sale—has on each one, after which life goes on, or better, it slips away.

The careful, technical perfection is not apparent and creates the impression of formlessness. Moreover, none of the people is of heroic stature, nor is there a main character. The entire group, a way of life, is the protagonist. The undramatic "life as it is" is made dramatic, and the proof is the performance itself and its repeated success with audiences, who are not jolted by shock but moved by compassion, admitted into an enclosed world and overwhelmed by the totality of experiences.

Bernard Shaw, who in *Heartbreak House* attempted a play in the Chekhovian manner, came closest to the structure of music, but his counterpoint is of ideas not of people. John Howard Lawson is thus correct in saying, "Shaw's characters discuss the social system; Chekhov's characters *are* the social system."

Once resolved, the dilemma presented new problems, and Chekhov could go no further. The form was distinct and permitted a *Cherry Orchard,* but not its repetition. He himself recognized its finality. He had in mind several plays on biblical themes in varying experimental techniques.

For the theatre after Chekhov, the problem was the extension of realism in combination with aspects of romanticism, a fusion of the two, in the manner of Giraudoux. In its resolution lies the possibility of a major advance in the contemporary drama.

The Comedy of Chekhov

Though the Moscow Art Theatre became known as the House of Chekhov, the playwright was not happy with Stanislavsky's interpretation. In a letter to the writer, Alexander Tikhonov, he wrote:[6]

> You tell me that people cry at my plays. I've heard others say the same. But that is not why I wrote them. It is Alexey [Stanislavsky] who made my characters into crybabies.

More vehement and more devastating, if true, was his complaint to his wife during rehearsals of *The Cherry Orchard:*[7]

> Nemirovitch Danchenko and Alexey positively see in my play something I have not written, and I am ready to bet anything you like that neither of them has ever read my play through carefully.

And Stanislavsky had the aplomb to say:

Right up to his death, Chekhov could not reconcile himself to the idea that *The Three Sisters* and *The Cherry Orchard* were sorrowful tragedies of Russian life.

Recently, an effort has been made to transform the "brooding despair" into comedy, and Chekhov would have been aghast, for now the reverse danger exists. The plays have been done with excessive clowning, the characters becoming boisterous buffoons—equally foreign to Chekhov's intention.

No one would deny that Chekhov was writing comedy. *The Sea Gull* and *The Cherry Orchard* bear the specific subtitle "A Comedy in Four Acts." But the word "comedy" is of course an elusive term. It includes everything from Aristophanic phallic pageantry to Hollywood gags, from Giraudoux's complex fantasy to Genet's sardonic nightmares. So elastic is the term that definitions are avoided. In looking for a common denominator, the assumption is made that comedies are plays in which major characters do not die, but this distinction is quite meaningless. Another definition holds that in comedy characters do achieve their goals, in happy resolution, and such is definitely not the case in any of Chekhov's plays. But if one assumes in comedy, as with Aristotle, baser characters whose faults contain something ridiculous, not painful or destructive, then Chekov falls more closely into line. However, like most great artists he resists any single classification. His comic art encompasses burlesque, broad farce, and gentle pathos. His short stories, another key to understanding him as a playwright, are likewise not of one pattern, but range from the earlier popular humor to "The Peasants" and "Ward No. 6," wherein, as in the later plays, he had arrived at a comedy delicate and lifelike, close to sorrow, containing farce and subtle irony, the ludicrous and the pathetic, but in which the whole is a comedy uniquely and irreplaceably Chekhov—a *comédie humaine*.

A few scenes from two plays suffice to indicate the

specific quality of Chekhovian comedy. From *Uncle Vanya,* the finely balanced love scene in Act Three is an excellent example. A touch of clowning can throw it into farce, and overcritical seriousness into tragedy. Sonya has foolishly confessed her love for Dr. Astrov to Yelena, who volunteers to speak to him in Sonya's behalf. Alone with the doctor, Yelena acquits herself of her mission quickly and ineffectively. When Astrov says he does not love Sonya, Yelena adds the one condition Sonya would be least likely to accept —that the doctor leave the house and never come back. He, however, has fallen passionately in love with Yelena, and interprets her motives as "a sly method of entrapping him," calling her the "bird of prey" (the Ibsen symbol). He will go away, but not until he is her willing victim. Yelena is taken aback by a situation that has gone too far, even though she has toyed with the idea of the doctor as the only attractive man in the area. She tries to withdraw, but the doctor *puts his arm around her waist.** He has again found his feelings, his ability to love, his joy in beauty. *He kisses her; at that instant Vanya enters carrying a bunch of roses for Yelena, and stands still in the doorway.* Yelena, *not seeing Vanya,* says, "Let me go!" *as she lays her head on Astrov's chest.* Astrov *holds her by the waist* and pleads, "Come to the plantation tomorrow . . . at two o'clock . . . Yes? You'll come?" What might have happened between the two is cut short as Yelena, *seeing Vanya,* now screams, "Let me go!" and *in great confusion goes to the window.* Before her next line, there must be a long pause. Astrov is not aware of Vanya's presence. Yelena has seen him over Astrov's shoulder. The doctor turns, sees Vanya, and moves away to regain his composure. Vanya stands there, the posies in his hand. The tension is broken by her next line: "This is awful!"—a maudlin understatement. Here is the usual situation of intrigue drama, this time the triangle without the husband.

* Words in italics on this and the following pages are Chekhov's stage directions.

The heroic protagonist precipitates a violent fight, challenges to a duel, or utters a *bon mot*. Vanya *drops the roses on a chair*. He is lost, confused, and *wipes his face and neck with a handkerchief,* muttering, "Never mind . . . no . . . never mind." Astrov says the most banal nonsense: "The weather is not so bad today . . ." and continues to prate about the weather. The other two pay no attention to him, so he walks out of the room.

Yelena *runs quickly up to Vanya,* not to console him nor to explain what has transpired, but to insist nervously, "You will do what you can to see that my husband and I leave here today! Do you hear? Today!" Again thinking only of herself. She waits impatiently. He says nothing, then slowly: "What? Oh, yes . . . very well." Now that he has spoken, from the agony of a man twice deceived, from deep within a shock more brutal than the awareness of the professor's duplicity, from the lonely heartbreak of an all too human figure, he adds, "I saw it all, Hélène . . . all . . ." How Chaplinesque! And the touch of her name in French! She ignores his reference and repeats, "I must get away from here today!" The professor and the others enter at this point. What a moment to begin the family council!

As they take their places, the professor blandly announces that he plans to sell the estate and invest the money in securities to yield a higher income for himself. This means negating all the work that Vanya and Sonya have done, and depriving the grandmother and the others of a place to live. Vanya, still trembling from the scene with Yelena, rises in fury and lets loose on Serebryakov all his previous failures to speak and act. He denounces the professor violently, shouts that the property legally belongs to Sonia, and in a blind rage, face to face with Serebryakov, says, "You are my bitterest enemy!" Yelena screams that she wants to leave the house immediately, the grandmother orders Vanya to obey so great a man of letters, Sonya huddles with her nurse for comfort. The professor, flustered by Vanya's tirade, calls him "a nonentity," and Telyegin, unable to bear the hurt to both, rushes out *in violent agitation*. Vanya, with the prophetic words, "You will remember me!" stalks out *through the middle door*. In *The Wood Demon*, he uttered the same cry and went out to commit suicide. Not so in the developed comedy of the later version. Sonya pleads with her father to try to understand her uncle and all the sacrifices he has made; Yelena begs him to go and appease Vanya. The professor leaves the room, followed by his wife. Suddenly a shot is heard off stage and then Yelena's scream. In dashes Serebryakov, *staggering with terror,* shouting, "Hold him! He is out of his mind!" He scurries to cover as Vanya and Yelena appear in the middle doorway. She struggles to take the revolver from him. He frees himself, runs into the room *seeking Serebryakov*. What a scene for melodrama!—the only violence in the entire play. Vanya shoots . . . and after a pause exclaims with deep humiliation, "Missed! Missed again!" Then, furiously, "Damn it!" He flings the revolver to the floor and *sinks exhausted into a chair,* muttering *in despair:* "What am I doing?" Yelena hysterically shouts, ". . . Take me away! . . . Kill me . . . I can't stay here!" Sonia whispers *softly,* "Nurse, darling," as the curtain comes down. How can this be taken otherwise than as comedy? The audience sinks back with relief . . . and laughs, laughs out of discomfort at Vanya's terrible inability to succeed in anything, even in hitting his *bitterest enemy* at close range. It is one of the most touching scenes in all theatre, comedy raised to the level of human pathos and suffering, all the characters victims of their inadequacies.

The final scene of the play has been most vulnerable to conflicting interpretations, for it lends itself to what one wants to find. After the professor, Yelena, and Astrov have taken their farewells, Sonya and Vanya are seated at the desk checking the accounts of the estate: ". . . Lenten oil, February sixteenth, twenty pounds . . ." Telyegin *softly plays on the guitar,* the old nurse *yawns* and *knits a stocking,* Vanya's mother *makes notes on the margin of her pamphlet*—all as they were at the beginning of the play. Sonya tells Vanya they will continue to work for others and have rest after they die, and *through her tears wipes away his tears with her handkerchief.* "Poor Uncle Vanya, you are crying. You have had no joy in your life, but wait . . ." Certainly not the usual end for comedy—tears, resignation, and soft music.

In the Soviet Union, the scene has meant joy in work, creative fulfillment through useful labor. Magarshack says it cannot be regarded as denoting the sad continuity of frustrated lives, but is a play of "courage and hope," in that the religious fervor of Sonya can now be devoted completely to others. Neither interpretation is valid if one does not divorce the scene from the totality of Chekhov's art. It is a sad scene, but the implications are comic. Sonya has no choice. Her religion is her only hold on survival. She can hardly be more devoted to others than she has been. She wanted Astrov, and missed all opportunities to get him by her ludicrous inadequacies. Vanya knows his life has been a miserable failure. Even his one good hate has failed him. But what can a good man do but go on—the long walk down the lonely road. So the two sit and check the pounds of Lenten oil.

"I am describing life, not blank despondency."

As for *The Cherry Orchard,* Chekhov wrote to his wife that he was at work on a play that would "definitely be funny, very funny, at least in intention," and later, of the finished script he said, "It is not a drama, but a comedy; in places even a farce." Typical is the love scene between Lopakhin and Varya near the end of the play. These two should get married. They are in love and well suited to each other. He has money and is a good man. She has the education he lacks, and the practicality to assist him on his way up in the world—a perfect middle-class home in the making. Moreover, she is leaving to become a housekeeper. Why not for him? Mme Raynevsky, as all are preparing to leave the cherry orchard after the sale of the estate, says to him, "I dreamed of marrying her to you, and everything seemed to indicate that you would get married," and adds, "She loves you . . . and I don't know why it is, you seem to avoid each other." He replies that he is willing, and "if there is still time," he is ready to "settle it straight off" and make her an offer. Mme Raynevsky calls Varya and leaves them alone. What follows is some eighteen lines of printed dialogue, a half-page, yet rich with the basic elements of Chekhov's comedy.

Lopakhin stands *looking at his watch,* waiting. Evidently he has other business to attend to and the affair with Varya must be done quickly. *Behind the door, smothered laughter and whispering, and at last, enter Varya.* The girls have been telling her about Lopakhin's intentions and probably teasing her. It is clear that both Lopakhin and Varya know what their meeting is about. What happens? She does not look at him directly, but starts searching among the boxes and packages, *looking a long while over the things.* Not a word is said. At last she breaks the silence with, "It is strange. I can't find it anywhere." She is still moving around, not looking at him, doing nothing to precipitate "an offer." His first words are, "What are you looking for?" The ice is broken, but in the wrong place. He has seized the opportunity to avoid the issue. Varya replies, "I packed it myself, and I can't remember." She is avoiding him and doesn't want to. Here Chekhov indicates *a pause.* What a taut and ludicrous moment as they now look at each other, quite unable to return to the subject of love or marriage! The fumbling with the packages has destroyed the mood, and so he says, "Where are you going to go now, Varvara Mikhailovna?" He accepts her departure, the very thing he wanted to prevent, and he makes it worse by addressing her by her formal name. The rest of the scene is a mounting tension of

commonplace comments, his final remark being about the
weather: "This time last year we had snow already . . . three
degrees of frost." Varya replies, "I haven't looked." Again *a
pause*. Will either one say something? She does. "And besides, our thermometer is broken." Details of domesticity
destroying her happiness. *A pause* again—the final one. Another chance. Will he come through? From outside, someone
calls him, and *as though he had long been expecting this
summons*, he answers and rushes out. *Varya sits down on the
floor, lays her head on a bundle of clothes, and sobs quietly.*[8]

Critics have talked of Lopakhin's peasant soul and his
innate fear of a woman his social superior. It is doubtful
if such was ever part of Chekhov's thinking. Lopakhin is
an accepted member of the household. In the first scene of
the play, his future marriage with Varya is an accepted fact.
He has been urged by the mother to ask for her hand. He
knows Varya would accept him. As a man of business he can
be decisive, but in tender and emotional matters he is inarticulate. Each hurts the other without wanting to, for
neither is able to achieve what he wants. As in all of Chekhov's comedies, the characters miss their opportunity. In a
sense they are fools, inadequate and overwhelmingly compassionate. This is what Chekhov meant by "life as it is." We
do not say the right word. We do not grasp the right moment. Life passes us by, and we are left—never completely
defeated, still struggling on—with our hopes as painful
memories.

Another example is the controversial scene in Act Three
when Lopakhin announces that he has bought the cherry
orchard. In most productions, Lopakhin, as Chekhov indicated, is the central character of the play, but this scene
has been variously interpreted in line with directors' prejudices. In the Soviet Union, he is made to be the spokesman
of a rising class, the progressive instrument of the once oppressed serf overthrowing the idle aristocracy. Another interpretation makes him a boasting fool, the insensitive

middle-class businessman lording it over his social superiors. Chekhov wrote, "Lopakhin is a merchant, of course, but he is a very decent person in every sense. He must behave with perfect decorum, like an educated man, with no petty ways or tricks of any sort." In the same letter to Stanislavsky, urging him to take the role, he added that Varya, a "serious and religious girl . . . would not be in love with a mere money-grubber." Why not take the playwright at his word? Chekhov was interested in people, not in political overtones.

When Lopakhin enters, the party is going on, a shabby imitation of former balls. He has come from the auction and is bursting with the news of his purchase, yet almost at once he is hit over the head by Varya, who intended the blow for Epikhodov. Mme Raynevsky asks him *with agitation* whether the sale has taken place. He wants to shout it to the world—a perfectly understandable behavior—but he is considerate and *embarrassed, afraid of betraying his joy,* and so evades an answer. Mme Raynevsky's brother Gaev, whose life has been part of the cherry orchard, enters, and she *impatiently* asks him to tell the news. *He does not answer her,* but bursts into tears and turns to the old servant Firs, and tells him about anchovies and herrings! When the sound of billiards is heard in the next room, the most pleasant sound in the world to him, Gaev stops weeping . . . and goes off to change his clothes! How more ludicrous can he be! Lopakhin had deferred to him, so now Lopakhin is the only one present who can answer. He says briefly, "It is sold." Mme Raynevsky asks, "Who bought it?" and his reply is again controlled and brief, "I bought it." Here Chekhov indicates *a pause.* Lopakhin has not been boastful nor tried to exhibit his new power. On the contrary, he has exercised remarkable restraint. But when Mme Raynevsky receives the news in tears and leans *against an armchair, unable to stand up,* and Varya *flings the keys on the floor,* he can hold back no longer. They have hurt him without meaning to. He will now hurt them out of his own goodness. He shouts to all to listen; he tells the details of the sale, he dances, he laughs, he stamps with his feet—he says all the wrong things, and he is wild with joy, even as Mme Raynevsky is *weeping bitterly*. He goes over to her and says, "Why didn't you listen to me? My poor friend!" and he bursts into tears too! He had wanted to help her—to help them all—but it just hasn't worked out. The great moment of victory has turned to farce, and Chekhov has Lopakhin, on the way out, *trip over a table, almost upsetting the candelabra* and nonplused, shout, "I can pay for everything!" Yes, he is insensitive to beauty (the symbol of the cherry orchard), but not because he is a boor; because money is his symbol, the symbol that has transformed his life. Money is power, and it has meant that he who "used to run around barefoot in winter," whose father "was not even allowed in the kitchen," is now lord and master of the estate. He is delirious with happiness, but his joy is based on what destroys those he loves. Again Chekhov, so warmly human, has given us the deep and disturbing comedy of pathos.

How was it possible for Stanislavsky, with the author on hand for consultations, and the author's wife an important member of the company, to distort Chekhov's plays? In an angry protest Chekhov wrote, "Take my *Cherry Orchard*. Is it my *Cherry Orchard?* With the exception of two or three parts, nothing in it is mine. I am describing life, ordinary life, and not blank despondency."

The "blank despondency" interpretation was a result of the success of *The Sea Gull,* the first play of Chekhov's produced by the Moscow Art Theatre. Stanislavsky had found it a perfect vehicle for his method of acting, which lent itself more readily to the serious portrayal of society in decay, lives misspent, and dreams unfulfilled. Thereafter he directed all of Chekhov's plays in the same gloomy style. Critics have fallen into line. They write of dynamic personalities helpless in a static environment, and Ronald Peacock, discussing *The Art of Drama,* deals with Chekhov as the negation of the dramatic. All agree that the form is unique. Why not then consider the comic element—an integral part of his art—as likewise unique? In comedy, characters as a rule are one-sided, very much as in romantic drama. Motivation is restricted to broad strokes. The protagonist has a single compulsive quality—a "comic flaw." He may be a *nouveau riche* who wants to absorb all aristocratic culture in one gulp, a charming old lady who likes to murder young men painlessly, a bachelor who insists on telling the truth at all times, an old man who wants a young wife, or a young girl who wants an old husband—and the situations are built around the dominant idiosyncracy.

Peacock supports this thesis, saying, "Comic personages, always near to caricature, appear as schematic human beings built up on one or two outstanding traits of physique or moral character or intellectual complexion." He adds, "The effort of the actor then contributes to the transparent fantasy. He is not required to sustain a convincing picture of a possible human situation, but to be effective . . . the comic actor must from his first entry be a calculated image."

Chekhov violates all these rules. His characters are not "schematic human beings," but multidimensional, seen from all angles, as fully drawn psychologically as the characters of Ibsen or Strindberg, and they remain "ordinary people." Perhaps here lies the basis of Stanislavsky's dilemma. The more deeply he became involved in the complexity of characterization, the more he lost the possibility of the comic. For the actor, to whom the "comic flaw" is a handle, it is doubly difficult to be ordinary and human.

Chekhov's people do not resolve their problems, but have to go on more aware of these problems. In *Uncle Vanya,* no one gets what he wants; no one changes his fortune. Serebryakov does not get the estate or the money he wanted; Astrov goes on unable to love; Sonya does not marry the doctor; Yelena is not relieved of the boredom with her husband; Vanya still supports the despised professor. It is a story of missed opportunities. Each person ends more isolated than before, and this is a key to the comedy, a comedy of inept people failing to achieve, of sensitive people surrounded by stupid ones, of good, selfless souls versus the self-centered; a comedy in which tears are always close to laughter. Some of the people do try actively to change the situation, but not with courageous dignity—yet with enough courage and dignity to be human and ludicrous. Does failure mean "blank despondency" and pessimism? To a certain extent, yes, but as a life element within the comic. Chekhov wrote, in a letter to Tikhonov in 1902:

> All I wanted was to say honestly to people: Take a look at yourselves and see how bad and dreary your lives are! The important thing is that people should realize just that, for if they do they will definitely create another and better life for themselves.

The final phrase may be undue optimism, but it is true that our own values are often not related to reality. There is laughter in the awareness of the absurd.

5. *The Drama of Discussion —George Bernard Shaw*

HEARTBREAK HOUSE

ON DECEMBER 9, 1892, Mr. J. T. Grein, the producer, offered a play at the Royalty Theatre in London that aroused greater furor than the private performance of *A Doll's House* three years earlier. On opening night, the Liberals and Independents "applauded furiously on principle,"[1] and the playgoing carriage trade "hooted frantically on the same ground." The author appeared before the curtain and made a speech urging support of the "New Drama." The play folded after two performances, but the uproar over it raged in the press for weeks, well fed with ammunition supplied by the playwright. The play was *Widowers' Houses;* the author, the thirty-six-year-old critic, pamphleteer, and unsuccessful novelist, George Bernard Shaw.

Lack of initial success did not deter Shaw. He enjoyed the notoriety and insisted publicly that the "English are only too anxious to recognize a man of genius if somebody will kindly point him out to them," a role he was eager to assume for himself. Grein's Independent Theatre, a group comparable to the Théâtre Libre of Antoine in Paris, had been launched to bring to England the realistic drama of the Continent, but one could not go on forever producing Ibsen, and Shaw had offered a native masterpiece, a "work of art pretending to be a better made play for actual use and long wear on the boards than anything that has yet been turned out by the patent constructive machinery." His boasted judgment has proved correct. Though one of the weakest of Shaw's works, *Widowers' Houses* has since been performed repeatedly in most countries of the world. Far more important, however, is the fact that it marked the advent of a powerful and influential figure in the theatre and that its opening night may well be considered the most revolutionary act in the English stage since the morality plays gave way to the robustness of the Renaissance.

Wit and Wealth

Widowers' Houses is a violent attack on Victorian morality. Presumably it deals with slum housing, but the problem is approached from the point of view of the rich. An attractive but impoverished doctor, Harry Trench, re-

lated to the aristocracy, falls in love with Blanche, daughter
of Sartorius, a self-made man who owns considerable real
estate in the poorer sections of London. Blanche has all the
education money can buy, and her father insists that she be
accepted socially without reservation. But when Harry discovers that his future father-in-law's income—and what
eventually will be his own inheritance—is derived from exploitation of the oppressed, he refuses to go ahead with the
deal. This is quite the usual situation of the current boy-
meets-girl melodrama. Sartorius could as well have been a
highwayman, a bank robber, or a peddler of dope. Instead
he lives by robbing the poor. Blanche should either declare
her love and follow Harry in his poverty, or Harry should
come into a fortune and defy the father. Instead, Blanche
scorns Harry's delicate scruples, and when Harry learns that
his own meager income is derived from the same source, he
declares his love all over again, and they decide to get married.

The play was attacked as "a rather silly play by a rather
clever man"; a "revolting picture of middle class life" which
aims "to show with Zolaesque exactitude that the middle
class even to its womanhood is brutal at heart." This had
been said of Ibsen, and Shaw was clearly following in the
tradition. But the critics added, "A discussion with open
doors of the pros and cons of slum landlordism." Shaw
answered them unequivocally. The point of view in the play
was "impartially socialistic," he said, and went on, "It is
impossible for any fictionist, dramatic or other, to make
true pictures of modern society without some knowledge of
the economic anatomy of it," and urged his critics to take
a course in political economy. Slum housing was only the
vehicle. The author was hitting at the very core of present-
day life. All wealth is thievery. It can be accumulated only
at the expense of the poor. The aristocracy hold mortgages,
and Sartorius and his agent Lickcheese do the dirty work.
Harry marries Blanche Sartorius because he realizes there is

no other way out. Her father is more honorable in that he is more honest. Harry had never bothered to find out the source of his own income.

Lastly, *Widowers' Houses* was not the frock-coated, beetle-browed Ibsen. It was gay, full of laughter and irrepressible wit. The author was a potent combination of Ibsen, Molière, and Henry George; the three factors of wit, socialism, and discussion he was to develop to the point where they became a meaningful extension of the modern theatre.

The First Decade—1890–1900

Shaw had found his forum, and for the next sixty years he turned out plays with remarkable persistency. The first decade is marked by a series of popular melodramas in the Shavian manner (*Arms and the Man, Devil's Disciple*) and two more important plays which advanced the Ibsen technique (*Mrs. Warren's Profession,* and *Candida*).

Whereas Ibsen was interested in the moral rehabilitation of man, Shaw dealt with the economic conditions that alter human relations. Poverty was the dread curse and any means to avoid it were justifiable. In *Mrs. Warren's Profession* Vivie, educated as a lady, with full regard for respectability and social standing, discovers that her mother's wealth is derived from operating a chain of successful bordellos. It is the same theme as in *Widowers' Houses,* with prostitution substituted for slum housing. In the one powerful scene of the play, Mrs. Warren answers her daughter's indignant questions with superb self-righteousness:

> . . . Where would we be now if we'd minded the clergyman's foolishness? Scrubbing floors for one and sixpence a day and nothing to look forward to but the workhouse infirmary. Don't you be led astray by people who don't know the world, my girl. The only way for a woman to provide for herself decently is for her to be good to some man that can afford to be good to her.

Shaw intended to shock his Victorian audience, and he carried it one step further when Vivie, now convinced, shouts in admiration:

> You are a wonderful woman—you are stronger than all England.

But though he did not hesitate to present the most ridiculous extremes of social hypocrisy, Shaw, at the conclusion of the play, returned society to its accepted foundations. Vivie rejects her mother in the last act and finds a less repugnant method of avoiding poverty.

Candida is the best known of the plays of Shaw's nonage, mainly because our most distinguished actresses have essayed the title role. Though the play follows more closely the tight Ibsen structure than any of Shaw's other works, it also marks a growing perfection in his own devices, discussion as drama, and inversion as wit, both of which make interpretation difficult and understanding consciously subtle. The apparent story is simple and conventional. Morell, the minister, is married to the gracious and capable Candida. The poet Marchbanks falls in love with her and we have the oft-repeated domestic triangle. But the Shavian variations are significant. Candida is the modern emancipated woman, the Hedda, who in English middle-class life has many outlets for her energy—mainly, managing her home and husband. She is the best the world has to offer, the epitome of the charming mother-wife, the contribution of English society to modern civilization. Her husband Morell is no stuffed shirt like Tesman. He is handsome and courageous, a Socialist who believes in the decency and equality of all people, who fights against injustice, and who is happy in his well-run home. Here, as in Ibsen, is the modern family, the cornerstone of society. Marchbanks, the intruder, is a derelict, a vagabond, a poet, a lost soul, and like other such characters in Shaw's work, a member of the aristocracy. But he is no serious romantic rival to Morell, for he is fifteen years younger than Candida and not a man with whom she would ever run away. The play is a series of discussions, mainly between the two men. They are the contrasting protagonists, each defending his philosophy of life and his love for Candida. Both should be strongly portrayed for the battle to be brilliant and equal. The meaning is rarely evident in production because the actress, as a rule, dominates the play.

In the final scene, when Candida demands that the issue be settled by each of them bidding for her, Morell offers all that bourgeois society considers decent and honorable:

> My strength for your defense, my honesty for your surety, my ability and industry for your livelihood, and my authority and position for your dignity.

Marchbanks can only bid:

> My weakness. My desolation. My heart's need.

It is a beautifully worked out finale to their three-act debate. Candida chooses "significantly":

> I give myself to the weaker of the two.

The poet flees into the night, and the married couple preserve the sanctity of the home.

On the surface the traditional has been upheld, even if it was on the verge of tottering for a moment, but closer examination reveals that the Shavian inversion has now been sharpened to an almost diabolical edge. The established home has triumphed, but it is a hollow victory. The stalwart husband is the weaker of the two men. The helpless youth, the inexperienced poet, is the stronger. As a result, the once harmonious marriage situation has been altered. Morell's declaration was a bit pompous, and now, his confidence undermined, he must continue to live with himself as well as with his wife. Morell is the Shavian idea, the Fabian Socialist who fights for social reform, dignity for all men. He is well-dressed, well-spoken, and a likely member of Shaw's own Fabian group, but he has been so concerned with the ills of society that he has not seen them in his own home. His wife has been nurse, cook, protector, button-sewer—the worker on whom his entire structure rests. He, the minister, has misunderstood the nature of the marriage contract. His strength is a fiction. He is thoroughly dependent upon the capable Candida, whom he loves, but with whom he has lost the poetry of love.

Marchbanks, on the other hand, is a romantic conception of Shaw's. Freedom from the enslavement of domesticity lies with the divine poet who rises above practicality. For him, life is nobler than "onions." He is the unique individual of Ibsen, the genius who is strongest because he stands alone. Yet his traumatic experience with Morell teaches him to do without love, without women. The secret in the poet's heart is that he can live without happiness. Both men have been drastically inverted as a result of their debate, yet the inversion has left them sad representatives of what they think they are.

More delightfully perverse is Candida. Always self-possessed, full of the instinctive wisdom of the home-builder, she turns out to be quite lacking in the faithful stability of English womanhood. She spurs on both men, yet she alone does not change. Candidly, she has been a bit of a vixen. Her treatment of her husband, under the unassailable masquerade of the "good woman," has been delicately dishonorable. She has seen to it that he never had a pretty secretary; she taunts him with the possibility of offering herself to Marchbanks, and in the presence of her lover requests a theatrical decision. Morell ends by falling flat on his lifelong illusions, leaving his wife queen of the household. He who would run the world cannot run his own house, his wife most subtly reminds him. To the poet she has been equally cruel, egging him on, then reminding him that he is fifteen years her junior, implying that anything serious between them had always been out of the question.

Yet everyone loves her. She is perfect. Her vices have made her more interesting as a woman. As a paragon of virtue, she was unendurable. Now she has revived interest in her marriage, and seduced her husband into courting her all over again. For this, women everywhere have worshiped her.

The Second Decade—1900–1910

With the turn of the century, Shaw found himself a successful playwright, well secured from the poverty he dreaded. His marriage and his plays had brought him enough money so that he could indulge in experimenting with the logic of his method.

One of his most ambitious efforts was *Man and Superman*. John Tanner, a composite of Bernard Shaw and Hyndman, the socialist leader of England, is an MIRC (Member of the Idle Rich Class), owns a fast sports car, has a chauffeur with whom he discusses philosophy, and writes revolutionary tracts. He would pursue science with the undivided discipline of a mind that is trying to bring enlightenment to the world, but instead he is himself pursued by Ann Whiteside, the eternal feminine, the goddess mother, the physical drive of sex. When John, despite his ability to dodge an answer and a woman, finally succumbs, the Life Force has overwhelmed them both. The play is a sparkling debate between the Passion for Truth and the Passion for Motherhood, for Ann has chosen the scientist John as the father of her Superman. Shaw, who prided himself on being the incarnation of the modern trinity—Socialist, atheist, and vegetarian—unfolds a peculiar justification of God, but his God is called the Life Force, an ineluctable power which is a combination of physical love, metaphysical disputation, and eugenics, beyond the reason of Tanner and the earthly drive of Ann. Its ectoplasmic image resembles more the Devil, and T. S. Eliot labeled "the potent ju-ju" of the Life Force a "gross superstition." Its purpose, like Solveig's in the last act of *Peer Gynt*, is to

see to it that there are more babies. But with Shaw they
must be better babies, ideologically preconceived.

The discussion is clearest in the Don Juan Interlude
of Act Three. The scene takes place in Hell, where for
more than an hour the Devil, an able advocate for himself,
Don Juan Tenorio (John Tanner), Ana de Ulloa (Ann
Whiteside), and the Statue (her father) discuss good and
evil, punishment, love, and happiness. It is the talkiest piece
in all dramatic literature. Though man, free from the womb,
may pursue intellectual interests, woman, creator of man,
must lure him back to re-enact her function. The genius is
the triumphant male achievement who rises beyond woman,
for though woman preserves life, genius is conscious of life.
But he discovers that whereas he advocates the Life Force
as its high priest, woman *is* the Life Force. It is a complex
variation on clever girl catches unwilling man.

In *Major Barbara,* Shaw returned to the jousts. Though
he continued to make genuflections to the Life Force in his
later plays, the anarchy of twentieth-century politics, with
its threat of world annihilation, forced him to treat immediate reality. In *Major Barbara* he is again concerned with
modern industrial society and the nonsense that surrounds
the virtue of poverty. In a lengthy preface, he wrote:

> Security, the chief pretence of civilization, cannot exist
> where the worst dangers, the danger of poverty, hangs over
> everyone's head, and where the alleged protection of our
> persons from violence is only an accidental result of the
> existence of a police force whose real business is to force
> the poor man to see his children starve while the idle
> people overfeed pet dogs with the money that might feed
> and clothe them.

And because he dealt with poverty, Shaw chose as his protagonist a millionaire, one who recognizes in "money the
first need and in poverty the vilest sin of man and society."
But Andrew Undershaft is not only wealthy; he has amassed

his wealth by manufacturing armaments, for "having grasped the fact that poverty is a crime," he knows that:

> When society offered the alternative of poverty or a lucrative trade in death and destruction, it offered him not a choice between opulent villainy and humble virtue, but between energetic enterprise and cowardly infamy."

Thus, Undershaft is the first Shavian inversion in the play. He is no villainous capitalist, but attractive, intelligent, and above all, honest. He is the businessman's morality, scrupulously direct, all the soporific platitudes removed. To him, money:

> represents health, strength, honor, generosity and beauty as conspicuously as the want of it represents illness, weakness, disgrace, meanness and ugliness.

And with his devastating logic he can prove it.

Barbara Undershaft is a major in the Salvation Army. She ignores money. She would save men by appealing to their common spiritual brotherhood. Her father would destroy men by inciting their common lust for wealth. Both are on fire with their gods: he with Mammon, she with the God of Love. With their first meeting in a long time, the conflict of opposites is on. Each would win the other for his god. To Barbara, the conversion of her father would be a major victory. To Undershaft, the bubbling, fresh, girlish personality of his daughter is wasted on a futile cause. He asks:

> Have you ever saved a maker of cannon?

Barbara is willing to try. They make a pact. Undershaft will visit the Salvation Shelter if Barbara will visit the munition works. Leading up to one of Shaw's superbly balanced aphorisms, Undershaft asks: "Where is your shelter?"

BARBARA: In West Ham. At the sign of the cross. Ask anybody in Canning Town. Where are your works?

UNDERSHAFT: In Perivale St. Andrews. At the sign of the sword. Ask anybody in Europe.

The second act is at the shelter. The souls Barbara saves are a sad indictment of the working class. Poverty drives them to accept religion and coffee. Undershaft, true to his word, comes to see, but the debate shifts to him and Adolphus Cusins, professor of Greek. Cusins is in love with Barbara and beats a drum to be near her. Andrew would even play a tenor trombone for the same purpose. The young translator of Euripides is the poet, the collector of religions, even the religion of Undershaft. He is the cultural, just as Undershaft is the economic, heritage of mankind. Barbara and his occasional ecstatic beatings of the drum are his Dionysian release, but he and Undershaft have a common purpose, the winning of Barbara.

For Cusins to win Barbara is difficult; for Undershaft it is quite simple. For the Salvation Army can carry on only with money, and they can get it from Bodger, the maker of whiskey, and Undershaft, the maker of cannon. When Andrew supplies whatever amount is requested, the rock on which Barbara stands crumbles beneath her. As she says:

> I was safe with an infinite wisdom watching me, an army marching to Salvation . . . and at a stroke of your pen in a cheque book, I stood alone; and the heavens were empty.

Barbara now knows that all is eventually Undershaft. He would even supply her with a newer and better religion, one that fits the facts. He would ruthlessly scrap anything that doesn't make money, as he would "an aerial battleship that turns out just a hairsbreadth wrong." Under these conditions, Barbara can no longer save souls. She takes off her uniform and goes to visit the factory.

In Act Three, Undershaft presses his triumph. His logic is incontestable. He says:

You can't tell me the bursting strain of a ten-inch gun, which is a very simple matter; but you all think you can tell me the bursting strain of a man under temptation. You daren't handle high explosives; but you're all ready to handle honesty and truth and justice and the whole duty of man, and kill one another at that game. What a country! What a world!

He, Undershaft, at least conforms to the world. But he can go on only if he has a successor, if there is a replacement to continue his line. He cannot find one in his own blood, for it has been corrupted by the very wealth he amassed; he needs as manager a foundling, one who has known no parentage, who can acquire the Undershaft philosophy and improve it. He discovers his man in Adolphus Cusins. What a triumphant future for cannon! The professor of religion wedded to the exploitation of death; the Euripidean, the representative of beauty and poetry, now business executive. And poor Barbara, major in the army of spiritual love, is to be the wife of a multimillionaire munitions-maker. It is the most ironic inversion of Shaw's own socialist thinking. He had intended to call the play *Andrew Undershaft's Profession,* in striking parallel to *Mrs. Warren's Profession.*

The Third Decade—1910–1920. Disillusionment

Wit and laughter and sparkling deviltry were futile weapons against the forces that drove a world to furious self-slaughter in 1914. The Undershafts were in the saddle, for the Cusinses had failed to bring enlightenment. The Victorian bubble burst, fragmenting its perspective, its morality, its ornate façade.

Shaw was sixty years old, alert, in full possession of his extraordinary talents, and bitterly disillusioned. In his preface to the *Quintessence of Ibsenism,* reissued after the war from which England had emerged victorious but crippled, he wrote:

Liberal ideals, Feudal ideals, National ideals, Dynastic ideals, Republican ideals, Church ideals, State ideals, and Class ideals, bourgeois and proletarian, all heaped up into a gigantic pile of spiritual high explosive, and then shovelled daily into every house with the morning milk by the newspapers, needed only a bomb thrown at Sarajevo by a handful of regicide idealists to blow the center out of Europe.

The artist as well as the statesman had failed to keep the world from spinning into reverse, and since he did not influence events, he denied the reality of events. Locked within himself, he made his poems and his music his own confessional, while he lived "without scruple on income he did nothing to earn." The mind and culture of Europe turned aimlessly, unclutched, while "barbarians . . . on the front bench in the House of Commons, with nobody to correct their incredible ignorance of modern thought," were heeding only "the upstarts from the countinghouse."

Shaw was still laughing, for laughter was his prop as well as his nature, but a bit grimly, for he no longer was sure he knew the answers, and in a world without confidence, without tenderness, he wrote *Heartbreak House,* a "Fantasia in the Russian Manner." He wrote the play before a shot had been fired. He did not release it until after peace had been declared because, as he said in the preface written in retrospect in 1919, he felt that war could not "bear the terrible castigation of comedy, the ruthless light of laughter that glares upon the stage."

In *Heartbreak House,* Shaw sums up his entire career. It is the best of his disquisitory plays, the one most perfectly constructed into a symphony of talk, and so rich and moving in its action that the outpouring of Shavian ideas on an endless variety of topics goes almost unnoticed. It is a picture of an entire era, of "cultured, leisured Europe before the war."

HEARTBREAK HOUSE

The scene is a house in the hills of Sussex. The room in which all the action takes place is in the form of the deck of a ship—as if, though rooted in rock, it is drifting, no longer in touch with the real world, a place where people can be themselves, where outside forces do not intrude.

ACT ONE—*The Disillusionment of Romance*

Ellie Dunn, an invited but ignored guest, is alone in the room until she is greeted by Captain Shotover, "an ancient but still hardy man with an immense white beard, in a reefer jacket with a whistle hanging from his neck"—the counterpart of Shaw himself.

The Captain engages in none of the surface amenities. He is truth, direct, unflinching. Ellie makes a good impression on him and he offers her tea, a thing he does only on special occasions. If there is any central character in this gallery of portraits it is Ellie, who both opens and closes the play. She is young and pretty, the daughter of a "poor but respectable man," and still believes in romance; she always carries a copy of Shakespeare with her.

The house belongs to the Captain, who lives here with his married daughter, Hesione. When his other daughter, Ariadne, Lady Utterwood, arrives, after having been away from home for twenty-three years, the Captain refuses to recognize her and vanishes brusquely from the room. Ariadne sounds the first despair when she says, "really very much hurt and annoyed and disillusioned":

> Oh, this house, this house! I come back to it after twenty-three years; and it is just the same; the luggage lying on the steps, the servants spoilt and impossible, nobody at home to receive anybody . . . and what is worse, the same disorder in ideas, in talk, in feeling . . .

And so throughout the play, like casual, seemingly offhand variations on a theme, bursting into brilliance mo-

mentarily with the whim of the conductor, characters make
remarks referring not only to themselves but illuminating
some aspect of contemporary life. For years, Ariadne has
lived with the thought of eventual return to her family,
only now discovering that her dream had more validity than
the fact. And she is rejected by the Captain, who insists she
"not try to ingratiate herself by impersonating" his long-
absent daughter, since he prefers Ellie's "Youth! Beauty!
Novelty! . . . badly wanted in this house." There has been
no youth of the world, old before its time. When the beautiful and glamorous Hesione enters, she nods to her sister
quite calmly, but Ariadne insists that she be greeted fer-
vently because one must behave "properly and decently."
Her mainstay is respectability, for she had married a member of the diplomatic service and lived the life of the empire-
builder, ignoring world changes but upholding the preservation of the proper.

Ellie is to marry Boss Mangan, the millionaire, her
father's employer, but confides to Hesione that she is really
in love with a Marcus Darnley whom she met in an art
gallery and who tells magnificent lies of adventure, of saving
the King's life at tiger hunts, and fighting for the Socialists
on the barricades even though he is of the nobility. All of
Shaw's Socialists are of the nobility, or at least of the upper
class. A handsome man of fifty enters, striking in appearance
with his mousquetaire mustaches. Ellie introduces him to
Hesione as Marcus Darnley, but he turns out to be Hesione's
husband. Ellie's is the second despair, her romantic love
smashed into disillusionment, and she says to Hesione:

> I have a horrible fear that my heart is broken, but
> that heartbreak is not like what I thought it must be.

The women leave as the shifting scene turns to Boss
Mangan and old Shotover. Here is the world antithesis:
Mangan, the captain of industry, the board of director's

man, so commonplace that he is indescribable, versus Shot-over, the captain of science, mind, reason, insight. The exchange between the two is sharp percussion. Shotover tells him not to marry Ellie Dunn, he is too old. At which Mangan, with assumed heroics, declares that what he wants he gets. Shotover punctures him with, "Talk like a man, not a movie," and advises him to marry instead a West Indian Negress. He himself was married to one for two years, a woman who redeemed him. Now, after an adventurous life, he is surrounded by "Respectability. Let it be a warning to all of you."

Randall Utterwood arrives, the fashionable West Ender, the brother of Ariadne's husband. He is also the diplomatic service, weak, ingratiating, a fool in the hands of women; he plays the flute when he wants to cry. Randall leaves to pursue Ariadne. Hector and Hesione, left alone, with reasonable sophistication discuss each other's extramarital adventures. Hector spends all his time making love to women he cannot love. He is the male counterpart of Ariadne, though he adds chivalry and heroism to a pursuit that is wasted. Shotover enters for a brief recapitulation with Hector in a scene that is the essence of Fabianism. Shotover is determined to kill all fellows like Mangan and Randall Utterwood because one is the distortion of love as the other is of money. Of Mangan, he says:

> Are we to be kept forever in the mud by these hogs to whom the universe is nothing but a machine for greasing their bristles and filling their snouts?

He will kill them by achieving the seventh degree of concentration and inventing a "mind ray that will explode the ammunition in the belt of [an] adversary before he can point a gun . . ." Mind over matter, the Fabian superman of intellect to eliminate the evil of the world, the idle waste of Utterwood and the coarse materialism of Mangan. The cruel paradox is that Shotover must hurry, for he is old and

"cannot waste time in talk"—the very activity of the Fabians. Shotover needs money to carry on with his plans and
his house, and he ends the first act with a cry for "deeper
darkness. Money is not made in the light."

The deck has been cleared. All are gathered. Ellie and
old Shotover are the two who have been hurt most.

ACT TWO—*The Disillusionment of Money*

Boss Mangan is alone with his fiancée, Ellie Dunn. The
house has had its effect on him. He tells the truth. He has
stolen the business from Ellie's father; as a matter of fact,
he always steals someone else's business. He advances money,
always that of other people, until a new business fails; then
he takes it over and makes the previous entrepreneur work
for him. He "takes no risk in ideas." All men are to him
"a heap of squeezed lemons." Ellie is not at all taken aback.
In the unexpected inversion, she replies that she is perfectly willing to marry him. Her mother had married a good
man and remained poor. She herself has been warned not
to repeat the mistake. It is a modern proposal of marriage.
But Mangan is not what he seems. He cannot even eat good
food but is on a severe diet. There is, in fact, no enjoyment in him, and so Ellie has her next disillusionment.
Now both romance and money have failed her. She hypno-
tizes Mangan and puts him to sleep.

Hesione rebukes Mazzini Dunn for wanting to throw
his daughter away on a beast, a ruthless captain of industry.
Mazzini quickly and calmly sets her romantic notions top-
pling. He, Mazzini, weak, a fighter for poetry and liberty,
runs the business. He knows and loves machinery. All Mangan does is see to it that they do not improve the quality
of the goods and make them too expensive. "He is down
on us for every halfpenny. We could never do without
him." Hesione explodes: "Then the creature is a fraud even
as a captain of industry!" and Mazzini answers:

I am afraid all the captains of industry are what you call frauds. Of course, there are some manufacturers who really do understand their own works, but they don't make as high a rate of profit as Mangan does.

Ellie and Hesione now discuss the problem of marriage. They represent two different approaches to love: Ellie that of poverty and simple respectability, Hesione that of riches and sophistication. Hesione is to Ellie the woman of assured beauty who manages men and people with superb grace. She is the last of the props, except Shakespeare, to which Ellie has clung, for Ellie needs strength "to lean on, something iron, something stony." She discovers that Hesione's magnificent black hair is false. After their exchange of hostilities, and then confidences, the two women fall into each other's arms, fast friends.

Mangan, having only pretended to be hypnotized, has heard the discussion about him and is furious. He would do anything to get away from this horrible house of truth, and he tries to flee but is forced to stay when a burglar is caught attempting to steal the family silver. Everyone assembles for a discussion of the problem of crime and punishment. (Shaw was to extend these ideas very soon in his preface to Lord Olivier's work on prison conditions, published separately later as *The Crime of Imprisonment*.) In *Heartbreak House,* with characteristic inversion, he drives home the point that the person who is robbed suffers most from the arrest and punishment of the evildoer. They therefore refuse to turn the burglar over to the authorities because they want to avoid "being dragged through the horrors of a criminal court and having all their family affairs in the papers." Instead, they take up a collection and would send the intruder on his way, but he turns out to be Billie Dunn, Shotover's former boatswain and the husband of Nurse Guiness. He never intended to steal. He prefers to be caught in the act. It is more profitable and less dangerous to have them take up a collection. The burglar fully understands society's reluctance to prosecute him, and knows the lack of harmony that prevails between the citizenry and the police.

Ellie is left alone with old Captain Shotover. She finds comfort in this sage who "has stood on the bridge in a typhoon for eighteen hours." Though "life here is stormier," he can weather it. In his presence, she speaks freely and with renewed conviction. Poverty and a soul don't go together, despite the popular prejudice. Souls are too expensive to keep. Mangan has money but no soul. Since he had robbed her father, she will therefore get the money back by marrying Mangan, and will maintain her soul. Shotover, however, can only ask questions and make pointed remarks. It confuses him to be answered and so he runs away, but Ellie holds him and he delivers his long speech of the play:

> . . . I see my daughters and their men living foolish lives of romance and sentiment and snobbery. I see you, the younger generation, turning from their romance and sentiment and snobbery to money and comfort and hard common sense. I was ten times happier on the bridge in the typhoon, or frozen into Arctic ice for months in darkness, than you or they have ever been. You are looking for a rich husband. At your age, I looked for hardship, danger, horror, and death, that I might feel the life in me more intensely. I did not let the fear of death govern my life; and your reward will be that you will eat, but you will not live.

Shaw's ever-repeated theme is the extent to which men will compromise to avoid poverty, which is, after all, the propulsive force of modern society and its basic weakness. Ellie is impressed by the Captain's words, but her most bitter disillusionment comes when he discloses that his search for the seventh degree of concentration is in reality an escape into—rum. He too is running away. His heart is broken, and "when your heart is broken, your boats are burned. Nothing matters any more. It is the end of happiness and the beginning of peace." Ellie has reached rock bottom—she wants nothing now and therefore she can find something beyond happiness. It is the same secret that was in the heart of the poet Marchbanks. Ellie and the Captain, the most conscious characters with the most distinct individual wills, have found each other. It is Ellie's final love scene. She will marry old Captain Shotover.

The curtain comes down on the second act with Hector's invocation to the heavens to "fall and crush."

ACT THREE—*The Wooing of Death*

The moon is out. It is later the same evening. All have reached an impasse in self-exploration, in turning themselves and others inside out. Solutions are offered. Hector would have them all destroyed because they are "useless, dangerous, and ought to be abolished." Lady Utterwood would have the house acquire horses, for there are only two classes in society: "The people who hunt are the right people, and the people who don't are the wrong ones"— Heartbreak House or Horseback Hall.

Mangan, for whom no one in this house has any respect, unveils a full confession. He is the secret power in the government, he really knows nothing about machinery, and to top it all, he has no money. Bigger men control him. He is merely the managerial instrument in the hands of what he terms "lazy, good-for-nothing capitalists." Though business and politics are in his hands, he really is nothing, he has nothing. He whom everyone has regarded as the arch capitalist is only a false front; he hates the real capitalists. And because he has finally spoken the truth, no one believes him. Ellie, still foundering, says, "There is nothing real in the world, except my father and Shakespeare." Everything else has proved false: Hector's romantic tigers, Mangan's money, Hesione's hair, and the Captain's concentration. At this point, Boss Mangan starts to take off his clothes. He may just as well be physically naked as morally.

All the themes have thus far been sounded separately or in various combinations. Shaw now pulls them together to merge in a final ominous discussion. Mangan is power, but he is like a child with a torpedo. Hector cries that they are England, a madhouse—and haunted. Mazzini plays a subdued note. He is the Liberal, the Labor Party. He has made speeches and written pamphlets. He had expected a revolution, but nothing has happened. "Nothing ever happens," he suggests mildly. Captain Shotover storms that nothing ever happens to the raw elements of nature, but the ship goes on the rocks, and that, not when the skipper is drunk but when he is drifting. England must learn "navigation. Learn it and live; or leave it and be damned."

The final full outburst is the message from the heavens. The enemy planes come flying over, dropping their bombs. Mangan and the burglar rush out to hide in the gravel pit. The others remain. Hector dashes all over the house tearing down curtains and turning on the lights, inviting the bombs to fall directly on them. Ellie and Hesione embrace in ecstasy. The bombs fall, not on the house, but in the gravel pit, destroying "the two burglars," Mangan and the thief, "the two practical men of business." The others have wooed death and failed. Their only joy was in the courage to meet disaster. They shout aloud, praying that the bombs will fall again, more successfully, tomorrow night. They stand in radiant expectation, having found a meaning, all that is left beyond hope. Not knowing how to live, they boast they know how to die. Ellie, in her final disillusionment, says with deep disappointment, "Safe! And how damnably dull the world has become again suddenly."

With wry laughter, Shaw thus pictured profoundly the saddest tragedy of our day, the final chapter in a dislocated world.

Shaw was sixty-five when he gave permission to present *Heartbreak House*. He continued to write vigorously for another three decades, but he contributed only one equally important play, *Saint Joan,* in which he returned to the past to reassert faith in the individual, in the Protestant right to divine truth directly and to act on it, to cast aside outworn heritage and to advance society with new methods, even though one be burned at the stake. It is Shaw's last finished discussion play, the finest dramatic debate in the language, with an epilogue that the world is not ready for its saints—Joan or Bernard.

An Intellectual Rebel in the Making

Shaw's work is an amalgam of three logically consistent elements: the philosophy of socialism (Fabian style), the method of dramatic discussion, and the device of using inversion as wit. Each is related to his life and times and deserves further consideration, for though Shaw left no disciples—his wit and personality were too unpredictable—his influence has extended, often unintentionally, into many avenues of the contemporary theatre.

George Bernard Shaw was born a Protestant in Dublin, most Catholic of cities. His father, a dealer in corn, was unable to support the family and retreated into drunkenness. Shaw, a total abstainer all his life, remarked later that he wrote with the same intensity with which his father drank. His mother decided to take the children to London, and they seem not to have minded being separated from the father. Shaw did some ghostwriting for music critics, but despite his firm efforts to be regarded as an unemployable he had to work for the Telephone Company for four years as a solicitor of line space. In his spare time he managed to write five novels, none of which achieved recognition, but his writing, together with his dress suit and his ability to play the piano, brought him into contact with the intellectual circles of London and kept him removed from the poverty he dreaded.

Through the intervention of William Archer, Shaw

obtained work as a theatre critic, and until he achieved independence as a playwright he alternated between music and drama criticism. In both fields he distinguished himself. In music, he championed the new work of Wagner; in drama, that of Ibsen. The theatricality of Wagner fascinated him, with its pyrotechnics of cloud-storming drama, its defiance of authority, and its music co-ordinated with the action. But more significant was his admiration for the hero individual, the superman, whom he incorporated into his own concept of progress. In Ibsen he found two essentials: the first, the idea that "bourgeois morality was largely a system of making cheap virtue a cloak for disastrous vices"; the second, the technique of Ibsen's middle period, "naturalism and the use of discussion replacing romance and melodrama" with what Shaw termed "natural history." *The Quintessence of Ibsenism* remains today one of the better insights into the work of the Norwegian playwright, even though it tells more of Shaw than of Ibsen. Likewise, his other dramatic criticism, published later in several volumes, is the most lucid that England has produced since Dryden. Shaw despised "Bardolatry" and "Sardoodledom": one, the false worship of Shakespeare; the other, the false worship of artificial form as commercialized by Victorien Sardou.

The third influence in the making of a rebel, apart from Wagner and Ibsen, was Karl Marx. When Shaw came to London, an impoverished young man, in 1876, socialist thinking was popular in liberal circles. Shaw took to it immediately and listened avidly to the lectures of Henry George about the principles of the single tax on land values and the unjust distribution of wealth. He had always been interested in economics, which, to him, was "what anatomy had been to Michelangelo." He spent hours in the British Museum reading *Das Kapital* in French, alternating it with the score of *Tristan and Isolde*—the God Hero and the economics of poverty! When the Fabian Society was formed in 1884, Shaw joined and became closely associated with

H. G. Wells, Sidney and Beatrice Webb, Graham Wallas, and William Archer.

The Fabians were well named—after the Roman general Fabius Maximus Cunctator, who fought all his battles by retreating. They believed that correct ideas would change the world, and that socialism would come about by education, by reform and patience, and the "inevitability of gradualism." The Fabian Society was intentionally small and never a rigid political organization. Each member possessed the right to disagree, and did. Shaw, for example, in opposition to the Webbs, insisted on a future society in which there would be equality of income for all.

The intention of the Fabians was to influence public opinion and to convince those in power, even the capitalists, to relinquish their control willingly. Reason and intelligence were the guides to social change. Once the truth was known, good people everywhere would unite to reconstruct the world. The anarchy of history would give way to guided planning. Thus, Bernard Shaw, music and drama critic, novelist and playwright, wrote tracts and speeches, books on political economy, and popular guides to socialism. He became the world's best-publicized Fabian, its spokesman and one-time president, and its philosophy is so deeply interwoven into his life and work that an understanding of him is inconceivable without a critical examination of this relationship. The immense library of Shaw's work is a history of Fabianism, its initial fervor, its success, and its disillusionment.

Shaw and Fabianism

The essential aim was cure by preachment. In a letter to Hyndman, the socialist leader, Shaw wrote:

> I am a moral revolutionary, interested not in the class war, but in the struggle between human vitality and the artificial system of morality.

This is close to the heart of Ibsen, with the difference that whereas Ibsen demanded a reinfused moral vigor, Shaw demanded reforms to alter the social artificiality. Ibsen would change man; Shaw, society. He prided himself on being a "revolutionary writer," and in the preface to *Major Barbara*, wrote:

> Here, I am . . . by class, a respectable person, by common sense a hater of waste and disorder, by intellectual constitution legally minded to the verge of pedantry, and by temperament apprehensive and economically disposed to the limit of old-maidishness; yet, I am, and always have been, and shall now always be, a revolutionary writer, because our laws make law impossible; our liberties destroy all freedom; our property is organized robbery; our morality is an impudent hypocrisy. . . . I am an enemy of the existing order for good reasons.

The early plays therefore deal with slum housing, marriage and divorce, prostitution, crime and punishment, but Shaw, as Fabian advocate, was striking at the root of social dislocation, the existence of poverty in the midst of plenty. Sartorius, Trench, Lady Roxdale, Mrs. Warren, Sir George Crofts, are all able to enjoy living comfortably because others are deprived of comforts. Again and again, Shaw struck at the curse of poverty.

> The evil to be attacked is not sin, suffering, greed, priestcraft, kingcraft, demagogy, monopoly, ignorance, drink, war, pestilence, nor any other of the scapegoats which reformers sacrifice, but simply poverty.

"Blessed are the poor" is hypocrisy. Without money, man is nothing, so Shaw became rich. At least, be honest about it.

> To teach children that it is sinful to desire money is to strain toward the extreme possible limit of impudence in lying and corruption.

The early plays were written to show that man cannot keep his money in one pocket and his ideals in another.

Since the Fabian believed social amelioration could be effected by the proper action in the proper direction by the proper people, Shaw was drawn to the unique individual. He understood the nature of drama as the conflict between the human will and the environment. Before he had written a single play, he wrote:

> . . . life consists in the fulfillment of the will, which is constantly growing, and cannot be fulfilled today under the conditions which secured its fulfillment yesterday . . .

This concept, in the nineteenth century, was a brilliant addition to dramatic theory. Shaw's protagonist became the superior soul who imposes his will on stubborn fact. Thus, Captain Shotover, seeking to discover a mind ray that will explode dynamite in the pockets of the capitalists by his willing it, is an extreme example of the will dominating nature. This is the essential romantic quality in Shaw and ties in with his theory of progress as the achievement of the great man—Andrew Undershaft, Julius Caesar, Napoleon, John Tanner, Joan of Arc, or King Magnus. It also gives the artist in Shaw the most magnificent role in history, the transformation of bewildering chaos into order. In his praise of Brieux, a defense of himself, he wrote:

> For it is the business of Brieux to pick out the significant incidents from the chaos of daily happenings, and arrange them so that their relation to one another becomes significant, thus changing us from bewildered spectators of monstrous confusion to men intelligently conscious of the world and its destinies.

This is Shaw, social reformer, but basically the artist.

Fabian socialism likewise determined the form of the Shavian drama. Ideas were in conflict; the debate was on. "After a century and a half of complacent vaunting of its own probity," the middle class was turning on itself "with accusations of hideous sexual and commercial corruptions." Since change was effected by revolutionary ideas, Shaw,

choosing the drama as the most direct forum, was compelled
to develop the dramatic values of discussion. He consciously
created a hitherto unexplored aspect of form, and its success is evidenced by the continuing theatrical power of his
work. Writing of Ibsen, he had said in 1891:

> Formerly you had in what was called a well-made
> play an exposition in the first act, a situation in the sec-
> ond, an unravelling in the third. Now you have exposi-
> tion, situation, and discussion; and the discussion is the
> test of the playwright. The critics protest in vain. They
> declare that discussions are not dramatic, and that art
> should not be didactic. Neither the playwrights nor the
> public take the smallest notice of them.

Though Shaw was too versatile to restrict himself to
any one formula, he extended the boundaries of the drama
most successfully in those plays wherein the conflict of ideas
is arranged in the heightened form of a musical composition, as in *Heartbreak House, Major Barbara,* and *Saint
Joan.* Not that Shaw's plays are merely debates; they abound
in the essentials of drama—character, situation, conflict of
aims, crises, resolutions, and a surprising amount of physical
action. But their special ingredient is the opposition of conflicting ideas. Shaw used the theatre, as all playwrights do,
to offer a philosophy of life, but his technique was to present a many-sided discussion, evoking by the brilliant interplay of challenging values a special level of response in the
audience. It is futile to say discussion is not drama. Shaw
proves the contrary.

Shavian Characters

Contrary to accepted criticism, Shaw could create characters. Joan and Candida are as intimately known as Mrs.
Alving or Mme Raynevsky; but it is true that his individuals become less important than the ideas they represent.
They cease to be three-dimensional as they shrink to the
one dimension of Shaw, and logically they should fade away

into pure idea, as they do in the remark of the Ancient in *Back to Methuselah,* "The day will come when there will be no people, only thought."

In *Heartbreak House,* we see the basic difference between Chekhov and Shaw. The play is Chekhovian in that it takes place in a country retreat, the people are cultured and leisured, and do very little and talk much. But in Chekhov, the characters feel from deep within themselves and their relations to others; in Shaw, they become figures in a morality play, a clash of concepts. Ellie could well be Everywoman, at least in aspiration; Hesione, Sophisticated Love; Ariadne, the Lady in the Manor House; Randall, the Empire; Hector, Romantic Heroism, with his Achilles' heel of unrequited pursuit; Mangan, Business and Realism; Mazzini Dunn, the Liberal and Technocrat; and Shotover, Aged Wisdom. In Chekhov, we are interested in people; in Shaw, in what they represent.

In most modern dramas, characters do not know what they want. They are victims of environmental forces, subconscious or psychic, which they little understand. In *Heartbreak House,* on the contrary, characters are fully aware of what they want. Like Mangan, they strip themselves naked, or almost so, in self-revelation. They know who they are. This is their comic tragedy, their direct realization of the world in which they live. This is the weird fascination of the house and its mystery. Here is truth, and knowing the truth, they have no way to turn, for the world is out of gear. The final despair is that truth and reason avail them nought. They can act only from impulse.

In the drama of discussion, there can be no heroes or villains. Since ideas are exposed and society is to blame, you cannot blame men. Shaw, therefore, tolerates all, and even leans over backward to show the virtues of the villain. The manufacturer of instruments of death becomes the most understanding Undershaft. Nor can characters end by dying, as Ibsen's do, for this would indicate that the idea they represent is dead. Shaw had remarked of Hedda Gabler that "the tragedy of Hedda in real life is not that she commits suicide but that she continues to live." It is therefore significant that in *Heartbreak House*, the burglar and the millionaire die. Their ideas are dead or dying, and Shaw is willing to let them go because they know no disillusionment and have not even the courage to despair. He blows them up with a bomb and twenty pounds of dynamite. But the heroes—at least the protagonist and antagonist, Ellie and Shotover, one young and compelled to live, and the other long past his time and a consort of the devil— remain alive, for they have only just begun their discussion.

Shavian Wit—The Device of Inversion

Just as Fabianism dictated discussion as the form of Shaw's plays, so did it give impetus to his wit. The device is simple. Juxtapose ideas, turn them inside out (the primary inversion) so that they are the opposite of appearance; then turn them inside out again (the second inversion), but in such a manner that they do not revert to what they were before but arrive at a point different from their origin. Stand an idea on its head, then put it back on its feet, but in unforeseen surroundings so that one is shocked into fresh observation and thought. Torn from its conventional associations, the idea seems strangely what it is not. Shaw employed this dialectic in single lines, characters, scenes, and an entire play, so that the paradox was built into a highly ramified structure, inversions tumbling over one another in varying weights and dimensions.

The inversion appeared in *single lines* such as:

Hell is the home of honor, duty, justice, and the rest of the seven deadly virtues.

Or:

The truth is, humor is one of the great purifiers of religion, even when it is itself anything but pure.

Inversion was also used in *character:* Don Juan is not the great lover, but is successful because he rejects his female pursuers; or Andrew Undershaft, armourer, is the most religious of men, for his religion is in tune with the modern world. And an *entire play* could be an inversion: Dick Dudgeon, the devil's disciple, proves to be the saint when he is willing to take another's place at the gallows, whereas the minister, devoted to peace, becomes a man of action and leads an armed band to the rescue.

The inversion of line, character, and plot produces a multiple impact, unexpected and disturbing. In *Everybody's Political What's What,* issued in 1944, the still belligerent nonagenarian said:

> Unless you state a thing irritatingly you might as well not state it at all.

and:

> It is always necessary to overstate a case startlingly to make people sit up and listen to it.

This is the protestation of the comic wit. Behind it lay the heartbreak of Shaw. He could not attack seriously because he feared being laughed at, and so he laughed in order to be taken seriously. In *The Quintessence of Ibsenism,* written before his first play, he said:

> The mask of laughter wears off the shames and the evils; but men finally see them as they really are.

In each play Shaw chose some aspect of morality and so twisted and distorted its common pose that people would at least question long-held dogma. The drama is a form of debate, the decision left to an aghast public who are barbed into viewing life from an unanticipated focus. It is a teaching device, and despite his abhorrence of teachers ("He who can, does. He who cannot, teaches."), Shaw was himself a teacher.

Inversion is a method which, like Fabius Maximus,

avoids the direct attack; the paradox of the ceaseless paradox is that it often gives the illusion of disbelief and of faith in nothing, but Shaw never wavered in his compassion for humanity, his love of people, his joy in nature, and his acceptance of social progress.

The Search for Art

No man has been called more contradictory names in his own lifetime, and by more distinguished men, than George Bernard Shaw. But of course Shaw's lifetime was almost a century, and so there was opportunity for successive generations with different vitalities to blast away. Ezra Pound called him "an intellectual cheesemite"; George Moore, "the funny man in the boardinghouse"; the verbose Winston Churchill, "the world's most famous intellectual clown and pantaloon in one, and the charming Columbine of the capitalist pantomime"; Yeats termed him "a barbarian of the barricades"; and the younger poet, Auden, said, "a Fabian Figaro." Shaw's wit was a prod to others to be as witty about him as he had been about everyone else.

Yet Shaw was bravely trying to create a work of art. With his first play he said:

> It is a propagandist play, a didactic play, a play with a purpose . . .

and then added:

> . . . you will please judge it, not as a pamphlet in dialogue, but as in intention a work of art as much as any comedy of Molière's is a work of art.

A work of art is not such by protestation of the artist. Shaw set up an artificial dichotomy between utility and art. Of Ibsen, he said:

> A Doll's House will be flat as ditchwater when A Midsummer Night's Dream will still be fresh as paint, but it will have done more work in the world; and that is enough for the highest genius.

The fusion of the two, art and message, form and meaning, the inseparable, indivisible substance of all great work, he rarely realized; but a *Heartbreak House* or a *Saint Joan* is enough for "the highest genius." As Sean O'Casey wrote:

> He was the greatest British playwright of his age; none equalled him then, none equal him now. None of those who learned from him have yet thrown a wider chest than his own.

His enduring frame of reference gave him the basis for superb comedy. You have to believe in a set of values before you can ridicule what has gone before or what is in effect today. Complete cynicism is never comedy. Shaw, like Molière and Aristophanes, was able to laugh at what was because he had a sense of what ought to be. And in advancing beyond Ibsen, he created a wider range for the unfolding of the modern theatre.

6. *The Theatre of Socialist Realism*
—Maxim Gorky

YEGOR BULITCHEV

A Writer Honored

In 1932, the world of letters acclaimed the fortieth anniversary of Maxim Gorky's first published story. The celebration was unprecedented in the Soviet Union. No writer in his own lifetime had ever received such public homage. Nizhni Novgorod, his birthplace, was renamed Gorky. Every city, large or small, had a street name changed to Gorky. The Bolshoi Theatre in Leningrad, which he had helped found, was now the Gorky Theatre, and even the Moscow Art Theatre, which by tradition had been associated with Chekhov and used the sea gull as its emblem, added Gorky to its name. Magazines, parks, amusement centers, rest homes, children, were named after him. Gorky, then sixty-four, still shy and retiring, somewhat taken aback by this over-abundance of devotion, contributed to his own celebration by announcing the completion of a new play. On September 25, it was performed at the Vakhtangov Theatre in Moscow. All the leaders of the Soviet government as well as of the arts were present. Delegates had been chosen from trade unions, collective farms, and youth organizations to repre-sent a cross-section of the entire nation. In addition to the resident diplomatic corps, distinguished foreigners attended, including writers from all over the world headed by a French contingent under the leadership of Henri Barbusse. Gorky himself was there. The play was his final major achieve-ment. Four years later he died, but in *Yegor Bulitchev* he had penned a powerful summation of his work, and as only a writer can, had honored those who came to do him honor.

"I dream him a new sun . . ."

Alexei Maximovitch Peshkov, who took the name of Maxim Gorky (Maxim the Bitter), had been born in poverty and risen "from below, from the nethermost ground of life, where there was nought but sludge and murk." At the age of four, he went to live with his ill-tempered and miserly grandfather, who on regular occasions beat him mercilessly. The boy knew neither love nor tenderness, nor the sense of being wanted. His mother blamed him for being the cause of his father's premature death from cholera, which Alexei himself had contracted first, and she also resented him as the burden that denied her her freedom. Years later, he wrote how he once, inadvertently, overheard his mother say:[1]

> I have sinned before God, but I cannot love Alexei
> . . . Is it not because of him that my hands are tied
> now? If it were not for him, how I could live! But with
> such a chain wound round my feet, I cannot jump too far.

Sent to work early, Gorky served as errand boy, dish-washer, and apprentice to an icon maker, and then ran away from home to wander as a tramp in the Crimea, the Caucasus, and the Volga regions. When he was hounded by the police for his political activities, he scampered about like a water rat, seeking refuge along the docks or in any hovel where he could stay for the night. At various times he worked as baker, stevedore, night watchman, clerk, and journalist, and he became so well acquainted with hunger, prison, and the loneliness of despair that he even attempted suicide. He had to write in hours stolen from work or illness, often wrapped in a carpet against the intense cold. Yet everything he wrote burns with a passionate zest for life and undeviating confidence in the future. His prose poem, much in the style of Walt Whitman, shouts a bold affirmation:

> Man! I dream him a new sun arisen in my soul . . .
> Onward he marches . . . free, proud Man . . .

"The terrific force of the theatre . . ."

Ten years after his first short story, "Makar Chudra," was published in an obscure periodical in Tiflis, Gorky was working on his first play, and so the 1932 celebration honoring his forty years of literary activity also marked his thirty years of association with the theatre. By 1902, he had achieved considerable success as a writer and could afford to live in the Crimea to relieve his pulmonary tuberculosis. There he sought out Chekhov, and the two who were to become the most important figures in the contemporary Russian theatre remained close friends, even though constantly critical of each other's work. Through Chekhov, Gorky came to the theatre, or rather, the theatre came to

him, for when Gorky was Chekhov's guest, Stanislavsky and
the entire company of the Moscow Art Theatre journeyed
to Yalta to perform for Chekhov, who had been too ill to
attend rehearsals. This new group of actors with their intense realism of production impressed Gorky with "the terrific force of the theatre," and he started work on two plays:
Meschane (translated as *Small People, Smug Citizen,* or
Petty Bourgeois), and *Na Dne* (*At the Bottom,* or *The
Lower Depths*). *Smug Citizen* opened first at the close of the
season in Petrograd. Gorky had just been elected to the
Royal Academy, and at the Czar's orders the election was
rescinded. Chekhov and Korolenko resigned in protest.
Demonstrations in Gorky's behalf took place all over the
country, especially among the workers, for Gorky had become a national hero in the revolutionary movement. On
the opening night, to avoid any popular uprising, "the
vicinity of the theatre and the theatre itself was guarded by
a special cordon of police, and mounted gendarmes were
stationed in the square before the theatre. One could think,"
added Stanislavsky in *My Life in Art,* "that these prepara-
tions were being made not for a general dress rehearsal but
for a general battle." The great director little knew that in
Gorky's play he was presenting a trenchant indictment of
existing society, an active philosophy of social discontent,
a condemnation of the waverings of the intellectuals and the
self-insulation of the middle class, which preferred comfortable living to militant struggle. To Gorky, the worthless
are those who live without an invigorating purpose, who
devote themselves to the emptiness of pleasurable pursuits,
ignoring human values. Nil, the railroad worker, is superior
to Peter, the self-pitying student, because Nil will fight for
what he clearly wants, whereas Peter is rendered immobile
by his constant rationalization.

Gorky was not satisfied with *Smug Citizen,* and indeed
it would hardly merit continued respect were it not for the
later plays. He wrote to Chekhov:

It seems flat and dull. I dislike it very much. This very winter I will write another play. And if that does not come off well, I'll write ten more until I get what I want! It has to be well balanced and beautiful like music.

"Creatures who once were men . . ."

That next play, *The Lower Depths,* did "come off well," and brought Gorky international recognition as a dramatist. Together with Chekhov's *The Sea Gull,* it remains the most memorable of Moscow Art Theatre productions, and of all their repertory is the most popular with Russian audiences.

Gorky's timing was courageous. Russia was on the eve of the 1905 Revolution. In depicting the poverty, terror, and degradation of human life, and the uncrushed will to create a better world, Gorky was a lone voice in the predominantly symbolist Russian literature of the turn of the century. The play was a success despite a rigorous police censorship, which deleted every line in the manuscript critical of the Czarist regime. Not until years later was the play presented in its original entirety.

The Lower Depths was well suited to the style of acting and production inherent in the Stanislavsky system. Despite efforts to be eclectic, the Moscow Art Theatre was at its best in straight realistic drama, and Gorky gave them life in the raw, challenging the full resources of the new group. At the first reading of the script, which was attended by Chaliapin and Andreyev, the company was spellbound by Gorky's voice as it revealed the awesome yet poetic drama of violence.

The play takes place in an underground basement where derelicts are crowded together. For the most part, they are discarded workers, though some still preserve the outward fiction of gainful production—the capmaker, the locksmith, the cobbler, the two longshoremen; the others have been cast off by society as no longer useful or profitable, or

they are the open enemies of constituted order—the thief,
the prostitute. They live like tethered animals—the life
Gorky had known, and of which he wrote:

> I was . . . the shrill cry of those who remain below
> and who let me arise to testify to their hardship.

In this crowded hovel, these dregs of humanity have
little left to live for, not even companionship among themselves. Compassion has given way to self-protection. They
live off the crumbs thrown to them, yet they go on living.
The itinerant Luka, a Christ of the poor, wanders among
them, and their hopes rekindle because he nourishes their
illusions of what they might have been. But then their
jealousies break out into murder, and the police come to
make arrests. In the confusion, Luka disappears and their
illusions, which he had sustained for a moment, evaporate.
They are now plunged into deeper despair.

Eugene O'Neill, a half-century later in *The Iceman
Cometh,* wrote of the need of the downtrodden to cling
to illusions, since in a callous world self-deception is a preferable opiate. To O'Neill, escape from reality leads to
belief in the illusory as more real than the real. Not so with
Gorky. In the final act, there arises from below life itself,
from the substructure of society, a powerful affirmation of
life expressed in the explosive words of Satin:

> Lies are the religion of slaves and the master of slaves!
> Truth is the God of the free man! . . . Man . . . there's
> the truth! Man himself pays for everything, and for that
> reason he is free . . . What is man? It's not I, nor you,
> nor they . . . no! No, it's you, and I, and they, the old
> man, Napoleon, Mohammed—all in one! (*Draws a human
> figure in the air with his fingers.*) Understand? This is
> something big! Here are all the beginnings and all the
> ends. Everything is within man—everything is for man!
> Only man exists; as for all the rest, it's the work of his
> hands and his mind! M-A-N! There's something magnifi-
> cent. It has a proud sound. M-A-N! You must respect

man, not pity him, not degrade him with pity! Yes, you must respect him! Let's drink to Man!

It was this burning fever in Gorky which impelled Chekhov to say of him:

> Gorky is a destroyer who must destroy all that deserves destruction . . . in this lies his whole strength and it is for this that life has called him.

"Freedom at any cost . . ."

As theatre, *The Lower Depths* was grim and overwhelming: the cellar, a parade of dark shadows, the washing back and forth of a section of society in which there was no individual protagonist but the mass itself. But whereas in similar plays such as *The Weavers* the group faces further extinction by the forces it rebels against, in Gorky the group congeals into a final cry of ultimate triumph in which each individual rises out of the mass a distinct and separate self.

For the Stanislavsky group, the production of *The Lower Depths* was a superb triumph. Chekhov was part of their own tradition; Gorky was the unknown, to be mastered. The actors went to the Khitrov Market to study the life of the underworld, and were surprised, wandering among "these creatures who once were men," to be greeted with respect and the oft-repeated question, "Why do you come to honor us?"[2] Face to face with these humble, weird, but courageous people, with death and starvation and despair present in every corner, the company was forced to discard what was left of its traditional theatricality. In presenting Gorky's play, the Moscow Art Theatre experienced one of the most meaningful stages in its evolution. Stanislavsky, who portrayed the role of Satin, responded as an artist to the inner core of the play when he said:

> It is said that the play is tendentious, that it has social and political notes. Be it so! For me, the actor, the play is *freedom*—freedom at any cost!

"The structure of music . . ."

The Lower Depths spread beyond the borders of Russia
and was produced in Europe and the United States; the
Reinhardt production in Berlin ran over five hundred
nights. Its success bolstered the realistic theatre, for the play
appeared not only on the eve of the Russian Revolution of
1905, but at the time when realism and its corollaries were
under sharp attack. Ibsen, Strindberg, and Hauptmann had
retreated to the fantasy of the subconscious. Gorky had no
need to retreat from life. He never wavered in his use of
realism. He was more interested in content than in form,
but the intensity of his beliefs drove him to transform material that was seemingly photographic and formless into
a distinct work of art.

The Lower Depths has the character of a tour de force.
Gorky never wrote another such play, nor has any other
writer, though the attempts have been legion. Zola had
borne the brunt of the enemy barrage, a straw man whipped
for his detailed account of the "slice of life," the "descent
into the sewer to take a bath." In The Lower Depths, however, Gorky fused this kind of raw material into a poetry
of spiritual awakening. The play is not purely documentary,
for out of its apparently unfashioned sweep rises a lyric
unity. There is a recurrence today of the Tobacco Road
school of drama, which often adds to its vulgarity a conscious
formlessness and an implication of philosophic subtleties.
In Jack Gelber's The Connection, lost souls awaiting their
shot of heroin are presumed to represent modern man, who
likewise seeks some "connection" to bring momentary release
from a senseless world. Such implications are farfetched,
imposed by critics too willing to escape from the conventional play. And vulgarity is not a substitute for dramatic
power. Gorky was never vulgar or concerned with violence
and depravity for their own sake. His passion and belief
raised reportage to drama. His was a sense of mission that

distinguished between good and evil without imposing judgment. *The Lower Depths* is a play Zola would like to have written.

Gorky did not need to visit the lower classes to report on their behalf. From their own ranks, he rose to sing of their redemption this side of eternity. That is why, though his fame is greatest as a writer of short stories and autobiographical novels, he was drawn to "the terrible force of the theatre," for there his social impact was direct and immediate. He said:

> I wrote plays because I had to. That is why they are so bad. But if I had studied the theory of drama, they would have been much worse.

Chekhov did not understand the final act of the play. He wrote Gorky that the work should have ended with the murder of Kostylov and the arrest of Vassya. He could not see that the cry of Satin in the more subdued fourth act is the inevitable resolution, the many themes moving into a unified affirmation. In his second play, Gorky had achieved "the structure of music."

YEGOR BULITCHEV

In the years that followed, though he continued to write for the theatre, Gorky failed to sustain his triumph. His novels were superior to his plays, and his political activity consumed much of his time. After world pressure forced his release from the Peter and Paul Prison in St. Petersburg in 1906, he journeyed to the Scandinavian countries and raised large sums of money to assist those still imprisoned. Gorky was also received warmly in the United States, and many meetings were arranged to welcome him until the Hearst press led a violent attack on him for traveling with his common-law wife. The scandal became so great that William Dean Howells and Mark Twain resigned from the banquet committee and no New York hotel would rent Gorky a room.

The Revolution found him on the side of the Bolsheviks, but he was shocked by the excesses of the armed proletariat at the storming of the Winter Palace. It took Lenin, an old-time friend, to win him back. To the early Soviet theatre he contributed little, and it was not until the worldwide celebration in 1932 that he revealed, with *Yegor Bulitchev*, another powerful work. A detailed examination of this play is essential in considering present-day trends in the theatre. It deserves to be better known in the Western world. *The Lower Depths* is too close to the influence of Chekhov; *Bulitchev* is the product of Gorky's maturity. It is assured, whereas the earlier play was still groping. *The Lower Depths* is a cry of rebellion, an inchoate, directionless struggle to free man, which in *Yegor Bulitchev* has crystallized into an awareness of responsibility. In this sense, Gorky has written a socialist play, perhaps the best that has come out of the Soviet theatre.

Yegor Bulitchev is in fact three plays, a trilogy composed on a grand scale, a document of history and people. The first play is called *Yegor Bulitchev and Others*[3] and depicts the rotting away of the merchant class just before the Revolution of 1917; in the second, *Dostigaev and Others*, Yegor's business partner resists the changes of the Revolution; the final play, *Somov and Others*, is the story of socialist construction. *Yegor Bulitchev* is unquestionably the best of the three.

The play opens with Yegor Bulitchev dying of cancer. He is a rich businessman, risen from the ranks of the peasantry, a big bull of a figure, stern, direct, dominating all around him. And all around him are contemptible: his business associates with their chicanery and double-dealing, seeking to take advantage of everyone, including Yegor in his illness; his wife, an ignorant, superstitious woman, groveling and whining in religious abjection; his children, already disputing the spoils; his sister-in-law, the abbess, venomous in her hypocritical platitudes; each a separate vulture hovering over the falling carcass, very much like *Les Corbeaux* of Henri Becque twenty years earlier, and *The Little Foxes* of Lillian Hellman a few years later. All are scheming for his money, all except three—Glasha, the housekeeper, who has been Yegor's constant companion and mistress; Shura, his red-headed illegitimate daughter for whom he has a deep and understanding love; and Laptev, Bulitchev's godson, a leader in the working-class revolution.

The time is the end of the First World War. The returning soldiers tell of the unrest at the front. At home, the political situation is chaos. Yet huge profits are to be made, and the Dostigaevs are eager for the loot. Yegor is beyond that now, a giant, crumbling with age, who senses the disintegration of all social and human relations and wants to pound his way through and know why. He is aware that all except Shura and Glasha are unscrupulous. He sees their villainy but he is caught by his own ignorance and helplessness. He submits to the cures of the tuba player, the village exorcist, and the witch healer; then, in his rage, turns them out. He roars against the duplicity of the abbess. He is sick enough to try anything, but too close to death to tolerate dishonesty. Typical is the scene with the tuba player. The cure consists of the patient's blowing four or five times a day on the tuba to eliminate noxious airs. Yegor asks the player's name, and when told it is Gabriel, bursts into guffaws and wants to know if the healer is a crook or just stupid:

TUBA PLAYER: A man can't make a living without cheating. You know that yourself.

YEGOR: You're right! It's wrong, but that's the way it is.

SHURA: Isn't it a shame to cheat people?

TUBA PLAYER: Why a shame? If they believe me?

YEGOR: (*Excited.*) That's also true. Don't you understand, Shura? It is true. That priest of ours would never admit it. He wouldn't dare!

TUBA PLAYER: You should give me more money for telling you the truth.

Yegor gives him more money, and orders Gabriel to blow his horn for all he is worth. The noise is weird and deafening. The rest of the family dash into the room, convinced that Yegor has gone mad. Shura orders the tuba player to cease, but Yegor shouts above the din.

YEGOR: No, no! Don't go away, Gabriel! Give it to them with all you've got! Blow! It's the day of judgment, the end of the world! Blow, Gabriel, blow!

The tuba player blows away. Yegor's face lights up with strange elation; the rest look on in bewilderment as the curtain falls on the second act. An old peasant superstition is transformed into the death knell of a society, and its own representative, Yegor Bulitchev, calls for its demise.

The third act ends with Yegor's death as the revolutionary forces are marching through the streets. Shura, at the window, calls out triumphantly for Yegor to come and witness the demonstration, but he can only mutter, "A Requiem. A Requiem Mass." He had wanted to welcome in the new, but he is tied to the past. His death is both personal and symbolic.

Yegor—"Not a typical merchant"

Like all of Gorky's work, the play is about people whose actions are conditioned by the social forces of which they themselves are an active element. Yet here, in addition, is a fuller canvas of society in collapse, with its abundance of dead mores, ignorance, and surviving folklore. The action is made up of the meaningful experiences of the day, yet towering above all is not a worker, a revolutionary hero typical of most Soviet plays, but a capitalist. Gorky had done the same before in his first novel, *Foma Gordeyev*, of which he wrote:[5]

> Foma is not a typical merchant. He is a healthy, strong individual who dreams of a free life and is crushed by the restrictive framework of the society he lives in.

The same is true of Yegor. He is surrounded by a savage environment; he himself is brutal, yet he has an insatiable faith that, rotten as the world is, new avenues will be opened up by man into which the love of life can pour itself more creatively.

Gorky's heroes are of protest and unrest: either tramps, cold, hungry, but free, who have no superiors to command them; or strong, positive, lonesome men like Yegor. Strange heroes indeed for a collective society, but Gorky had one foot in each world, and his impressionable years had been spent under the czarist regime. From his youthful world he retained a belligerent humanitarianism and a respect for knowledge. In Yegor, these are transformed into the elements of modern tragedy—man struggling with hostile forces, sensing alternatives, willing to yield yet unable to do so, forced to fight to the end, succumbing only to death.

The tragic overtones make a sympathetic protagonist of Yegor. He is rude and insulting to his wife; he once had an affair with his wife's sister, the abbess; he has long carried on an affair with Glasha; he had married for money; his illegitimate daughter lives in the household; yet we admire Yegor and dislike his wife, for she is hypocritical, self-righteous, ignorant and weak, whereas he is direct, honest, lusty, bursting with life even in death. He has mastered the world of the merchant and found it wanting. He probes for new values, and is all too human—with too little and too late. He refuses to succumb to deception, religious chicanery, superstition, not because he is aloof and beyond them, but because he is part of them, has lived with them, and has risen by his own strength to reject them.

The Insistence on Realism

Gorky's preoccupation with content gave rise to a theory of literary and dramatic form. In the Soviet Union, the first-felt freedoms after the Revolution let loose a wild flurry of experimentation rejecting the old and honoring the new, regardless of merit. It is doubtful if the theatre anywhere had witnessed such variety and exuberance. Whatever art forms were considered a protest against bourgeois restrictions were now honored. Even the dignified Moscow Art Theatre was frowned upon as old-fashioned and non-revolutionary. Holding the limelight were Evreinov with almost "pure theatricalism," Tairov with his "aesthetic principles," Meyerhold with his "bio-mechanics" and constructivist stagecraft, the poet Mayakovsky with his futurism, and Andreyev and his mad masochism. The growth in the theatre was phenomenal, for the theatre was held to be a collective art, close to the people. Everywhere new theatres sprang up—children's theatres, peasant theatres, folklore theatres, and theatres of the national minorities. Each factory and collective farm had its own producing organization. Theatrical practice reached a magnificence unequaled—became so superb, in fact, that hollow plays, long since forgotten, gave off a false luster of inherent worth. Theatre exceeded drama and transformed mediocrity into apparent genius.

It was at the height of this eclecticism that the debate on what socialist art should be reached its climax. Gorky, the recognized dean of Soviet letters, offered his definition of socialist realism, the official artistic expression of the Soviet world. It was in this spirit that *Yegor Bulitchev* was written.

Socialist Realism—The Unity of Opposites

In the Western world there has been much discussion as to the nature of socialist realism. The best explanation is in Gorky's own words:[6]

Within the romantic school, one must distinguish two sharply divergent tendencies: passive romanticism, which either attempts to reconcile people with reality by coloring it, or else attempts to divert people from reality and lure them to fruitless preoccupation with their inner world with thoughts about "the fatal riddle of life," about love and death, about problems which can never be solved by speculation and contemplation, but only by scientific research. Active romanticism on the other hand attempts to strengthen man's will to live, to rouse him to rebellion against reality with all its tyranny.

But the "active" romanticism that Gorky warmly endorsed for its positive approach to life was a still undeveloped art form. He continued:

From all this, we may be fairly certain that in our literature we have not as yet had the sort of romanticism which advocates a creative attitude to reality, which glorifies labor and the development of the will-to-live, and advocates the building up of new forms of life, and which also preaches hatred of the old world.

Gorky then examined realism, which likewise has two divergent schools—critical realism, and socialist realism. The former, the dominant literary trend of the nineteenth century:

. . . exposed the negative side of life, was defeatist, and stressed the infirmity of the individual's social existence and the utter futility of life.

Gorky, himself a writer of this school, respected the work of past realists. In his speech at the First Congress of Soviet Writers, he said:

We have no intention of underrating the great work of critical realism, and we appreciate its accomplishments in the very art of writing. But we must remember that this realism can only assist us in depicting the defects of the past, that we may better struggle against them and overcome them. However, this form of realism did not and cannot assist in the formation of the socialist individual,

for it confined itself to criticism alone without attempting
to formulate any positive belief.

What critical realism lacked was the confidence and direction of active romanticism. The synthesis of these two gave
rise to socialist realism, which "participates in shaping the
new mode of life to make of literature a fighting weapon of
socialist society."

In Marxist dialectic, Gorky had effected a unity of opposites, and fallen victim to a political concept of art. Of
the two words "socialist realism," one is political, the other
literary. The ingredients of the new art form come from
both worlds: faith in the individual's present ability and
future potential; faith in man's reasoned power to organize
a better existence; glorification of labor; concern with folklore and the art of the people; and the participation of
literature in the work of improving and forming a collec-
tivist world. The artist is no impartial observer. Art is an
element in the social revolution.

All of which is plausible politics but unproductive art.
No Soviet play has achieved international acceptance. The
merger of politics and art has not been a successful one.
Richelieu, decreeing the form of French neoclassical drama,
produced a Racine but stifled the theatre thereafter. The
emphasis on reason and control and a set of rules eleminated
extravagance and imagination. The Soviet decree, however,
contains an additional dilemma, since Marxism predicates
the inevitability of communism. Good and evil are stereotyped, and the results preordained when history predicates
a happy ending. The socialist hero must triumph, if not for
the moment, then eventually. Tragedy is therefore diluted,
if possible at all. Thus, socialist realism in turn stifled the
artist by imposing a formula, and resulted in a long series
of mediocre melodramas.

Despite Gorky's expressed intentions, *Yegor Bulitchev*
has little to do with the new theory. It is a play in the tradi-

tional realistic style. Though the communist world has as yet contributed no major play, it does have a unified faith and a developing myth to bolster it, and out of this may come a ritualistic drama. In recent years the insistence on socialist realism has subsided and it may one day be honored in the breach more than in the observance, for the artist, like Gorky, needs his own search for freedom.

Gorky was too strong an individualist to accept conformity. Many of his short stories attest to the shortcomings in human beings and the "incomprehensible spite of people," and he could not engage in blind adoration of the ideal proletarian. His participation in the definition of an art form may well have been his effort to find a balance between the world he dreamed of and the Soviet world in which he found himself, a personal act of expiation. He sought beauty and truth in this life and embraced a materialism which includes "man's reason and imagination." He is much closer to Dostoievsky, whose appeal to God's grace he rejected. Though hailed by Soviet society as its apostle, Gorky belongs to the mainstream of Russian literature.

7. The Relativity of Truth—Pirandello

HENRY IV

TO GO from the work of Strindberg, Chekhov, Gorky, and Shaw to that of Luigi Pirandello is to explore the full range of possibility in form and meaning in the contemporary theatre. Ibsen and those who fought at his side stormed the citadel of romantic intrigue and vacuous formula plays, to establish the theatre of psychological insight and integrity in human relations. No sooner was realism triumphant than it was attacked from all quarters as limiting the vision of man to the earthly and confining it to the middle-class living room. If Ibsen is realism's affirmation, Pirandello is its negation.

Italy has produced few playwrights of distinction. Pirandello is the exception. Though it has had a long and diversified history, the Italian theatre has been more derivative than creative. The grandeur that was Rome inspired the essayist and the architect, one the moralist, the other the builder. The playwright provided spectacles to win popular support for military and political ventures and became the hired publicist of emperors. Even the mighty Seneca is a rewritten version of Greek tragedy, and Plautus and Terence are clever adaptations of Menander. The finest theatre was the *commedia dell'arte,* in which superb actors performed folk comedies in the provinces and for which no playwright was needed. Not until the Renaissance, almost a millennium after the fall of Rome, did Italy become the center of a new world that found its fullest expression in painting, sculpture, and poetry. The theatre, however, produced little of enduring value. The best plays of the period were those of Machiavelli, whose *Clizia* and *La Mandragola* are vitriolic satires on marriage and the customs of the newly risen merchant class; the best productions resulted from the experiments in stage architecture and design of Serlio and the Bibbienas; but nothing in the theatre could compare with the work of a Dante or a Michelangelo. When the Renaissance, born in Florence, moved across Europe, Italy fell back to the Middle Ages and for three centuries, caught between two worlds, consoled herself with her poverty and her ancient glory, while the ideas which were unnourished seeds in the Italian theatre rose to splendor in Spain, France, and England.

Finally, under Garibaldi, Italy reawakened a pride in

her national destiny, and it was then natural that the theatre also should attempt to catch up with the latest developments in more industrialized countries. Realism was at its height in Paris and Berlin at the end of the nineteenth century. The Italian writers copied it and called it *verismo,* or truthfulness to life. Giuseppe Giacosa led the way with such plays as *Come le foglie (Like Falling Leaves),* a family drama modeled after Ibsen, in which a businessman, having achieved success, watches his family life disintegrate as his wife falls in love with a painter, and his children, indifferent to success, move toward bohemian pleasures. His hopes and careful plans vanish like falling leaves. Giacosa is much better known for his librettos of Puccini's operas. Giovanni Verga, another Verist, tried to outdo Tolstoy and Strindberg in brutality and violence on stage. *La Lupa (The She-Wolf)* has Nenni split open his mother-in-law's head with an ax as she attempts to seduce him. Verga's fame is more securely based on his Sicilian novels. Ibsen would not have been proud of his Italian disciples.

Realism failed because it was foreign to Italian soil. The psychological problems arising from industrial growth were alien to a basically peasant economy. And tradition and religion prevented the acceptance of the individual freedoms required of a militant middle-class society. Sentimental medodrama and lurid adventures proved more popular—for instance, D'Annunzio's *Più che l' amore (Beyond Love),* in which a superman kills a lioness in Africa, cheats at cards, and violates his friend's sister. Not until the First World War did the Italian theatre achieve an indigenous form and international distinction.

Italy's effort to become a major world power had ended disastrously, and the inglorious defeat led to a disillusionment far more widespread than in other nations. The heroic tradition of the past could not be reactivated with an unwilling nation. In the attempt to discover herself, Italy found life degrading and reality meaningless. An abortive revolution aroused many to renewed action, but soon resulted in a discontent with politics and made the people an easy prey for Mussolini. Bitter young artists rejected the older romanticism with its mock heroics that lulled the dreamer into docility, and embraced Futurism, which spread to every country of the Western world. It demanded a complete break with the past, which had enslaved the present with its failures, and called for a worship of science and the machine. It sought an inner dynamism and violence of movement. Though the main appeal of Futurism was to the painter, an offshoot was the *teatro del grottesco*, whose manifesto in 1915 depicted the agony of the generation living through the horrors of war, still chained to symbols of the past. Its leading playwright was Luigi Chiarelli, whose daring and experimental *La maschera e il volto (The Mask and the Face)* was a savage denunciation of Italian honor and of the stupidity and corruption of a depraved society. Paolo, the main character, declares extravagantly that he would kill his wife should she ever be unfaithful, but when he finds himself a cuckold, he cannot carry out his boasts. He spirits his wife away and announces that he has drowned her. After his acquittal he is idolized by all the ladies, who fall at his feet. They offer themselves to him because he has honored them by annihilating infidelity. Then an unrecognizable corpse is found in the river, but on the day of the funeral Paolo's wife returns. He is now in danger of going to jail for perjury, for declaring himself guilty of a crime he never committed. Happy to be reunited with his supposedly dead wife, he runs off with her. The demands of the code of honor are subjected to excoriating cynicism. The mask of the title is the face man presents to society, in contrast to the unmasked reality of his inner self. The irony lies in the possible punishment for something he has not done and in the mores of the past, which encourage dishonesty and deception. The grotesqueness of the play is the nightmarish quality it gives to society's dance of death.

In the rejection of realism, the Italian theatre found its direction. The theatre of the grotesque leads directly to Pirandello, the only writer gifted with an intellectual precocity and theatrical sensitivity to carry the fight against realism to its logical absurdity.

Appearance and Reality—"The theatre and reality cannot meet without destroying each other."

From his native Sicily, Luigi Pirandello inherited an awareness of violence in man's life, a cynicism about politics, and a hatred of the poverty that throttles the poet. A series of tragedies in his personal life added to his disillusionment. His family had been well-to-do and owned a prosperous sulphur business, which enabled him to study philology at the University of Rome, and later continue his research in philosophy at Bonn, where he absorbed the metaphysics of Kant and the dialectics of Hegel.

As if by design, both his family and his wife's suddenly lost all their money. A mine disaster and a bankruptcy left them penniless. Pirandello's wife was giving birth to their third child at the time, and the shock was too great; she became mentally unbalanced. Pirandello was too poor to send her to an institution, and for seventeen years he lived in their small, crowded quarters with a screaming and jealous wife, who rebuked him unjustifiably for neglecting her and having affairs with other women. He earned a meager living by teaching in a girls' school near Rome.

Pirandello wrote poems and a novel before he turned to the theatre, but it was his plays that finally brought him international fame and a Nobel Prize for literature in 1934, which enabled him to place his wife in a sanatorium. With the exception of *Liolà*, his work reflects his deep sadness, his preoccupation with death and suicide, and his gloomy meditations on the futility of existence. He once wrote, "I have tried to tell something to other men, without any ambition except perhaps that of avenging myself for having been born." He saw petty man as a mockery of God's intention, and declared that "the divine spirit enters into us and becomes dwarfed into a puppet." Yet by combining the theatre of the grotesque with his flair for *commedia dell'arte* improvisations, he created a bizarre and influential form for his speculations on the nature of reality. His first important play, *Six Characters in Search of an Author,* was produced in all Western capitals and given a major production by Max Reinhardt. From Mussolini, he received a theatre of his own, and the freedom for further experimentation. He himself directed many of his works and toured Europe and South America with his company. He wrote little in his later years and again sought new forms, for his earlier insistence on the unknowability of truth and the relativism of knowledge was difficult to dramatize in fresh and ingenious methods once a formula had been established, but the plays which are typical are landmarks in the theatre of ideas.

Così è, se vi pare, translated as *Right You Are, If You Think You Are* or *It is So! (If You Think So),* tells of Signor Ponza who will not permit his wife's mother to visit her, a seemingly usual domestic problem, but the officials of the town are aroused when complaints are made that the mother-in-law has to shout to her daughter from the street below. Ponza explains that his wife is not Signora Frola's daughter; he now has a second wife. His first wife, who *was* her daughter, has died, but the Signora refuses to believe this. She explains that Ponza is deluded. He has never recovered from a dream that his wife died, and they have had to perform the marriage ceremony twice. He thinks his wife is another woman, but his second wife and his first are really the same person. The relations between mother and son-in-law are pleasant and without hostility, each one doing his best to preserve the other's illusion. Only because the neighbors have interfered, must a decision be reached. The villagers demand an end to uncertainty. Is she or is she not the daughter of Signora Frola? In the final scene, the wife comes down for her only appearance before the gathered populace, and says, slowly and clearly, "I *am* the daughter of Signora Frola," and as all sigh with relief, she adds, "*and* the second wife of Signor Ponza." Then she continues, "And as for myself, I am nobody!" The Prefect exclaims, "No, no, madam—for yourself, you must be either one or the other." Her answer is, "No! I am she whom you believe me to be." Laudisi, the philosopher-narrator, makes the final comment —"There, my friends, you have the truth!"[1]—and bursts out laughing. The laughter is Pirandello's, for he had once written, "Ask the poet what is the saddest sight and he will reply, 'It is the laughter on the face of man.' " All truth is relative. Each one has his own truth. Appearances are faulty, and lying a necessity. In an early essay on humor, Pirandello had said:

> The harder the struggle for life and the more one's weakness is felt, the greater becomes the need for mutual deception. The simulation of force, honesty, sympathy, prudence, in short, of every virtue, and of that greatest virtue veracity, is a form of adjustment, an effective instrument of struggle . . . And while the sociologist describes social life as it presents itself to external observation, the humorist, being a man of exceptional intuition, shows—nay, reveals—that appearances are one thing and the consciousness of the people concerned, in its inner essence, another. And yet people "lie psychologically" even as they "lie socially."

How can one ever penetrate another's identity? Why pry beneath the assumed self to uncover a self equally indistinct? Ponza and his family managed to maintain their illusions peacefully. Society, in insisting on *the truth* and invading the inner privacy of self-isolation, becomes absurdly cruel and worthy only of the philosopher's laughter. The wife negates herself, caught between two truths and society's insistence on clarity—a sacrifice to the social lie.

The form is unusual. The characters are shadows without any specific psychological individuality. The flow lies in the continuing debate as to the nature of reality. *Six Characters in Search of an Author* is a more highly developed and far more theatrical treatment of the same theme. It is Pirandello's best-known play and has become incorporated into the repertory of most theatres, and yet it is the most complex for it plays the same action on many levels simultaneously. It is a play within a play within a play, performed on a bare stage, the first of a trilogy in which the actors move on stage, in the auditorium, in the boxes, in the lobby, and often in the aisles. Pirandello called it a "comedy in the making," to indicate that what happens is improvised, though actually it is a carefully planned sequence of revelations. The haphazard appearance has the form of *commedia dell'arte,* as though life were being re-enacted in the process of living, yet the audience is made fully aware of the artifice of the theatricality. The comedy is a ludicrous tragedy of those who have not yet lived out their lives, the sad and pathetic fate of those who are trying to escape from disaster and are searching for the means to do so, as Pirandello himself must have tried while living with a demented wife and teaching to stay alive.

Six characters interrupt a rehearsal of a Pirandello play to ask the director and actors to act out their lives, because the author who created them has failed to complete his work, in much the same way that God left man ignorant of his destiny.

Since actors in the truth of their realization become other characters, the intruders may be able to witness what will happen to them, for as Pirandello said in his preface to the play, "born alive, they wished to live." What a perfect situation for a treatment of the many aspects of appearance and reality! The audience is one reality; the rehearsing actors another, with the stage as the instrument for transforming appearance into a different illusion of reality; and lastly, the characters created in fiction, who now want to know how their lives will end—all three interchanging their respective concepts. The six characters are bound together by a common origin, "each with his secret torment . . . and mutual entanglement." Pirandello had found them alive, but now they must carry on by themselves, and so he has them enter the theatre, where art can hold the flow of life for observation.

As the six characters relate their past, interrupted first by the actors and then by one another, Pirandello has set the stage for dialectical fireworks. The claims of realism are subjected to the most devastating attack. When the Stepdaughter relates the details of the scene with her father in the house of prostitution, the Manager orders her to stop because "you can't have this kind of thing on stage." She insists on telling the truth, instead of permitting the Manager to go back to rehearsing a "cerebral drama" of Pirandello's. The Manager says the actors have to create for the audience the illusion of reality, at which the Father, in deep distress, reminds them that creating that illusion is only a game for them, whereas for his family, there is "no other reality outside of this illusion. What is a game of art for you," he declares, "is our sole reality," and adds that what the actors feel today may prove an illusion tomorrow, since it varies "according to will, sentiments, which in turn are controlled by an intellect" that likewise varies. Were it ever fixed, then the "fatuous comedy of life" would end.

The intricacies multiply, for the actors are listening to characters whom they are asked to make real even while their own reality is questioned. Moreover, every individual is changing from moment to moment. The Stepdaughter calls the Father "immoral," and he is angry at being so pigeonholed. Adjectives that characterize a man, such as "honest" or "brave," only limit him in the fluidity of life, imprison him within the confines of false denotation. Conscience is multiple, and motives are so mixed that we have only the illusion of being unique personalities, and to judge us by one deed is to deny continuity. In any single deed, only part of a person is involved.

If motives are so complex, how can they ever be acted out on stage, and how can art give form to that which escapes definition? How can all avenues to understanding be presented in the flowing minute of truth, and how can one judge reality if each character is gifted with varying capabilities of articulating the truth? The Father is able to express his consternation. He is voluble and communicates an insight into his motives, but the others are mute. How can their inner motives be known?

The life of the six characters before they came on stage was sordid. The Father, believing his wife to be in love with his clerk, had set up a separate home for them. The wife had three more children before the clerk died. One day, in a brothel, the Father almost committed incest with the Stepdaughter, but was prevented by the intervention of the Mother. Now, filled with remorse and guilt, he is anxious to take them all back. The children sit around, silent and embittered. The Stepdaughter challenges the Father's motives. Though the actors never take up the story and continue the lives of the characters, they themselves begin to move forward in the present. The younger son hides behind the trees, and a revolver shot is heard. The actors rush to pick up the body, and as the boy is carried off, the Manager asks if he is *really* wounded. A few of the actors exclaim in horror that he is dead, while others remark calmly that it is only make-believe, only pretense.

THE FATHER: (*With a terrible cry.*) Pretense? Reality, sir, reality!

THE MANAGER: Pretense? Reality? To hell with it all!

Pirandello's keen intellect fashioned a masterful fantasy aimed at eliminating the pretensions of realism. Out of his own despair, he preceded the negativists of France by two decades. He invented a form as loose and unconfining as the subject matter of his discourse, and succeeded in holding within his art the endlessly escaping formlessness of reality. He went beyond science, which has been able to capture and analyze only one minute corner of the complicated labyrinth of living. Positivism clings to a self-delusion, the last stage of which is insanity.

Pirandello equaled the magician's trickery of *Six Characters* in his finest play, *Henry IV,* in which a tighter structure lessens the complexity but concentrates the dramatic power.

HENRY IV

Henry IV of Germany, who went to Canossa, lives in a modern villa. The past is relived in the present. The Henry of the play had fallen off a horse during a carnival, and when he recovered consciousness, in his traumatic shock he thought of himself—or pretended to think of himself—as the character in history whose costume he had worn. The masquerade turned into reality. What he presumed to be, he became, at least in his own mind. A wealthy relative has surrounded him with all the trappings of historical accuracy, even to a retinue of valets who pamper his whims and serve as court attendants. But the historical throwback is deliberately incomplete. The audience knows the action is of today. The servants, though in clothes of the eleventh century, smoke cigarettes when the Emperor is not in the room, and are caught in their own fantasy between the selves they are in real life and the selves they are performing—puppets who have the form without the content. Above the throne in the main salon are life-size portraits of Henry IV and of the Marchioness Matilda of Tuscany, his consort, who interceded with Pope Gregory VII to lift the decree of excommunication, but the portraits show young people in carnival outfits, like two mirrors "which cast back living images in the midst of a world" that is dead. Arriving to visit Henry for the first time in eighteen years are Donna Matilda, her lover Belcredi, her daughter Frida, who is now the living figure of her mother in the portrait, Henry's nephew, who maintains the household, and a psychiatrist. Donna Matilda is the woman he loved at the time of the carnival and Belcredi was then his rival. They have come to see if he can be restored to normal living. They don robes to represent their counterparts in Henry's court. The Emperor enters with regal ceremony. He *is* Henry IV in every outward detail, and he pleads with Donna Matilda to intercede with the Pope, but in Frida he sees the woman for whom he made his sacrifice and he begs to be permitted to "love her as she deserves." In Belcredi he senses an enemy. Henry leaves, and the first-act curtain comes down with the question of his madness unresolved.

The rest of the play proceeds in continuous time sequence. Matilda and Belcredi are certain that Henry has recognized them; Frida is frightened by his advances; the doctor requires further proof. Frida puts on the robes her mother wore at the time of the portrait, and with that gesture bridges eight hundred years by losing herself in the role of Matilda of Tuscany—or she may be only part of a game, neither self in entirety, but elements of both personalities in conflict, like the valets of the King. When the guests leave, Henry turns to his attendants, and to their utter amazement speaks no longer as the Emperor but as a man fully aware of where he is and who he is. He strips off the masks of everyone, revealing the lies and deception that are hidden beneath. Why have they come to make fun of him? They want to investigate their own guilt, and to "infuriate a poor devil already out of the world, out of time, out of life." The servants, listening to his rational comments, are puzzled as to what their role should be with an apparently sane man, and embarrassed by the ridiculousness of their own previous actions. Henry is delighted with their confusion, but his thoughts revert to his visitors. He had forced them to put on their masks to "satisfy [his] taste . . .

for playing the madman," and now he will watch them take their masks off.

The audience is still uncertain about Henry, for Pirandello was obsessed by the absurdity of using labels to define a personality that is fleeting, insubstantial, ever changing. Henry is angered at their use of the word "mad," their hope to "crush a man with the weight of a word," just as the Father was in *Six Characters*, who refused to accept a single adjective to define his personality. Henry says that he has played his part consciously, knowing that civilization fears the madman, who shakes the foundations of convention and logic, a logic that "flies like a feather" and wafts back an illusory truth. It was they who had come to see Henry IV, they who had made a dead man order the live about. As a child, he knew other truths from other appearances. He lived in the world of imagination and to him the moon in the pond was real, but they forced on him conventional truths and tore him from his dreams. He will have his revenge at last. He will expose their imposed truths, for —and he is now conventionally rational—he knows that Belcredi was an accomplice in bleeding the horse in order to cause his fall at the carnival eighteen years before, and has taken his place with Matilda. He will make them regret their intrusion into his present world. Now that he is no longer mad, the pleasure of reliving history is no longer his. Besides, his valets know all about it. But just as he resolves to discard his play-acting, Old John, a servant, enters with a lamp to perform his role as amanuensis to the Emperor. Henry remarks that a jest may be the truth if one plays it *as if* it were true. For Old John's sake—or perhaps he may have reverted to his former condition—he becomes Henry IV and dictates his memoirs.

In the final act, Frida and her fiancé have taken their places where the portraits formerly hung. They are now Matilda of Tuscany and Henry IV. When the King enters, they step out of the frames in a planned shock treatment to throw him back to the twentieth century. Frida, however, is frightened and Henry takes her in his arms. She shouts for help, and the others rush in. He discloses his secret. He had recovered many years back. There was no need for a psychiatrist to examine him. Why should he have returned to their world—to friends who had deceived him, to a woman who had given his place to another, to a banquet table from which all the crumbs had been cleared away? Because of the ugliness of the real world, he had decided to stay in his make-believe world. They who came to cure him are the real madmen, for they have submitted to being part of his pretended world. At last, he can open the windows and breathe life and remain in the embrace of Frida, the woman he lost, who has returned as lovely and as young as when he first loved her. Sanity is tolerable if he can roll back the years and resume his life before the accident at the masquerade. Has he gone mad again? He pulls Frida close to him. The others move to separate them. In the confusion and shouting, Henry draws a sword and kills Belcredi. History has avenged the crime on itself. As Belcredi's body is carried off, Henry is left alone with his followers. Now that he has committed murder, his only salvation is to pretend madness again, and for the rest of his life.

Henry IV is the traditional well-made play with variations. The unities of time, place, and action are rigidly adhered to—the one-set throne room, the constriction of time to a few hours, and the movement focused on one action: the arrival of the guests and its fatal consequences. In *Six Characters*, Pirandello had achieved a new form through his imagination and his skill in manipulating, on many levels, an obvious artificiality that gave him freedom to explore the philosophical problems incorporated in the technique itself. The form got out of hand in the later plays, and the machinery overwhelmed the content, so that the characters ceased to be self-propelled. Strindberg, to focus on a world of dreams, had initiated a style that mastered time by eliminating it. Brecht, to reach objectively dispassionate judgment, had evolved an epic form that was integrated with his intention. Pirandello, after many efforts at an illogical structure that would match the relativity of evidence, which became increasingly obscure, reverted to a traditional form, and the result was his most complete drama. He had sought to eliminate time by becoming absorbed with it, and this involvement produced a distance between meaning and structure.

Henry IV is a mordant view of man. After the protagonist has forsaken his madness to face reality, he retreats to madness to preserve his sanity. When outsiders compelled him to, he played the game, but in seclusion from them; now he chooses to return, for reality is too painful to endure. Behind his own mask lies the terrible anguish of loneliness. All mutual relations are freighted with deceit and misunderstanding.

> Without wanting to, without knowing it, in the strife of their bedeviled souls, each of them, defending himself against the accusations of the others, expresses as his own living passion and torment the passion and torment which for so many years have been the pangs of my spirit: the deceit of mutual understanding irremediably founded on the empty abstraction of the words, the multiple personality of everyone corresponding to the possibilities of being to be found in each of us . . .

Nor is there much to cling to, since appearances are false, and reality but shifting quicksands which suck in appearances and disfigure them to make any truth unrecognizable and unknowable. Pirandello was caught in the quicksands himself, for if complete relativity embraces all of life, it includes the philosopher and the poet who can never achieve harmonious relationship. If the mind can reach no truth, even a changing one, then the poet's form is inaccessible to hold that change, and the play becomes a montage of merging shadows and ceases to be drama. Pirandello was impatient with formal art, though he borrowed from it when necessary. The artist gives form to the indistinct and endless flow of life, but the logic of Pirandello, even as poet if not philosopher, is that there can be no form, yet he must strive to create it. The result is anarchy. Pirandello was well aware of his dilemma. He wrote: "All that lives, by the fact of living, has a form, and by the same token must die, except the work of art which lives forever, insofar as it *is* form." The artist holds life-in-motion motionless. The philosopher denies even that possibility. Pirandello's problem is insoluble.

The same is true of personality. Given only an unyielding moment to adhere to reality, its accepted qualities fragmented, a human personality becomes, like the plays themselves, a combination of specters in conflict with different parts of itself. The result is a soulless void, an overfine distillation that evaporates into emptiness. Overratiocination can eliminate art, and the cerebral dramas of Pirandello become self-conscious artifacts. It could not be otherwise. Taking the props out from under life leaves no positive basis on which to reconstruct.

Mussolini's publicly displayed friendship for Pirandello was not for what the playwright had to say, but for his name, which the Duce used to bolster a faltering dictatorship. Pirandello has been accused of being pro-Fascist, and he did make statements approving the seizure of Ethiopia. But Mussolini certainly found little comfort in Pirandello's plays. Men must live with some truth and be willing to die for it, if a society is to survive. Pirandello's work, however, is devastatingly nonpolitical, and his continuing negativism can arouse little public enthusiasm. Herein lies his limitation. There is no indignation, only controlled description, and the warmth supplied by logic burns all too quickly. His fecund imagination reached beyond instituted order, whether of state or temple, to view man in proportion, in hope of touching certainty, but he found none though his search was heroic. He turned away from realism because, he said, "The theatre and reality cannot meet without destroying each other."

Modern psychiatry and physical science, in accepting the relativity of knowledge, have made Pirandello's meaning less startling. His form still reigns wherever the playwright attempts to portray varying levels of consciousness. Anything is called Pirandellian if the actors on stage are halted by a narrator who talks to the audience about the meaning of reality. But today, in the face of an equal lack of assertion and of helplessness at the prospect of megaton bombs, Pirandello's wanderings at the edge of infinity give him an increasing voice in the contemporary theatre. He has influenced many writers: Evreinov in Russia; the German expressionists of the postwar period; Eugene O'Neill; many of the French playwrights, among them Cocteau, Anouilh, and Ionesco; and in his own country, Ugo Betti. Forgotten for a time in the prosperity of the twenties, he has resumed his leadership in the anti-dramas of despair, and though Pirandello may not inspire hope, he does attempt to illuminate the destiny of man.

8. The Theatre as Temple—T. S. Eliot

THE COCKTAIL PARTY

THE PRESENT-DAY THEATRE is deeply concerned with the relation of God to man. O'Neill struggled to find a modern and more scientific God. Sartre demonstrates how deeply he is disturbed by devoting an entire play to the proof that God does not exist. Beckett, more responsive to the separation of man from man, writes of a God who never appears yet for whom inarticulate and helpless man must go on waiting. None of these playwrights represents the established orthodoxy. Today, there is a movement, increasingly strong in the theatre, for the religion of the past, a retreat from worldly preoccupation and a return to the solace of the church.

The most gifted of such playwrights is Paul Claudel, whose *Le Soulier de Satin (The Satin Slipper)* is a modern masterpiece in which the entire universe becomes a stage for man's ascent to divine love. Claudel is closely followed by Mauriac, Bernanos, Montherlant, and in England, Graham Greene, all devout Catholics or converts to Catholicism. The most distinguished international reputation, however, has been achieved by T. S. Eliot. Hailed by many critics before his death as the greatest living English poet, he has long held sway in university circles and intellectual magazines as the arbiter of literary taste. His influence has been limited but deep. With *The Cocktail Party*, his first play in eleven years, he made a successful entry into the popular, competitive commercial theatre. After its premiere at the Edinburgh Festival in 1949, the play was acclaimed in New York and had an unprecedented run for a serious verse drama. Its success was all the more significant because Eliot had written but two previous plays—one, *Murder in the Cathedral,* performed occasionally in England and experimentally by the Federal Theatre Project in the United States; the other, *The Family Reunion,* a minor piece reserved for church production. But it was *The Cocktail Party* that became the basis for extended discussions on the importance of the theatre as temple.

A Puritan Royalist

Thomas Stearns Eliot was born in St. Louis, Missouri,

of a well-to-do middle-class family that boasted descent from
Isaac Stearns, one of the original settlers of the Massachu-
setts Bay Colony. He studied philosophy and literature at
Harvard, the Sorbonne, Oxford, and several German uni-
versities, returning later to teach at Harvard, but taking
up permanent residence in England. During the First World
War he was a schoolmaster and banker, later devoting his
time to editing and publishing. In 1927, at the age of
thirty-nine, he announced his intention to become a British subject, and declared a few months later, in the preface
to *For Launcelot Andrews,* that he was "a classicist in literature, a royalist in politics, and an Anglo-Catholic in religion," a statement which he carefully deleted from the
revised edition in 1936. The years between the Kaiser's
invasion of Belgium and the beginning of the Depression
were decisive ones for Eliot's thinking. The author of "Pru-
frock" and *The Waste Land,* the voice from "the other side
of despair," the venerated poet of postwar disillusion, was
now confirmed in his convictions. A descendant of the persecuted Puritans was the champion of the Crown and the
Church of Rome.

"They are hunting me down; I must move on . . ."

   Though his plays are few in number, Eliot from his
earliest writing was drawn to the theatre: "The ideal medium for poetry . . . the most direct means of social 'useful-
ness' for poetry is the theatre."[1] Many of his essays deal
with dramatic theory and criticism. His own preferences
were for medieval morality plays; for Dante's *Divine Comedy,* which he termed the greatest drama of all time; the
Restoration plays, which he termed virtuous; and neglected
Elizabethans. *Everyman* is, for him, a model of religious
exhortation; Dante is the poetic expression of the philosophy
of Thomas Aquinas; the bawdy outburst of the Restoration
is a Puritan's consolation; and such figures as Ben Jonson,
who likewise was converted to Catholicism in his maturity,

are examples of a classical style, patterned structure, and a dominant rhetoric.

In 1926, Eliot attempted his first play but completed only sparse fragments. This was *Sweeney Agonistes,* a combination of Aristophanes, Milton, and the jazz hall. It opens with two prostitutes who fear the arrival of the dangerous Pereira, speaking in a staccato dance rhythm that is repeated later in the dull conversation that opens *The Cocktail Party:*[2]

DUSTY: How about Pereira?
DORIS: What about Pereira?
        I don't care.
DUSTY: You don't care!
        Who pays the rent?
DORIS: Yes, he pays the rent.
DUSTY: Well, some men don't and some men do
        Some men don't and you know who.
DORIS: You can have Pereira.
DUSTY: What about Pereira?

Doris cuts the deck of cards and draws the two of spades, the coffin, reannouncing the note of fear. The vacuous businessmen with obviously Jewish names are interrupted in their party with the girls by the arrival of Sweeney, who recounts the story of a man "who did a girl in" and kept the corpse in the bathtub for days. All break into a chorus in triple rhythm to a background of percussion knocks on the door:

> When you're alone in the middle of the night
> and you wake in a sweat and a hell of a fright . . .

It is likely that the dreaded Pereira is coming.

The rhythmic combinations disclose an abundant talent, but the disconnected fragments are distorted far beyond their meaning. The metaphysical bursts, clashing with coarse reality, give rise to elusive and obscure interpretation. *Sweeney Agonistes* was not intended for production, although Eliot's admirers have since staged it many times, adding with directorial skill a sequence lacking in the original. It reads well as an exercise in metrical orchestration and also has value because what it tells us of Eliot's development, his strained early efforts to evolve a new dramatic form by blending an imitation of Greek tragedy, popular dance rhythms, and brutal, elemental caricatures. In published form, the play is prefaced by two important quotations—one, from the *Choephori* of Aeschylus:

ORESTES: You don't see them, you don't—but I see them: they are hunting me down, I must move on.

and the other, from *St. John of the Cross:*

Hence the soul cannot be possessed of the divine union, until it has divested itself of the love of created beings.

Herein lie the continuing elements of Eliot's later plays: the sense of evil, of fear, of persecution by supernatural forces, atonement and absolution, reaching for identification with God, and the rejection of human concerns.

Eight years later, in his next effort in drama, Eliot wrote a series of liturgical chants for *The Rock,* a religious pageant produced to raise funds for the "Forty-five Churches of the Diocese of London." The poetry of these choruses is more dignified, but the underlying message is the same—the need for religion in a world of selfish material pursuits. Genuflections to the glory of God are mixed with acid comments on the pleasures of the middle class, such as the cynical epitaph:

And the wind shall say "Here were decent
   godless people
Their only monument the asphalt road
And a thousand lost golf balls."

"We have lost our way in the dark . . ."

Eliot's first full-length play was written the next year, in 1935, when the now established and authoritative poet

was forty-seven years of age and his contempt for bourgeois
insensitivity had mellowed into a confirmed religious prose-
lytism. *Murder in the Cathedral* deals with the assassination of Thomas Becket, Archbishop of Canterbury in the
twelfth century, by the agents of Henry II. The Chorus of
the Poor, the Archbishop's faithful followers, witness the
action as the Four Tempters (later, the Four Knights who
commit the murder) offer Thomas the manifold temptations of this world to recant in his opposition to the King
—riches, physical comforts, worldly power, and the greater
religious power of martyrdom. Thomas chooses death, even
though:[3]

> The last temptation is the greatest treason.
> To do the right deed for the wrong reason.

To him, in imitation of the Passion of Christ, martyrdom
is a spiritual fulfillment preferable to worldly compromise.
The play has all the elements of Greek tragedy—chorus,
declamation, single protagonist in bold relief, and a para-
basis in the form of a Christmas sermon. It has been successful in production, the most stirring of Eliot's plays, for
it offers mass chant, a church interior, and a religious awe
which does have historical relevance. It is full of pageantry
and the solemnity of Thomas' faith. He is human enough
to waver momentarily, but only because his choice of martyrdom may be ascribed to a desire for self-glorification. The
weakness as drama is the confusion between heroism and
holiness. Thomas embraces death with joy. Anouilh, a more
practical dramatist, faced the same problem of the diminish-
ing role of the individual. Once his Becket decides to defend the honor of God, he becomes static and immune to
worldly matters. Anthony Quinn, who played the King in
the Broadway production, had the more dramatic role.
When he left the cast, Laurence Olivier shifted from Becket
to the King. Anouilh has portrayed the conflict between
two men. The King, in search of love on earth, finds it in

Becket, but Becket does not respond and the King must destroy his Archbishop. Becket, never fully satisfied with sensual pursuits, finds an honor he can defend even with his life, but his long-sought dedication to a cause is an inner non-dramatic passion. Eliot, on the other hand, never mentions love or honor. His Thomas is concerned with the propagation of the faith. The symbol of the Cross becomes a coruscating condemnation of secular power. Anouilh triumphed in the human struggle of the King. His play is in witty prose. Eliot triumphed in the victory of God. His place is in austere verse.

Eliot's later plays attempted the same message—in modern apartments with twentieth-century characters. *The Family Reunion,* written at the time of England's deepest crisis in 1939, is a modest chamber piece completely divorced from national events. Henry, Lord Monchensey, returns to his country home to find solace from the haunting obsession that he has murdered his wife by pushing her overboard on a transatlantic liner. He discovers through Aunt Agatha and Mary, the rejected girl who has always loved him, the catharsis he seeks. His mother, still alive, has been overpossessive; his father never loved her, and had gone away entertaining thoughts, as Agatha discloses, of:[4]

> how to get rid of your mother . . .
> You were due in three months' time;
> You could not have been born in that event.

Harry's guilt feelings are the projection of his father's unfulfilled will, and his resentment against his mother's destructive love has been transformed into hatred of his own wife. Finding himself "happy for the moment," he does not marry the understanding Mary, but goes off on some unknown missionary task,

> To the worship in the desert, the thirst and deprivation,
> A stony sanctuary and a primitive altar.

The Chorus, this time, consists of the four uncles and aunts, stupid and thick-skinned, who never see the Eumenides that pursue Harry, and keep chanting:

We have lost our way in the dark.

Though Eliot enthusiasts have called the play "the greatest English tragedy since the Elizabethans," it is unfortunate dramatically. The combination of classic myths and modern settings is rarely successful. Greek legends had meaning to a Greek audience and grew out of an accepted religion. When these legends are transferred to the modern world, they become dislocated. Cocteau, Sartre, and Giraudoux, stemming from Racine and a French neoclassic tradition, used the Orestes story familiar to their audiences, for a modern connotation. O'Neill labored formidably to create an Aeschylean trilogy, but the result is a psychological and physical, not a religious, drama. Eliot used a classic form—chorus, Furies, verse—but the relevance has been skimmed from the myth; the Eumenides get tangled up in the ancestral drapes. The Orestes theme with a religious resolution—Thomas Becket with a sprinkling of Freud.

THE COCKTAIL PARTY

None of these plays would have gained Eliot more than casual sway in the theatre were it not for *The Cocktail Party,* ten years later.

The play opens with an embarrassed cocktail party in the London drawing room of the Chamberlaynes—"embarrassed" because Lavinia, Edward Chamberlayne's wife, has just left him and he has been unable to reach the few guests to call off the affair. Present are Mrs. Julia Shuttlethwaite, a chattering overseer of everybody's affairs; Alexander MacColgie Gibbs, a world traveler, who can always put you in touch with somebody somewhere; Peter Quilpe, a young writer; Celia Coplestone, Edward's mistress; and a mysterious Unidentified Guest who, after the others have gone, arranges to have Lavinia return. Act Two takes place in the office of the Psychiatrist, Sir Harcourt-Reilly, who turns out to be the Unidentified Guest. He is the propelling force of the drama—the voice of T. S. Eliot, an amalgam of priest and doctor who reconciles the estranged couple and sends them back to bored domesticity. For Celia, he offers a different course, which only the elect can pursue: to renounce worldly pleasures and go off to Africa as a missionary. In Act Three, two years later, the same characters as in Act One reappear at the Chamberlaynes, except for Celia. We discover that Celia has died, crucified in the jungle, at which news all drink a toast and leave. Edward and Lavinia then await the guests for another, and apparently less disturbing, cocktail party.

Apart from the quality of the verse and the dramatic power the play possesses in production, it is essentially a "message" play, of particular importance in the contemporary struggle for values.

"Private shadows . . ."

In *The Cocktail Party*, Eliot reaffirms his belief in the nobility of salvation for the chosen few. Earlier he had written of William Archer: "He used some deplorable terms such as 'humanitarianism.'"[5] In *The Cocktail Party* he repeats his opposition to social and human adjustment and maintains that the highest duty of man is to God, the supreme achievement a mystical identity with Him, reserved for the aristocracy of spirit. For the rest of mortals—even the educated middle class, including prosperous lawyers like Edward Chamberlayne—there is nought to life but muddling through with coarse insensitivity. The cocktail set is equated with the temptations of Everyman in a modern morality play. The characters wear evening clothes but the solutions are those of St. Thomas—Aquinas or Eliotus.

In Eliot's three plays, the protagonists make the same

choice in almost the same words. Harry, released from his fears, says:

> I have not yet had the precise directions.
> Where does one go from a world of insanity?

and then decides he will become "the missionary out to the world." Thomas Becket takes for granted his martyr's crown. Celia, facing the Psychiatrist-Priest more in a confessional booth than on a professional couch, says:[6]

> . . . I want to be cured
> Of a craving for something I cannot find
> And of the shame of never finding it . . .

and is told that the path she is to choose

> . . . requires faith,
> The kind of faith that issues from despair.

Harry's fate we never learn. Thomas is assassinated, and Celia slain by those she would convert, but all three have renewed their religious conviction.

To Eliot, the world of sense and science, of reason and logic, of social reality, is trivial and illusory. The only reality is of the divine essence, a Platonic divorce from actuality, the imposition of a transcendent, inexplicable reality beyond the immanent. Over and over again in *The Cocktail Party* recur such lines as:

> I was saying what is the reality
> Of experience between two unreal people . . .

or:

> Perhaps the dream was better. It seemed the real
> reality . . .

Harry, in *The Family Reunion*, says:

> The things I thought were real are shadows, and
> the real
> Are what I thought were private shadows.

Negation of this world leads to adventure in the world of "private shadows." The Psychiatrist says to the chosen Celia:

> You will know very little until you get there;
> You will journey blind. But the way leads towards possession
> Of what you have sought for in the wrong place.

And she replies, most illogically, out of desperation rather than conviction:

> I don't in the least know what I am doing
> Or why I am doing it. There is nothing else to do:
> That is the only reason.

To which the answer is:

> It is the best reason.

"I must . . . atone . . ."

To achieve an Eliot peace on "the other side of reason" requires suffering. This is essential if one grants the premise of Original Sin. Man is evil, born in guilt, both he and Nature imperfect. Only through expiation, rigorous ethical discipline, can some element of grace be achieved. This philosophy is a throwback to the thought of the Middle Ages. It makes of suffering a desirable good. Thus the Confessor-Psychiatrist, quite jubilant—or at least unperturbed—over Celia's horrible fate, says:

> She paid the highest price
> In suffering. That is part of the design.

Those who are privileged to be martyrs, who atone for all men, must in turn experience the concentrated suffering of all humanity. This accounts for Eliot's being drawn to Thomas Becket, and to Celia, who on the conference couch impresses the doctor deeply when she says:

> And I feel I must . . . *atone*—is that the word?

Atonement in this highly personalized sense renders the world unnecessary to the protagonist. He has a completeness in his own destiny. He is always alone, terribly alone. Celia, disclosing her symptoms, says:

> It isn't that I *want* to be alone
> But that everyone's alone.

He who finds atonement separates himself from his fellow men, but for all men there is neither companionship nor communication. The entire universe is one "huge disaster." Harry, in *The Family Reunion,* even after he has found a temporary peace, says:

> What you call the normal
> Is merely the unreal and the unimportant.
> I was like that in a way, so long as I could think
> Even of my own life as an isolated ruin,
> A casual bit of waste in an orderly universe;
> But it begins to seem just part of some huge disaster,
> Some monstrous mistake and aberration
> Of all men, of the world, which I cannot put in order.

Eliot's early reputation after the First World War was based on his remarkable ability to articulate this bottomless despair. The grinding emptiness of worldly existence, the dread and futility of uprooted loneliness in "The Hollow Men" and *The Waste Land* of 1922, fell on the willing ears of a postwar youth sick and lost. But Eliot was lonely not because his beliefs had failed, but because he was still in search of belief. He had not participated in the war:

> I was neither at the hot gates
> Nor fought in the warm rain
> Nor knee deep in the salt marsh, heaving a cutlass
> Bitten by flies, fought.
> ("Gerontion")

He had never accepted the world and then found it wanting, but he had accepted desolation and disorder as the natural fate of sinful man. Advancing toward religious conversion, he was consistent in embracing communion with God as the most lonely of all experiences.

Such despair bathes itself in the mystery of the supernatural. In all of Eliot's plays there are the ineffable vapors of vagueness and violence. Even in the opening chit-chat of *The Cocktail Party*, Julia says:

> There's altogether too much mystery
> About this place today.

In *The Family Reunion* there are endless references to cold, gloom, blood, sacrifice; and in *Sweeney Agonistes* an entire page consists of the words "dead," "coffin," "death," winding up with, "Life is death."

"Why speak of love?"

Concern for the few implies contempt for the many and for life itself, since the few are destined for happiness elsewhere. Most people—all those not elected to suffer martyrdom—are fit only for:

> Birth, and copulation, and death.
> That's all, that's all, that's all . . .
> *(Sweeney Agonistes)*

And of these, birth is an evil, copulation a sin, and death a welcome guest. Thus, in *The Family Reunion,* in her final round with Mary as they exorcise the spirits, Agatha sings:

> A curse comes to being
> As a child is formed.

Most revealing is the lot of the husband and wife in *The Cocktail Party*. Early in the play, in discussing his own marital infelicity with the Unidentified Guest, Edward says:

> Why speak of love?
> We were used to each other . . .

Such an adjustment would be understandable were Celia
not in the picture. A maladjusted couple have separated and
there evidently are no offspring. But when Celia rushes
back to Edward to talk things over, now that he is free, he
states that Lavinia is returning. Celia is hurt, particularly
when he adds:

> It is not that I am in love with Lavinia.
> I don't think I was ever really in love with her . . .

What about his love for Celia? Is that too an escape and a
deception? He confesses that if he ever loved anyone it is
Celia, but adds:

> It never could have been . . . a permanent thing . . .

Celia persists:

> Oh, Edward! Can you be happy with Lavinia?

And the reply is Eliot's own bitter antihumanitarianism:

> No—not happy: or, if there is any happiness,
> Only the happiness of knowing
> That the misery does not feed on the ruin of loveliness.

Edward will not enjoy the passionate fullness of Celia's
love for fear of its aftermath, for fear of life. Going back
to Lavinia will be miserable, but at least that relationship
never had its moment of love! Celia's affair with him, on
the other hand, is charged with the potential of smashing
his smugness and of sanctifying her in life, but Eliot never
gives them a chance. When Lavinia reappears, the scene is
not unpleasant; it is ugly. Edward despises her:

> In a moment, at your touch, there is nothing but ruin.
> Oh God, what have I done?

then adds the symbols:

> . . . The python, the octopus . . .

strangling every bit of himself out of what he could be.
    This is the reconciliation effected by the Psychiatrist,

who gives it his blessing and divine approbation. He tells Celia, who has a right to know, that married couples can be:

> . . . contented with the morning that separates
> And with the evening that brings together
> For casual talk before the fire.
> Two people who know they do not understand each other,
> Breeding children whom they do not understand
> And who will never understand them.

Celia, quite naturally puzzled, hesitates briefly and then asks:

> . . . Is that the best life?

And out of the cold, puritanical repressiveness comes the answer:

> It is a good life.

Eliot goes on, in explanation:

> . . . in a world of lunacy,
> Violence, stupidity, greed . . . it is a good life.

Surely not a very inspiring God offers such a dread appraisal of life and marriage. One feels that Sir Harcourt-Reilly knows it is not a "good life," for in reviewing the case with the old windbag Julia, who turns out to be one of his confidential agents, he permits his disturbed conscience to entertain some doubt, when he says:

> . . . what have they to go back to?
> To the stale food mouldering in the larder,
> The stale thoughts mouldering in their minds.
> Each unable to disguise his own meanness
> From himself, because it is known to the other.
> . . . I have taken a great risk.

Self-adjustment to disgust is all Eliot will permit the Chamberlaynes, a choice of lesser evils in a hierarchy of evils. Edward discovers he is "a man who finds himself incapable of loving," and Lavinia, "a woman who finds that no man can love her," and the Doctor counsels that "the best of a bad job is all any of us can achieve."

Nowhere in Eliot's plays or poetry is there the passionate exaltation of mutually creative physical fulfillment. Nowhere do men and women enjoy the awakening of the senses. The display of emotional freedom in Tennessee Williams is a protest against society's repression of sensuous pleasures. In the tender moments of Anouilh, the beautiful love of Orpheus and Eurydice is too all-consuming for this world and leads to death, but their joy is beyond pain. With Eliot, the lusty vitality of Shakespeare gives way to a repugnance to sex. In one of his early poems, written in French, "Lune de Miel," Eliot describes the intimacies of a honeymoon couple—the cheap hotel, bedbugs, sweat, animal odors, and the lovers lifting up the sheet to scratch their swollen legs.

In the plays, Harry spurns Mary, with whom a healthy life is possible, and Celia, so capable of worldly pleasures, is sent off to her crucifixion. Eliot had the wit to caricature himself, when he wrote:

> How unpleasant to meet Mr. Eliot!
> With his features of clerical cut,
> And his brow so grim
> And his mouth so prim
> And his conversation so nicely
> Restricted to What Precisely
> And If and Perhaps and But.

Creating Character—"We have wasted such a lot of time in lying."

It is somewhat unfair and also irrelevant to accuse Eliot of not creating character, for his people are arranged arguments in the unfolding of a thesis, figures in a morality play. Someone has remarked that the only real persons in *The Family Reunion* are the two brothers who never appear. In *The Cocktail Party* there is more conscious effort at character delineation, but since Eliot's ideal is man alone, unconditioned by events, he is little concerned with change in people. Freedom, to him, comes through separation from one another, not through drawing together. Celia has need for the infinite, which cannot be restrained by the limitations of conjugal love. Eliot's scope is ambitious, but the religious becomes drama only when it is engaged in human struggle, when there is interaction with worldly temptations, the pitting of man against God.

Of the minor characters in *The Cocktail Party,* Julia and Alex are upper-class idlers who turn out to be secret aides of the Doctor. How they make this transition or why they possess the virtues that entitle them to the confidence of the Doctor is never explained, but they do serve to merge their vague outlines into a choral background when, together with the Doctor, they chant the liturgical farewell. Peter Quilpe, the young writer in love with Celia, is dismissed even by the characters in the play as too trivial. His fate is to write for Hollywood.

As for the Chamberlaynes, Lavinia is the frustrated, unhappy wife of a successful lawyer. Edward is the frustrated, unhappy husband of a pretentious society woman. Eliot is always on the point of saying something significant about them, but never does, as at the moment when Lavinia returns, for instance. She herself suggests the possibility:

> I shall always tell the truth now.
> We have wasted such a lot of time in lying.

Lavinia has been to see the Psychiatrist, and so now we expect some refocused insight into character, or at least something more profound in their marital maneuvering, but all she says is:

> And now I see how absurd you are.

What a dour gathering of unpleasant people!

Celia comes closest to being sympathetic. One would like to know her better but never gets the chance. At the edge of revelation, the doors close abruptly. She is physically attractive, young, has responded almost poetically as Edward's mistress. But just as she is beginning to emerge, she reports to the Psychiatrist, has her interview, and vanishes from the play. She does not appear at all in Act Three. In lieu of her appearance, her death should have particular meaning to the others. She should be the central character even though not present, for she had had the spark of living and was not sunk in the banalities of bourgeois intrigue. She understood and forgave both Edward and Peter. She was noble in confronting her Confessor. She had the potential of a superior human being, but she has died on an anthill in an African jungle. What is the effect on the others? Lavinia looks at the Doctor and says:

> What struck me though
> Was that your face showed no surprise or horror . . .
> I thought your expression was one of . . . satisfaction!

Edward also is pained at the wastefulness of Celia's past two years, but again the Doctor consoles with:

> You think her life was wasted. It was triumphant.

Julia adds that Celia "chose a way of which the consequence was crucifixion," at which Alex opens a bottle of champagne reserved for a special occasion and all drink. Celia's death is a cause for jubilation.

In the novels of Graham Greene, like *The End of the Affair,* the martyrdom of the mistress has a miraculous effect on all who came into contact with her. Her sacrifice has spiritual meaning for others. Greene is concerned with creating modern miracles, the continuing renovation of the Church. But with Eliot, the Chamberlaynes go on giving parties, Peter works for the cinema, and the Doctor waves his benediction. Nothing has changed. In Eliot's hagiology, new saints arise, but God's order is maintained. From the point of view of drama, Celia's death has been in vain. With

Greene as with Eliot—just as with the socialist realism demanded of Soviet playwrights—the nature of tragedy is limited by a predetermined miraculous end. In Eliot, martyrdom replenishes the presence of God on earth; in Afinogenov, the death of the hero advances the cause of socialism. Both are happy endings, but one has to be sympathetic to the particular faith to enjoy them—and the formula does become repetitious. One has to believe in limitations on human freedom to accept the conclusions.

Yet in Eliot's transcendent logic, Celia is a masterful creation. She is capable of both profane and divine love. Christian freedom to her is the freedom "to divest herself of the love of created things." She reaches *beyond* man to be most *to* man. Life, which is God-given, she returns to God so that all men will have no fear of death.

In the cocktail set, which by extension is equated to the whole of society, Edward, still clinging to some sense of social responsibility, says to Reilly:

> It's about the future of . . . the others.
> I don't want to build on other people's ruins.

Lavinia concurs, but the Psychiatrist dismisses any trace of human compassion by saying abruptly:

> Your business is not to clear your conscience,
> But to learn how to bear the burdens on your conscience.
> With the future of others you are not concerned.

Each man is to work out his own destiny and not worry about his brother.

Sir Harcourt-Reilly is the unique character, for his decisions redirect the lives of other people. So important is he in production that Alec Guinness was imported to Broadway to repeat his Edinburgh triumph. Reilly is essentially the Voice; there is no action on his part. He dispenses advice. Even though the other characters do not change, they have changed emotional reactions. Reilly does not. He is the Unmoved Mover—in three disguises: the Unidentified Guest, the Psychiatrist, and the Family Guardian. He is Eliot's original contribution, for he is Eliot himself. Edward finds him offensive for intruding in his personal affairs and for his tone of the cross-examining attorney, an annoying mixture of schoolteacher and pedant, with an ever-present self-assurance of superior wisdom. Reilly even gives advice on what and how to drink. When Edward asks him what he will have, the reply is gin and water, a powerful combination which may be all right for the busy Psychiatrist, but Reilly also has the unpleasant habit of telling the host:

> And I recommend you the same prescription . . .
> Let me prepare it for you, if I may . . .
> Strong . . . but sip it slowly . . . and drink it sitting
>   down.
> Breathe deeply and adopt a relaxed position.

The gin is part of the ritual. As a person, Reilly cannot be judged; he is too intangible. He can be valued only by his counsel. As an actor, he has to skip nimbly from Psychiatrist and guest to high priest and confessor. Even in production, vague and abstract lines in the office walls and furniture convey cathedral overtones. The realistic first-act drawing room fades into the inner sanctum of religious truth. As the Chamberlaynes leave, Sir Reilly stands over them in holy benediction and chants:

> Go in peace. And work out your salvation with diligence.

After Celia has accepted her fate, Alex and Julia enter and together with the doctor proceed to the libation. The scientist's consulting room resounds to the chorus of voodoo incantations, as though the three were dancing around the victim they have prepared for human sacrifice. The rhythms of *Samson Agonistes* are used for the sermon on the couch.

"I am not sure I grasp it myself . . ."

At the time of the New York run, it was fashionable to admit being puzzled by the profundity of the play. Eliot himself is responsible for encouraging his reputation for obscurity. Sir Reilly admits:

> And when I say to one like her
> "Work out your salvation with diligence," I do not
>   understand
> What I myself am saying.

Eliot has sown the seeds of ambiguity. Examples of his repeated contradictions are too numerous to permit a detailed discussion. It is difficult to argue with a man who says he doesn't know what he is talking about, or whose equivocations are designed to prevent his being pinned down. In reviewing *Notes Towards the Definition of Culture,* E. M. Forster writes:[7]

> The very title of the book is ominous. It is not about culture nor about a definition of culture, nor does it even offer notes on a definition. It offers "notes towards the definition." By its caution and astuteness, the title forestalls possible objections. But what cumbersome English!

And to further the air of mystery, Eliot adds in the text itself:[8]

> The way of looking at culture and religion which I have been trying to adumbrate is so difficult that I am not sure I grasp it myself except in flashes, or that I comprehend all its implications.

The Verse Drama—"to get at the permanent and universal"

One further point remains to be discussed in the theatre of T. S. Eliot—its form, the verse drama. Ever since the reaction against the realistic theatre at the end of the nineteenth century, some have contended that the speech of everyday living limits the scope of the drama; that the

essence of reality, the freedom of fantasy, the revelation of
the subconscious, cannot be adequately expressed in prose;
that to restore the dignity of language and the heritage of
the theatre the verse drama is needed. Eliot was a consistent
champion of this school. In several essays and particularly
in "A Dialogue on Dramatic Poetry," he states his case:

> Only prose drama can give the full gamut of modern
> feeling, can correspond to actuality. But is not every
> dramatic representation artificial? And are we not merely
> deceiving ourselves when we aim at greater and greater
> realism? Are we not contenting ourselves with appearances
> instead of insisting on fundamentals? . . . The tendency,
> at any rate, of prose drama is to emphasize the ephemeral
> and superficial; if we want to get at the permanent and uni-
> versal we tend to express ourselves in verse.

Insight is not a question of form. Appearances expressed in
prose may reveal more of fundamentals than verse that distorts reality. Eliot himself indicated the reverse of his own
contention when he said:[9]

> All poetry tends towards drama, and all drama towards
> poetry.

The deciding factor in whether a play should be written in verse or prose is what the play has to say. Form is
a means of enhancing, intensifying, and supporting the
content. Every poet finds his material demanding its own
outlet, as Eliot well knows. Of Shakespeare, he wrote:

> . . . the novelty of form has been rather forced upon him
> by his material than deliberately sought . . .

And:[10]

> Any radical change in poetic form is likely to be the
> symptom of some very much deeper change in society and
> the individual.

Since Aristotle, it has been generally accepted that the noble
drama of "persons of great renown and prosperity" deserved

verse, whereas plays of ordinary people, usually comedies, were of coarser nature and were relegated to prose. Prose was confined to the immediate, restricted by the details of environment; poetry permitted greater freedom on higher levels of abstraction.

The middle class for centuries had been held unfit material for drama. Between *Shoemaker's Holiday* and *Ghosts* came a long period of gradual change in attitude toward the acceptance of bourgeois drama as significant, although even today, with most plays devoted to problems of the middle class, few grant them the dignity of verse. This attitude is derived from the Elizabethans. Poetic receptivity was then a court prerogative. When the rabble came on stage, poetry shifted to prose. Much of this prejudice persists today. Maxwell Anderson prefers the verse form, yet in *Winterset*, which deals with the poor and the criminal, the verse is considered superimposed, whereas in *Elizabeth and Essex*, which deals with kings and history, it is hailed as eminently appropriate. The realistic play added to the confusion by writing bad prose resembling a social polemic or political tract. Not until Ibsen—and later, in Chekhov and Shaw—did the prose drama of the middle class achieve an artistic unity. And Synge and O'Casey found in the routine lives of Irishmen the glow of poetic speech. Poetry belongs to no single class, nor is it more fit in the mouth of a king than on the lips of the grave-digger. It is a function of the theme.

The theme of *The Cocktail Party* would hardly lend itself to the use of verse were it not for the Psychiatrist, who adds enough of the mystic and religious to justify it on traditional grounds. Yet the strange result is that the drawing-room set is not elevated; rather, God is lowered to a professional, practicing middle-class psychiatrist.

Nor is the verse itself of distinguished quality. The content rebelled against lending itself to what it could not be. In the theatre, the listening audience can barely detect the verse form. Try saying aloud some of the lines already quoted, such as:

> There's altogether too much mystery
> About this place today . . .

ignoring the arrangement printed for the eye. For the most part, the result sounds like normal conversation in a somewhat accentuated rhythm. True, Eliot, who as a young poet was brilliantly inventive, is still capable of acutely arresting repetitions, sharp and unusual opposites, and a literal precision of phrasing, yet in *The Cocktail Party* there are few quotable lines. The verse is not functional.

Eliot maintained that *Everyman* has all the essential elements of drama, being both religious and dramatic (though the latter is questionable); that *The Divine Comedy* is the greatest written drama (though never intended for the stage); and that the Mass is the highest moment of dramatic experience. Thus, in writing his own religious play, he employed verse not as it was dictated by what must be said, but mechanically, as an obligation, to add a cloak of otherworldliness.

The poetry retards the play and eliminates what little action there is. In production, the play becomes a succession of words, not deeds, and the actor is preoccupied with the novelty of saying verse lines as though they were prose. For Alec Guinness, as Dr. Reilly, it was a personal triumph; as the Voice—removed, alone, with no developing relationships with other characters—he could deliver his lines as monologues, as pronouncements. The rest of the cast always seemed a bit nonplused.

The Political Program

It would be pleasant to limit discussion of Eliot to his work in the theatre, even though his plays are a conscious expression of a unified program. One is always on safer ground in dealing exclusively with aesthetic problems, but a playwright who writes with his whole being shows his political thinking as well. Of course one does not go to the theatre with a textbook on Existentialism to decipher Sartre, nor read about Marxism before seeing a production of Brecht. A play must stand on its own merits as a dramatic experience. But it is a two-way exchange of ideas between playwright and spectator, for the audience brings to the theatre its own critical bias, whereas the thinking of the playwright determines his characters and the situations in which they are involved. The creative problem is how to rise beyond polemics and propaganda and achieve drama.

In writing of T. E. Hulme's book *Speculations,* which had considerable influence on Eliot and Ezra Pound as well, Karl Shapiro declared, "In it is laid down almost every precept of modern poetics: the political reactionism, the religious fundamentalism, and the hatred for 'romanticism,' spontaneity, and freedom."[11] In *The Idea of a Christian Society* and *Notes Towards the Definition of Culture,* both written in the same period as *The Cocktail Party,* Eliot formulates a politico-religious program, a "healthily stratified society" in which

> public affairs would be a responsibility not equally borne: a greater responsibility would be inherited by those who inherited special advantages . . . the governing elite of the nation as a whole would consist of those whose responsibility was inherited with their affluence and position.

Eliot knew the world is in search of order and that the times are out of joint. "We haven't left them such an easy world to live in," says Gerald to Charles in *The Family Reunion,* and Harry shouts out:

> It is not my conscience
> Not my mind that is diseased, but the world I have
>   to live in.

Eliot also knew that:

We cannot restore old policies
Or follow an antique drum.

("Little Gidding")

He was disturbed that today "everyone is being too conscious and conscious of too much. Everybody is conscious of
every question and no one knows any answers." He advocated a rigid, semi-theocratic society in which the elite of
money, blood, and spirit direct the destiny of the nation.
Eliot was never in favor of popular democracy.

Van Wyck Brooks, in *A Forward Glance*, the final chapter of his literary series on American cultural history, attacks the dehumanization of literature. He accuses Eliot of
representing the reverse of all that is noblest in the American tradition, labeling him, in Jefferson's phrase, "a traitor
to human hope." This is strong condemnation and not unexpected from a liberal humanitarian; however, Eliot could
defend his position just as ardently. One does not have to
love democracy to be a playwright. And the belief that the
superior few are responsible for progress finds strong support. But whatever may be his political views, the dramatist
must have compassion for man or at least for a few men.

In *The Cocktail Party*, the Unidentified Guest tells
Edward that the crisis in his life may lead to his finding out
what he really is, for he is nothing "but a set of obsolete
responses," but then the Guest adds, "The one thing to do
is do nothing." A philosophy of negation, a noncreative
resignation, runs counter to the dramatic. The entire play
becomes non-action. Therefore *The Cocktail Party* might
be considered the epitaph of a sick world anxious to crawl
back to its womb in the Middle Ages. Eliot's later plays,
A Confidential Clerk and *The Elder Statesman*, repeat the
same theme and add little to his stature as a playwright.

The theatre is a response to people's needs and an articulation of human aspiration; therefore form and content
must have meaningful relevance. Eliot does fill a definite

need today. To a troubled world, he offers assurance. To those fearful of decision, he offers a salutary avoidance of responsibility. To those disturbed by scientific materialism, he offers a prestige defense of the continuing and beneficent presence of God. The Cross is the symbol of man's freedom and faith, the solution to all ills. As a playwright, however, his zeal to proselytize defeats him. His stage is a platform for consultation and decisions, the unfolding process of pre-destination.

9. Irish Romantic Realism—Sean O'Casey

RED ROSES FOR ME

A NATION coming into being turns backward, glorifying its roots, and on the other hand turns forward, glorifying its people. An historic sense uncovers legends of the past and also the drama of the simple folk of the present. The hero of bygone days offers symbolic identification. The implied greatness of the common people nourishes hope in the immediate struggle. Such has been the case with Ireland and her great poets of the theatre, William Butler Yeats and Sean O'Casey. Yeats is the romantic fantasy of the myth of the hero; O'Casey, the realistic fact of the people's daily lives. But the opposing forms are rarely complete in themselves, for the myth and the fact are endlessly interwoven. These two poets are so identified with the awakening of the nation and so richly endowed with the gift of fancy that Yeats is never far from reality and O'Casey is always close to the ideal.

Beyond any Class

Ireland is a poor country, and even now, years after her political separation from England, removed from the industrial prosperity of her neighbors. There are few rich, and many peasants and workers. Her theatre has not been confined to the problems of the middle class, which dominate Western culture. Yeats sang of kings and *The Countess Cathleen*, O'Casey of Joxer and the urban proletariat.

Not until Ibsen did middle-class drama achieve stature, three hundred years after the Renaissance. It remains our heritage today, and contemporary playwrights, whether Priestley or Carroll, Sartre or Bernstein, Lillian Hellman or George S. Kaufman, follow in the tradition—more refined, more clever, more repetitious. Even T. S. Eliot was compelled to use the upper-middle-class cocktail set in drawing his modern saints.

So widespread has this influence been that the problems of the executive or the suburbanite are now implicitly assumed to be universal. In the United States, with its high standard of living, this assumption has some degree of truth. Class lines are indistinct, and with few exceptions even the workingman and the farmer think and act as members of the middle class. Add the leveling process of the mass media of communication, and values become stereotyped and general. Such is not the case in other countries. In Europe, Asia, and Latin America, there is a sharp cleavage between the peasant-worker and the propertied group. Yet few plays have been written about working-class characters. Zola, drawn to playwrighting where his success was least, as was the case with Diderot, spearheaded the call for life as it was, rather than as it was presumed to be. The result was sociological studies of the drab and the sordid wherein the hungry and the forgotten were not dignified with, but were cast beyond, human tragedy. In Hauptmann's *The Weavers*, the revolt of the workers is blind and bestial, a savage protest against unbearable suffering. Even in *The Lower Depths,* a compassionate Gorky treats of the marginal and the derelict.

Not until after the First World War was a workers' theatre developed. The movement was most intense and organized in Germany; it spread throughout Europe and the United States but was quickly dissipated, two decades of so-called "proletarian theatre" producing little that was enduring. Hitler in Germany and the end of the Depression in the United States swept the theatre back to its preoccupation with middle-class themes.

Almost alone, then, Sean O'Casey wrote consistently of the poor and the humble and offered them the dignity of drama, perhaps because the soil of Ireland was more congenial to the poet, perhaps because the realist in O'Casey had a touch of the divine, or perhaps because, like so few of the proletarian playwrights, he invested his characters with laughter and sorrow, with balance and insight, that raised them beyond any class into the common struggle of all humanity.

The work of Yeats belongs more to a Continental tradition superimposed on Ireland. He fashioned a mythology and language with little relevance to the needs of the living theatre. O'Casey, closer to the ground, created new myths of heightened power for an industrial era. Both made major contributions, but the work of O'Casey has special importance in any consideration of freedom of form and meaning in the contemporary theatre.

O'Casey's Early Work—"I knock at the door . . ."

Sean O'Casey was born in the slums of Dublin, where survival meant a rugged back and callousness. His entire life was a series of contradictions Sean was sickly, half-blind, and oversensitive. Only the patient care of a devoted mother and the chance fortune of an excellent doctor in the local clinic saved the lad from total blindness. The family was Protestant in intensely Catholic Dublin. The father was a worker who accumulated a good library of the classics and avidly read the philosophers and social thinkers, but his untimely death split the family. The sons drifted away into marriage and the army. Sean was forced to give up his schooling and go to work—as stock clerk, hod-carrier, bricklayer, dock-worker—to help support his mother and save pennies to buy Shakespeare and Balzac, and prints of Van Gogh and Goya. From his father, from his brothers, from his own associates, he drank deeply of working-class politics. He participated actively in the complex confusions of the Irish liberation movement, went to jail, wrote songs, issued leaflets, and suffered the blistering disappointment of the enthused when the Irish leaders proved themselves no different from their British predecessors. O'Casey moved more and more toward a confirmed socialist philosophy.

His early plays, among which are the two best-known, *Juno and the Paycock* and *The Plough and the Stars,* depict intimately the life of the poverty-stricken, courageous, drunken, vacillating, bickering urban proletariat of Dublin as they are caught in an awakening Ireland. O'Casey lived with its pains and sorrows, its dreams and its hopes, its militancy and its desertions, and wrote about it. His own six-volume autobiography, beginning with *I Knock at the Door,* is a richly told tale of his interest in poetry and politics and of the social background of our times. He is not the middle class looking in, but the working class looking out.

O'Casey was drawn to the theatre from his earliest years. His brother Archie, an employee of a Dublin newspaper, was active in an amateur group that played in union halls, unused stables, or a former parish dispensary. Archie "was . . . completely gone on the stage, and Sean was following close behind," writes O'Casey in *Pictures in the Hallway,*[1] and adds:

Archie lived and fought and died and lived again in the toils of the great persons, treading out their glorious lives, gorgeous before the footlights. The theatre housed the quick, the rest of the world encased the dead.

Sean became an actor and played Gloucester to Archie's Henry the Sixth, Brutus to his Mark Antony, or even Mc-Clusky to his Salem Scudder from *The Octoroon* of Dion Boucicault. He joined other groups, increasing his knowledge of stage technique, but the theatre was not lucrative and the hours were long, usually after a hard day's work elsewhere; most often the groups fell by the wayside. One experience was most fruitful. A group had taken over a hall that had been a Methodist church, but when their theatre did not pay, they converted themselves into a gambling club for the playing of House, a form of Lotto, most of their customers being "turbulent dockers and carters." As O'Casey writes about it:[2]

> Sean's job was to come in at nine in the morning, clean up the medley of chalk, cigarette butts, cartons, and other rubbish scattered over the hall, wash down all the benches, trim the lamps, and leave everything ready for the night's session when he left at five in the evening. For the first time in years, he was able to feed himself regularly, though simply, for he devoted most of what he got in buying a complete set of Balzac, and a new set of Shakespeare's Works,—all second hand . . . Well, God's help, as an Irish proverb says, is as near as the door; and so it proved to be, though it required the help of some hundreds of dockers, carters, and labourers to open the door and let Him in; and it was often a queer thought to Sean that he owed a new lease of life to the folly and thoughtlessness of these uncultured, uncouth, brave men. From the hard toil of these rough men, dishevelled in body and mind, out of what they earned so hard, he lived, ate of bread and meat, and nourished his sensuous being in art and literature. And worst of all, in his thoughts, he never thought of thanking them.

His ambition and love was the growing and already famous Abbey Theatre; Sean watched it from the street at night, hung around its alleys, finally became part of it, and in 1923 they accepted his first play, *The Shadow of a Gunman.* But life with the Abbey proved as riotous and raucous as less literary days, reflecting the basic contradiction of the theatre, for the Abbey was as tumultuous a marriage of opposites as Ireland herself.

The Abbey Theatre

Of all the independent and free theatres that sprang up in the early years of the century, following the example of the Théâtre Libre and the Freie Bühne, the Abbey of Dublin was the only one that did not grow out of the movement for a realistic theatre, or at least not completely so. Antoine and Brahm and Stanislavsky were in revolt against traditional theatres, which were inadequate to cope with modern psychology and group interrelations. In Ireland, however, there had been no other theatre of any consequence. The Irish started fresh but muddled, their philosophy of the theatre breaking into partisan sniping.

Some years before, in 1899, the Irish Literary Theatre had been founded, with Yeats and Edward Martyn as the leading spirits, and two more contradictory figures would be hard to conceive, at least harnessed under the same roof. It was like putting Maeterlinck and Mayakovsky in the same theatre. Martyn was the rebel, the realist; Yeats, the conservative romantic. Martyn was interested in social problems, Yeats in Irish folklore. Yeats had even proposed that the theatre be set up in London with English actors. Martyn, who had written one good play, *The Heather Field,* that could serve as the cornerstone of Irish realism, wanted a theatre that would actively participate in rousing the Irish people, in the spirit of Ibsenism. After a few stormy seasons they split apart, and the Abbey Theatre came into being under the aesthetic guardianship of Yeats and with the generous financial support of Miss A. E. F. Horniman. But the influence of Martyn could not be denied; it was linked to the pressing political upheaval and it crept in, though uninvited.

Such ill-mated dual tendencies were possible in Ireland in 1903 because the struggle for social betterment coincided with the fight for independence; interest in Irish legends and historic glory joined hands with interest in a shilling more a week. When, however, the Free State was formed and the revolutionary fervor became riddled with compromise, the Abbey retreated to the quaint historicism of Yeats and lost its public. O'Casey's was the fresh, invigorating blood that could have saved the theatre, for *The Plough and the Stars* caused riots and fights in the streets, the sure sign of an Irish theatrical success. But his relentless insistence on continuing the fight was bound to run afoul of the cautious leadership.

When his *The Silver Tassie* was rejected in 1929, he left the Abbey Theatre and Ireland, and became a voluntary exile in England. Yet though he had nothing but contempt for the petty administrators of the Abbey, he respected and admired Yeats, who to everyone's surprise became a member of the Seanad Eireann (Irish Senate), combining the spirits of Dean Swift and Cathleen ni Houlihan with practical affairs of state. Yeats defended O'Casey's play, but their differences were too wide for reconciliation and O'Casey said fare-thee-well to Inishfallen.

Red Roses for Me has been selected for detailed analysis here. The earlier plays have been seen often and are well known, whereas *Red Roses,* after its opening in Dublin in 1943, had to wait thirteen years for an American production. A mature working-class play, it offers an opportunity to examine the strength and the weakness, the confusions and the power, of a distinct theatrical contribution.

RED ROSES FOR ME

ACT ONE—*"A bit of a wash for the Blessed Virgin . . ."*

The first two acts take place in the living room of the Breydons' two-room flat in the poor tenement district. The dilapidated, ill-furnished quarters are brightened by the ardent cleaning of Mrs. Breydon and the gay-colored, carefully guarded flowerpots. Even in the set, O'Casey searches for sharp contrast, the conflict of opposites.

As the curtain rises, young Ayamonn Breydon, dressed in a bright green doublet and a crimson velvet cloak, sword in hand, is standing on a chair in the center of the drab room reciting lines from Shakespeare, his mother prompting him. Ayamonn is a railroad worker, but his interests are poetry, music, and painting. This is a recurrent theme with O'Casey —the interest of the common man in the best in art and literature. Ayamonn is to do a scene in the union minstrel show. He knows it will be difficult to put over, for the workers are reluctant to accept Shakespeare "out of all that's been said of him":[3]

> They think he's beyond them, while all the time he's part of the kingdom of heaven in the nature of every man. Before I'm done, I'll have him drinking in th' pubs with them.

Ayamonn's mother upbraids her son for trying to do too much:

> Less than two hours' sleep today, and a long night's work before you. Sketchin', readin', makin' songs, an' learnin' Shakespeare: if you had a piano, you'd be tryin' to learn music. Why don't you stick at one thing, and leave the others alone?

But his reply is:

> They are all lovely, and my life needs them all.

The workers are demanding an extra shilling a week, and the show is to raise funds for use in case a strike is called. Ayamonn is in love with Sheila Morneen, a Catholic, the daughter of a police sergeant. Thus, in the first few lines the theme is set on its various levels—Ayamonn's cultural hunger, the threatened strike, the religious and class differences between him and Sheila.

The women of the neighborhood, all in rags and all Catholics, bring in the statue of the Virgin and plead for a bit of Mrs. Breydon's Hudson soap to give the Blessed Virgin "a bit of a wash." Sheila enters to tell Ayamonn that she cannot go with him on their planned outing tomorrow because her family, opposed to her being with him, insist she attend a retreat of the Daughters of St. Frigid. He protests that he has given up a workers' meeting to spend his one free day with her. The lovers' quarrel is interrupted in turn by Old Brennan of the Moor with a young singer who shyly offers the lovely Dublin ballad "Red Roses for Me"; Roory, the Fenian, who rants about an independent Ireland; Mulcanny, the atheist, who rails about science and a materialistic interpretation of religion; and the old women, returning in hysterics because the Virgin, Our Lady of Eblana, has disappeared from her niche in the church. Sheila leaves in anger, and the first act ends with Ayamonn and Roory singing a song to Irish freedom.

ACT TWO—"*Let us bring freedom here . . . with silver trumpets blowing . . .*"

The second act is a development of the events in Act One in the conventional realistic form. As a matter of fact, they might be considered as two scenes of a single act with a brief time interval. Brennan of the Moor slips into the room with the stolen Virgin, all washed, gilded, and sparkling. He is secretly going to put her back in her place and create a minor miracle. Mrs. Breydon leaves to assist at the last rites for a dying neighbor. Roory, Brennan, and Mulcanny engage in a bitter argument over King versus Pope. Sheila returns and urges Ayamonn not to take part in the strike. She has heard there will be trouble, and has been assured that if he refuses to join the strikers, he will be made a foreman. He condemns her for trying to persuade him to be a blackleg. The Protestant Rector visits Ayamonn to urge him to prevent any violence. A committee of workers reports that the strike has been called and that Ayamonn has been selected as one of the speakers. He leaves to join his comrades as the ladies in the house sing a paean of praise in honor of the returned and washed Lady of Eblana.

ACT THREE—*"Another world is in your womb . . ."*

The third act is the controversial shift to an expressionist set. It takes place on a street leading to the bridge over the river Liffey. The outline of the city in the distance is gray and gloomy, dominated by the silver spire of the church and the red pillar of Nelson's statue. Men and women sit huddled in dark corners, their bodies weary, their faces expressionless. The three women who carried the Virgin are dressed in black, specters in the eerie night scene. Eeada is selling cakes and apples; Dympna holds a basket with "decadent blossoms, and a drooping bunch of violets hangs from a listless hand"; Finnoola is pregnant. The theme is anounced with the opening words of Eeada:

> This spongy leaden sky's Dublin; those tomby houses is Dublin, too—Dublin's scurvy body . . .

and Dympna's echoing refrain:

> A graveyard where the dead are all above th' ground.

The Rector and the Inspector enter, the officer clad in his brilliant uniform. He has come from church and is on his way to join the troops to head off the demonstration.

A lounger spits on the Inspector's shining boots. The Rector says:

> Things here frighten me, for they seem to look with wonder on our ease and comfort . . .

as the two move on and pass over the bridge. Brennan enters, sits down on the walk, and sings a merry ballad for the pennies that are tossed to him. Ayamonn and Roory come in at the last bars of the song. The night gathers. Ayamonn speaks to the huddled derelicts:

> Rouse yourselves; we hold a city in our hands!

But the chorus, low and bitter, replies:

> It's a black and bitther city.
> It's a bleak, black, and bitther city.

Roory will have none of them. They are unworthy of battle. Misery has put them beyond the fight. He would have gun peal and slogan cry to startle them from their desolation, and he leaves in disgust. Ayamonn, alone in the darkness, speaks to these shadows of men and women. He visions their future, their glory on earth:

> Friend, we would that you should live a greater life; we will that all of us shall live a greater life. Our strike is yours. A step ahead for us today; another one for you tomorrow. We who have known and know the emptiness of life shall know its fullness. All men and women quick with life are fain to venture forward.
> (*To Eeada*) The apple grows for you to eat.
> (*To Dympna*) The violet grows for you to wear.
> (*To Finnoola*) Young maiden, another world is in your womb.

The scene brightens, and the city is bathed in brilliant colors; the hollow men now stand stalwart, warriors in the light. The shrouded figures of the three women turn fresh and young, cloaked in silvery mantles. Ayamonn dances on the bridge with the transformed beauty of Finnoola. He starts the song, and all join in:

We swear to release thee from hunger and hardship,
From things that are ugly an' common an' mean;
Thy people together shall build a brave city,
The fairest and finest that ever was seen!

Ayamonn leaves, and just as quickly as the city of the future
burst into color, it now sinks back into gloom. In the distance, the sound of marching feet signals the beginning of
the demonstration. The song "Free City" is heard. Softly,
then less hesitantly, the people on the bridge join in.

ACT FOUR—*"We honour our brother . . . for the truth forever before his face."*

On the grounds surrounding the Protestant church, the
Rector, an admirer of Ayamonn's, is under fire for his refusal to oust Ayamonn as a vestryman, despite the threats
of his moneyed pew-holders. Mrs. Breydon and Sheila enter,
followed by the crowd that is to join the demonstration.
Ayamonn holds one side of the stage, the Inspector the
other. The Inspector warns that any violence will be crushed
by violence. As the crowd leaves, the Rector gives Ayamonn
his blessing. Shouts and shots are then heard. The frightened, dispersed mob comes rushing back across the church
grounds in panic and fear. Finnoola reports that Ayamonn
has been killed in the charge of the mounted police. The
curtain lowers for a brief time interval, and rises on the
same set.

It is now evening, and the body of Ayamonn is carried
into the church. Old Brennan of the Moor is alone in the
growing darkness. A dim light from the interior seeps
through the slightly open door as he sings a farewell song
to the fallen hero.

The Theme—*"We who have known the emptiness of life
shall know its fullness."*

This brief account of the plot gives little idea of the
scope and dramatic power of the play. It is not unusual in

what it has to say; it follows the pattern of the strike plays so common in the early thirties, repeated here in the three-fold form: (1) the Temptation of Ayamonn, (2) the Vision of the Future, (3) the Death of the Leader. What makes the play distinctive is the way in which it is said. Most strike dramas followed a formula and became repetitive before they were mature. O'Casey offers a sweeping pageant of a world in which individual characters are sharply drawn with the exuberance of Shakespeare's chronicle plays, which go beyond political partisanship. A lowly hero has the sublimity of kings.

The strike has always captured the imagination of playwrights, for it is the moment when battle lines are drawn, when words give way to action, when opposing forces are engaged in a test of strength and endurance. O'Casey does not portray the strike itself. That would be cinematic rather than theatrical. He is concerned instead with the strike as the moment of change. The leader is gone, his cause defeated, but the effect on others is renewed courage and a resolve that his death shall not have been in vain. Even the lethargic *lumpen* proletariat are aroused. Sheila and the Rector, most removed from union issues, are the most trans-formed. Ayamonn's evocative hope for all mankind:

> We who have known and know the emptiness of life shall know its fullness . . .

is echoed by the Rector in his farewell words at the funeral:

> We honour our brother, not for what may have been an error in him, but for the truth forever before his face.

In the symbolic reference to the protagonist's death lies the heart of a playwright's philosophy. There is no sharper contrast in the contemporary theatre than that between T. S. Eliot and Sean O'Casey. Celia Coplestone of *The Cocktail Party* dies to replenish the love of God for all men. Ayamonn dies to renew faith in man's progress on earth.

Both deaths are blood sacrifices that must have meaning if they are not to be wasteful and nontragic. But meaning is conditioned by belief. George Steiner, in *The Death of Tragedy*, states that:

> . . . in the very excess of his suffering lies man's claim to dignity . . . Man is ennobled by the vengeful spite or injustice of the gods.

Such irrational, unjust destruction leads to the mystery of tragedy and the greatness of man. Steiner claims that the possibility of full tragedy ended with Shakespeare's time; yet Eliot and O'Casey conform to all his definitions. When he says, "Tragedy is irreparable. It cannot lead to just and material compensation for past suffering . . . Oedipus does not get back his eyes or his sceptre over Thebes," he is on solid ground, but when he adds, "Better plumbing can resolve some of the grave crises in the dramas of Ibsen," he ignores the social implications of all tragedy. Hedda Gabler might have avoided suicide in the hands of a capable psychiatrist, but her disaster is an individual problem; a way of life is not at stake. It *is* with Oedipus. He does not get back his eyes, but Thebes is relieved of the curse. Evil has been purged and harmony prevails. Society cannot endure with parricide and incest, even though they be unintentional. So it is also with the starkest tragedy of all theatre, *King Lear*. The kingdom is reunited and the venom removed from the state.

In tragedy, the individual bears with him the possible doom of many. The mores of a people hang in the balance. The Greek world was more unified, and the transgression of Oedipus, though rooted in the past, threatened a civilization. Today, the possibility of tragedy is diminished but to those with a common belief, it exists. To the devout, Celia's suffering in *The Cocktail Party*, out of proportion to her guilt, is a joyous vindication of faith that was endangered. Such is also the case with Ayamonn. Not the nature of tragedy, but the issues involved, have changed. When Lady Gregory read to O'Casey the script of *Singing Jailbirds,* Upton Sinclair's play, he rebuked her for admiring "the worst play ever written signifying its sympathies with the workers," and added:[4]

> The Labour Movement isn't a mourning march to a jail house! We are climbing a high hill, a desperately steep, high hill through fire and venomous opposition. All of those who were highest up have dropped to death; lower down most of the climbers have dropped to death; lower still, many will drop to death; but just beneath these is the invincible vast crowd that will climb to the top . . .

O'Casey offers an alternative to anarchic individualism. To him, the good of all lies beyond and within one's own self-interest. Ayamonn is not a loose fragment fighting against all to better himself. He would achieve individuality through identification with the group. As O'Casey often repeated, "Life depends on co-operative and collective energy."[5]

This is well illustrated by the love of Ayamonn and Sheila, a love deepened, broken, reborn by the specific obstacles that beset them. Ayamonn's thoughts are of Ireland and his fellow workers. He never holds himself apart and beyond them. Even his interest in Shakespeare is linked to his desire to get them to talk of poetry in the pubs, to make Shakespeare part of their lives. Sheila is the bourgeois world. She is the daughter of a police sergeant, wooed by the Inspector of the Guards—none of them very rich or important people, but middle class in thought. Sheila is concerned with self, which includes her lover but implies his advancement at the price of hurt to others. She would have him desert his comrades to save their marriage. With more money, a little better home, a status a notch above that of the railroad workers, they can be happy. All she asks is a prettier skirt, a nicer shawl:

Ayamonn, my love . . . now, really, isn't it comical I'd look if I were to go about in a scanty petticoat . . . and my poor feet bare! Wouldn't I look well that way!

and Ayamonn quietly answers:

With red roses in your hand, you'd look beautiful.

To Ayamonn, her request is treason. To her, it is the logic of life. This same conflict of moralities is expressed in the scene between mother and son. There are no secrets between them. Mrs. Breydon warns of the dangers that lie ahead with Sheila:

She's a Roman Catholic; steeped in it, too, the way she'd never forgive a one for venturin' to test the Pope's pronouncement.

Ayamonn's answer is sprightly:

Life and all her vital changes'll go on testing everything, even to the Pope's pronouncement.

Patiently, the mother persists:

She's the child of a sergeant in the Royal Irish Constabulary, isn't she? . . . and the bigger half of Ireland would say that a man's way with a maid must be regulated by his faith an' hers, an' the other half by the way her father makes his livin'.

And then she adds, not out of reproach but in helpful advice, that which touches him most, for it springs out of a consciousness of class:

. . . but many have murmured again' a son of mine goin' with the child of a man crouchin' close to their enemy.

The "enemy" is the employer. To a militant European trade unionist, Ayamonn's acceptance of Sheila's advice would mean catastrophe. O'Casey writes in his autobiography of a visit he attempted to pay to O'Brien, once a fiery leader of the labor movement and now a government official. Frustrated by his inability to get to see O'Brien, he noted the fawning office staff, the plush carpets, and the chauffered Cadillac waiting outside. A youthful world of hope collapsed around O'Casey, and he never forgot the incident.

The conflict between Sheila and Ayamonn is a major dramatic theme, but O'Casey unfortunately does not give it full play. Every time the lovers have a scene together, some interruption cuts short the relationship. O'Casey is anxious to include too much.

The Characters of the Play—"most potent when local"

Like the structure of the play, the characters are a combination of the real and the ideal, most pronounced in the case of Ayamonn. The name is Gaelic, taken from a Fenian streetcar conductor who made a deep impression on the young O'Casey. References to Gaelic legends and the use of Gaelic names—Sean O'Casey himself had changed his name from John Casside—are indications of the interrelationship of the workers' movement and the fight for Irish independence, which embraced even an independent language. Ayamonn is thus ardent Fenian and trade union leader.

He is the centralizing force, the unity of many opposites, which in him and through him are reconciled. Roory and Mulcanny and Brennan o' the Moor, as well as Sheila and the Rector, circle around him. He is understanding and tolerant of what divides one from the other, but he is uncompromising in his own faith in what is right. He grants others the right to be heard but he does not forsake principle. He rejects Roory's ironclad, fiery Catholic patriotism, which would "burn the books" and choke off the right to dissent. He dreams of a world without fear:

> Roory, Roory, is that th' sort of freedom you'd bring to Ireland with a crowd of green branches an' th' joy of shouting? If we give no room to men of our time to question many things, all things, ay, life itself, then freedom's but a paper flower, a star of tinsel, a dead lass with gay

ribbons at her breast an' a gold comb in her hair. Let us
bring freedom here, not with sounding brass and tinkling
cymbal, but with silver trumpets blowing, with a song all
men can sing, with a palm branch in our hand, rather than
with a whip at our belt, and a headsman's axe on our
shoulders.

When Sheila complains that art, poetry, union meetings,
and Shakespeare mean more to him than she, he replies:

You're part of them all, in them all, and through them
all.

Yet this very strength and nobility of Ayamonn is a
weakness of the play. He, like Act Three, gets out of hand.
Poet, painter, actor, and worker, he leaps beyond the local
issue of a shilling more a week, and with the color of the
poetry, the flood of images, and a touch of Irish fantasy is
transformed, like the city itself, into the legendary ideal.
He becomes the hero-saviour, Wolfe Tone and Brian Boru.
No such excess enters in the earliest and most successful of
his plays, *Juno and the Paycock* and *The Plough and the
Stars,* equally rich in speech and song, but rooted in the
living room, as local and detailed as the broken furniture,
the light under the Virgin, or the mug of ale, yet typical because they are so real.

O'Casey of the smells and sounds and breath of Dublin
moved away from his early realism and has been wrestling
with two forms ever since. Clifford Odets has said:[6]

A comparison of O'Casey's two sensibilities . . . forces
upon us the conclusion that he is most potent when local,
particular, and concrete.

The first two acts offer full testimony that when O'Casey
so wills, he can create living characters. Mrs. Breydon, like
Juno, is the patient, strong, suffering woman, shielding and
protecting her own yet giving generously to her neighbors,
understanding her son's drive and ambitions yet straining
to preserve the unity of the home; O'Casey's women give

life and nurture it well, wise enough to let the young sport
where they will, even though doomed to lose their own because they have given too wisely and too well. And in the end
when Mrs. Breydon loses her son, she has no regrets, no
tears, but an unswerving faith in the nobility of his life, "for
fine things grew thick in his nature." Hardship and poverty
and understanding have driven all the pettiness out of her.
When she stands at the grave of her son, she says:

> Isn't it a sad thing for him to be lyin' lonesome in th'
> cheerless darkness of th' love-long night!

and there is more poignant suffering and heartbreak than
if she had bathed herself in an agony of tears.

The Rector is a recurrent figure in O'Casey's plays,
—the man of Christ caught between his love for the people
and the demands of his wealthy parishioners. O'Casey had
no love for the institutionalized church, but he had deep
respect for the priest or minister who labored in defense of
the poor. In *The Star Turns Red,* the Brown Priest of the
People is opposed to the Purple Priest of the Politicians.
The Rector of St. Burnupus, the Rev. E. Clinton, is a
warmly sympathetic character. He performs his duty in
urging Ayamonn not to participate in the strike, for he
would avoid bloodshed, but faced with Ayamonn's determination, he gives him his blessing. He rejects the efforts to
remove Ayamonn as vestryman, and over the opposition of
his pew-holders he conducts the funeral services. To those
who would deny Ayamonn his burial rites, he says:

> It is a small thing that you weary me, but you weary
> my God also . . .

The Structure of the Play

The shift to expressionism in the third act is not integrated schematically, yet theatrically it is starkly beautiful,
and a magnificent interlude, wild and extreme, lavish and
colorful, with a bravura logic of its own. It could well stand

by itself as a modern ballet. The first half of the play ends
with the declaration of the strike. It is as though the tocsin
had sounded, ominous and expansive. The living room can
no longer confine events. They have moved beyond the
individual to the mass. Ayamonn no longer belongs to himself but to the people of Dublin. Personal problems are dissolved in a moment of history.

Why should Ayamonn sacrifice his painting, his songs,
his acting, his love for Sheila? The explanation could be
made in realistic scenes with friends, but the bold sweep of
the scene on the bridge is a demonstration—in motion, in
song and pageantry, in color and light and dance—of
broader issues. "A gold-speckled candle, white as snow, was
Dublin once," and shall be again. Standing with these
shadows of people, the city increasingly "bleak, black, and
bitther" like a "batthered, tatthered whore," a streak of
fading sunlight playing on his head, Ayamonn calls forth
the hidden splendor of the city. The scene brightens, the
houses are purple and silver, the loungers slashed with
bronze and scarlet, stirred by the beauty they have never
seen before "for their tired heads have haunted far too low
a level," as Ayamonn dances with Finnoola in two pools of
light, one of gold, the other of violet. It is his dream visualized. All the others have paraded across the bridge, ignoring those huddled there. Ayamonn alone stays to bring them
life as he hurries onward to his death.

Qualitatively, life has changed and so does the form of
the play. Expressionism lends itself to mass movement, to
precise intellectualization, to dealing in concepts. O'Casey
is seeking a merger of two forms. His success is debatable,
for the shift is sudden and unanticipated. In production it
raises the directorial problem of uniting the warm intimacy
and biting realism of the Breydon household with the
delicate fantasy of the dream, yet as experiment in modern
theatre the play challenges respect. O'Casey's own artistic
restlessness and the insatiable demands of what he had to

say could not be held within the severe restrictions of the Ibsen form.

Language and Laughter—"You envy-stippled titivated toad . . ."

The clash of extremes in O'Casey is further evidenced in his use of laughter and his use of words. He has been brought to task for putting comedy and tragedy too close together, breaking in to destroy mood, yet this practice may well be characteristically Irish—volatile, bubbling with an outward gaiety, hiding the poverty and pain with an arrogant pride and an unexpected metaphor. O'Casey's resources are so abundant that he is prodigal. The result is looseness and extravagance. Art can be severely styled, holding its stresses with delicate balance, saying less in order to say more; or it can be richly detailed, saying all to avoid omission, flowing intricately into every corner of space, outwardly expressive— the classic versus the baroque. O'Casey is the full decoration, the gay panoply, the brilliantly hued.

The final scene of *Juno and the Paycock* is unforgettable. Juno, who has tried to hold her family together, sees everything crumble around her—her income lost, an only son murdered, an unmarried daughter pregnant, a worthless husband drunk in the pubs. She leaves her home with the anguished cry:

> Sacred Heart of Jesus, take away our hearts o' stone, and give us hearts of flesh! Take away this murdherin' hate and give us Thine own eternal love!

The room is silent and deserted, echoing the distraught plea of a brave woman who has failed; then the door opens, and Captain Boyle and Joxer enter and end the play with a riotous, incoherent drunken scene. Yet the laughter they produce is all the more reckless and nervous for the tragedy that lies behind it.

So too with speech. No other poet in the English language would be forgiven such exaggeration. He is music and song and dance, and his unabashed people revel in a multiplicity of over-pouring images. The language is free, often coursing into channels of limpid beauty that give pleasure in the pure joy of uttering them.

Yet herein he makes his own pitfall, for he is so fond of the sound of words, so in love with Shakespeare for a twist that a phrase contains, so thirsty to pour new and heady wine into old bottles, that he is carried to excess; often his overweighted lines taste flat despite their effervescence. Thus, Ayamonn talks repeatedly of "a gold canoe dipping over far horizons," or of "time's grey finger putting a warning speck on the crimson rose of youth." But nothing can equal the overstated epithets of *The Star Turns Red,* like "you envy-stippled titivated toad" and "you pale hypothesis of a needless life." O'Casey is most Irish when he is deflating the big words of small men and the pettiness of boasting heroes.

The Romantic Realist

This conflict in speech, in form, in incident, is the motivating contradiction in O'Casey, which on the broadest level is reflected in his characters and his philosophy—the endless war between the dream and the fact. In Ibsen, this contradiction results in negation and suicide. In O'Casey, there is hope and confidence. Breydon dies to forge a new world; Solness dies because his world is dead. But the present and the future do not merge easily. O'Casey is the materialist with a dash of Shelley—the earthbound trade unionist with his head in the stars. In the early plays, the realist is triumphant, held in check by the discipline of form. As the dream demands more room, the front parlor is pushed aside and the universe becomes the stage. The first act of *Red Roses for Me* ends in the romantic style with a hymn to freedom, as do the plays of Schiller, wherein the local incident gives way to broad generalities.

The problem in O'Casey is how to achieve a fusion, how to harness this romanticism. His partial failure gives a sense of incompleteness, often of awkwardness, yet this very dynamic contradiction, even unresolved, is the source of his power and his poetry. Perhaps it accounts for the fact that though he disagreed with Yeats, he felt a deep kinship with the dean of Irish poets. There is much of Yeats in O'Casey, and even more of Molière. George Jean Nathan has aptly said: "O'Casey is a Molière full of Irish whiskey."

10. The French Theatre —Giraudoux, Sartre, Camus

THE MADWOMAN OF CHAILLOT
THE DEVIL AND THE GOOD LORD
CALIGULA

IN THE PAST THREE DECADES, Paris has been the center of the most vital theatre in Europe, varied in its forms, bold in innovations, and rich in the diversity of ideas. The date for this resurgence may well be May 3, 1928, the opening night of *Siegfried* by Jean Giraudoux, directed by Louis Jouvet. The animated discussions that followed, the laudatory articles in the press, the conversations in the streets, indicated the pride Paris felt in sharing a work of art. The French take their theatre seriously. Other playwrights responded as though, long quiescent, they needed the stimulus of one success to rouse their creative fervor.

Behind Giraudoux lay a great tradition. When, out of

the Renaissance, the French nation was born, its highest cultural expression was in the drama of Corneille, Racine, and Molière. In 1636, the famous controversy over *Le Cid*, in which every man of letters participated, was the most thoroughgoing debate that had ever taken place on the nature of drama. Corneille was accused of having violated the Rules presumably laid down by Aristotle for the only noble form for tragedy. Richelieu, prime minister and second-rate playwright, was responsible for the decision declaring Corneille guilty. As a result, a most rigid literary form was officially established. Racine alone was able to achieve lyric beauty and dramatic power within its severe demands; Corneille retired from the theatre. Not even socialist realism in communist countries has been as rigorously upheld as the classical mode that dominated Europe for two centuries and remains today, preserved in the Comédie-Française, the glory of every Frenchman. It stifled creative freedom, but it did set artistic standards that are unconscious measuring rods compelling a standard of perfection in all other forms.

It took the French Revolution to loosen the hold of classicism on drama. In France, as elsewhere in Europe, cardinals and statesmen are often poets and critics. Diderot, an unsuccessful playwright like Richelieu before him, called for the elimination of the Rules and the introduction of new techniques more applicable to a middle-class society. Victor Hugo followed with flaming manifestoes on the freedom of man and the worth of the individual. Then romanticism was born, the classical unities of time and place were disregarded, and the universe became the scene of action in the Faustian style. But the fire of romanticism burned out quickly, and its place was taken by trite formula plays and intrigue melodramas. Vitality in the theatre came from writers in other countries, from Ibsen, Strindberg, and Chekhov. Realism, the new movement, had begun in France with the theatre of Antoine, but it never took firm roots. Its value lay in stimulating experiments such as the Théâtre Libre, which led eventually to the Vieux-Colombier and the emergence of creative directors. Jacques Copeau had resisted both factual representation and the theatre of illusion, and initiated a bare stage of austere spiritual intensity. From the combination of Antoine and Copeau arose the "Cartel" of Charles Dullin, Georges Pitoëff, Louis Jouvet, and Gaston Baty, the Famous Four, each with a distinct concept of staging and design. The classical theatre no longer barred the way. The director was ready, but the writer was lacking. He appeared after the First World War.

Twice invaded by a mechanized foe, her voice in foreign affairs reduced to secondary importance, her youth destroyed, and her future a prospect of declining stature, France was forced to re-examine her long-accepted dependence on honored tradition. The playwright responded not with a specific faith nor an emotional rallying cry of superiority, but with an intelligent illumination of events. The first of the new voices was Jean Cocteau, who teamed with Jouvet, the director, and Christian Bérard, the designer, to dramatize the Gods as *The Infernal Machine* who destroy Oedipus— an oblique analogue of present-day man. Though the odds are against him and he is ill-matched for the struggle, the simple, rustic Oedipus outdoes the Gods by accepting his fate and entering into the glory of legend. It is a comforting thought to Frenchmen, though nothing more than a victory through resignation.

An effort further to redefine the relation of God to man and reaffirm religious faith is represented in the works of André Obey, Henri de Montherlant, Georges Bernanos, François Mauriac, and above all, Paul Claudel. On the other hand, more worldly matters were reflected in the philosophical theatre, which ranges from the *No Exit* of Sartre, and the *Saul* of André Gide to the experimental plays concentrated in the pocket theatres of the Left Bank. Wit, reason, delight in language, and a fascination with ideas are common to all.

The playwright's approach to understanding encompasses the cynicism of Anouilh, the vengeance of Genet, the disorder of Adamov, and the piety of Mauriac.

Of all the playwrights, Jean Anouilh has long held the widest audience. He was completely devoted to the theatre and turned out more than twenty plays in as many years, two or three sometimes running during a single season. His dramas are carefully constructed, and abound in clever dialogue and unrelenting pessimism, as in *The Waltz of the Toreadors.* His theme is usually the triumph of stupidity and dullness over those with purity and idealism. He is never too intense or overserious, but toys with ideas, delighting in the nuances of conversation about love and sex and even God. The rare exception is *Poor Bitos,* an unmitigated portrayal of hatred and the evil of money, developed in a dream sequence of Robespierre's reincarnation. *Becket, or the Honor of God* is a more serious effort to discover an honor for which man can offer his life, but Anouilh's charm and popularity lie with the earlier plays like *Antigone* and *The Lark.* The only writer who has equaled his success, and has also held the stage for a quarter of a century as a significant figure of the theatre revival, is Jean Giraudoux.

Jean Giraudoux: Fantasy and Style—"There is no theatre which is not prophecy."

Giraudoux was born in 1882 in the village of Bellac. Though he traveled extensively as a member of the Ministry of Foreign Affairs, he regarded the provincial setting of his birth as his spiritual home, an ordered microcosm of the world at large. Giraudoux received the thorough and formidable education of a French man of letters. He became a student of German literature and spent many years in that country as a representative of his government. He was deeply concerned with the enmity of the two nations, their antipodal cultures, and the necessity of their fusion. Giraudoux's first play, *Siegfried,* is the oft-repeated drama of traumatic amnesia in which a French soldier, found naked on the battlefield, is returned to Germany by mistake. Despite the heritage of his birth, Jacques becomes the famous writer, Seigfried. In the end, when Geneviève uncovers the inner self of Jacques within Siegfried, she becomes enamored of German culture and says to the restored Frenchman, "Siegfried, I love you." The surface differences and the basic similarities of two nations are resolved in the admiration of the best in both—a hope for future peace and a one-world philosophy to eliminate hate and to find the common identity of man. The Siegfried-Jacques theme so dominated Giraudoux's early thinking that he repeated it in his novels and essays.

His own life was likewise a marked duality between the career statesman and the dedicated writer. He rose to be Minister of Propaganda and remained in office until the German Occupation. He knew practical politics, the corruption in high office, the absence of idealism, and the inevitability of war, yet he devoted years to effect a common understanding among nations. This is the theme of one of his most magnificent plays, *La Guerre de Troie n'aura pas lieu,* known in English in Christopher Fry's adaptation as *Tiger at the Gates.* The title (The Trojan War Will Not Take Place) is not intended as irony. Rather, it is Giraudoux's philosophy that the individual must attempt to reorder his relation to destiny, and though the result may be tragic, at least he experiences a moment of doubt and the recognition of possibility. The Gods cannot decide for man. When the decision is left to Zeus as to whether Helen shall be returned to the Greeks, he answers in the evasive words of a Talleyrand, "Separate Helen and Paris without separating them." The Messenger of the Gods adds that everyone must leave and permit the negotiators to face each other alone: "And let them arrange matters so that there will be no war. Or else, he swears to you, . . . there will be war." Not the equivocation of the Gods but the will of two men has to decide between war and peace, between love and hate.

Hector, the warrior, returning in triumph from foreign conquest, wants no more war, and convinces the Trojans not to fight and to give Helen back to the Greeks, but he still has to persuade Ulysses, ambassador of the Achaeans. The scene between the two is a brilliant debate on man's role in face of the inevitable. Ulysses, out of his long experience, knows that on the eve of any war "two heads of the hostile peoples meet alone in some neutral village, on some terrace on a lake shore . . . and agree that war is the worst plague of the world . . . and they are truly full of the desire for peace, and they part, shaking hands, feeling like brothers . . . and the next day, war breaks out." The exchange that follows removes any doubt that Hector's logic has convinced him:

ULYSSES: You know what made me decide to go, Hector?

HECTOR: Yes, your noble nature.

ULYSSES: Not exactly. Andromache's eyelashes dance as my wife Penelope's do.

Like all great generals, he prefers the physical pleasures of peace. As Ulysses departs, the poet-demagogue, Demokos, demands that Helen remain in Troy. Hector strikes him down, and as the mob gathers Demokos shouts that he has been slain by the Greek, Ajax. The lie of the poet turns the delicate balance. Ajax is murdered and the War Gates reopen. By his one rash act, Hector has undone all his efforts for peace, and is indirectly responsible for the war to come and the ruin of Troy. To add to his discomfort, Helen is seen in the background in the arms of Troilus. Man must act to redirect history even though the Gods are beyond reason and his destiny may have already been decided. Today, with the world's most powerful leaders reiterating their determination to maintain peace, the parallel is most alarming.

Giraudoux did not live to see the end of the Second World War he had sought to avoid, but he did succeed in establishing a new tradition in the French theatre. In Louis Jouvet, he had found a director with the scenic imagination to realize the beauty of language and prophetic fantasy of his plays. The two formed an intimate and continuous relationship that gave the playwright a brilliant company and an available theatre.

Man's conflict with God is further developed in *Ondine* and *Amphitryon 38* (so called because Giraudoux had uncovered thirty-seven other versions of the Alcmene story). In both plays, goodness triumphs. Though the gods would have it otherwise, Ondine remains true to her love, and Alcmene true to her husband. Jupiter seduces the mortal of his choice, but he is forced to assume the form of the husband whom he would cuckold; Alcmene, the following morning, is unaware of any guilt. Ondine, the nymph of nature, is rejected by Hans, who chooses the dull domesticity of Bertha. He has to make a decision between a great passion and a conventional marriage. He compromises the ideal, as most men do, but with Ondine the ideal remains pure, for she is not a creature of the earth but the spirit of the sea. When the Fisherman comes to claim the life of Hans, her lover, in accordance with the pact she has made she pleads for his life, even though she hears in the distance the church bells ringing for his wedding with Bertha.[1]

ONDINE: Don't judge men by our standards, Old One. Men don't deceive their wives unless they love them . . . It's a form of fidelity, their deceit. It's only because he wished to honor me that he deceived me. It was to show the world how pure I was, how true . . .

SECOND FISHERMAN: He has made you suffer, my little Ondine.

ONDINE: Yes, I have suffered. But remember we are speaking of humans. Among humans you are not unhappy when you suffer. On the contrary. To seek out in a world full of joy the one thing that is certain to give you pain, and to hug that to your bosom with all your strength—that's the greatest human happiness.

Hans says later, without rancor, "I was caught between the whole of Nature and the whole of Destiny, like a rat."

This preoccupation with the slim chance of success in the struggle against destiny is worked out on a lighter note in *La Folle (The Madwoman) de Chaillot,* a fantasy about the polarity of good and evil. In the Jouvet production, Christian Bérard designed the sets, adding visual fantasy in the expressionistic café in the Plâce de l'Alma of Act One and the dungeon bedroom of Countess Aurelia in Act Two. Though the play lacks the lyric intensity of *Intermezzo* or the philosophic inquiry of *Sodom and Gomorrah,* it is, for sheer exuberance and theatrical delight, one of the finest moments in the theatre.

THE MADWOMAN OF CHAILLOT

Outside the café gather the President, the Prospector, the Baron—the wicked of the world, the financiers who seek only profit. Interrupting them are the Ragpicker, the Street Singer, the Flower Girl, the Deaf Mute—the poor of the world, interested only in human happiness. The polarity is simple and seemingly trite, but is transformed into drama by the cleverness of the dialogue and the ingenuity of the events. The wicked would tear down the city of Paris because they have discovered oil beneath its streets. The Madwoman, Countess Aurelia, enters, a garish figure with an immense train gathered up with a clothespin, ancient button shoes, and a hat in the style of Marie Antoinette. She is mad because she is so sane. She refuses to leave her own world of beauty to endure the reasonable world of selfishness and falsity. The President knows the danger she represents, for he says, "Wherever the poor are happy and the servants proud, and the mad are respected, our power is at an end." A young man half-dead from drowning is brought in by the policeman. He has been an agent of the Prospector's, blackmailed into blowing up the city hall, but he has preferred to jump in the Seine. When he is revived, the sergeant questions him. The Countess demands that he be consoled instead, since "when people want to die, it is [the sergeant's] duty as a guardian of the state to speak out in praise of life." The officer stumbles, finding it difficult to do this, at which the Countess takes over and describes her own adventure in life: "I have my cats to feed, my dogs to pet, my plants to water. I have to see what the evil ones are up to in the district, those who hate people. I watch them sneaking off in the morning to put on their disguises—to the baths, to the beauty parlors, to the barbers . . . and when they come out with blonde hair and false whiskers to pull up my flowers and poison my dogs . . . I am ready." In these little things lie her identity with nature, her joy in being alive, the delights which complicated modern life has suppressed.

Irma, the waitress, is a lesser Aurelia, but also an angelic figure; she can hear the deaf mute talk. She is the pure in heart, the Ondine, or the Agnes of *Apollo of Bellac*. The Ragpicker tells the Countess what is happening in the real world. "Little by little, the pimps have taken over. They don't do anything. They don't make anything, they just stand there and take their cut"; of his lowly associates, he adds: "We are the last of the free people, it's the end of free enterprise." They inform the Countess of the plot of the evil men, and she devises a counter-plan to destroy them.

Act Two takes place in the underground bedroom of the Countess Aurelia. She has invited her friends, three other madwomen of Paris, to get their approval to destroy wickedness. They improvise a mock trial in which the Ragpicker stands for the accused. He ardently defends the rich, but is declared guilty by the assembled poor, at which he shouts, "I am never guilty! I am the law. When I speak, that is the law! When I present my backside, it is etiquette to smile and apply the lips respectfully. It is more than etiquette, it is a

cherished national tradition guaranteed by the Constitu-
tion."

In stylized groups, the Presidents, the Prospectors, the
Press Agents, the Prostitutes, and all those who curry favor
with them, and follow in the quest for oil, are sent to their
doom in the cavern below. The obsession with material
values has turned them into nameless, mechanical figures
who are defeated by their lust for wealth. When all have
gone, the Countess says, "They've evaporated. They were
wicked. Wickedness evaporates." Her friends rejoin her and
announce that the leaves are in bloom again, the birds are
flying again, life is good again, and Pierre and Irma are in
love. As they look at each other and hesitate, the Madwoman pleads, "Kiss him, Irma. Kiss him while there is still
time, or in a moment his hair will turn white and there
will be another madwoman in Paris." There is little time
to assert human values and they must not be denied. The
pleasures of the passions are marred by the intervention of
reason.

The play has to be seen and heard. It is a triumph of
sophisticated urbanity, which through fantasy has more to
say about social problems than the fanatic intensity of the
reformer. Giraudoux is never out of control, never too passionate, never the crusader. The appeal is to the senses, to
the intellect and the imagination, in a bizarre masque of
seeming improvisations. The language is precise, and like
so many French plays, full of brilliant talk, the resolution
by debate, the model conversation that can settle even affairs
of the heart. For this he has been called "precious," the master of style, too concerned with nuances of phrase and imagery. But though he is essentially a stylist, he goes beyond
preciosity into drama that may lack tragedy but assumes grandeur. Sartre condemned Giraudoux for not being a "committed" writer. Giraudoux replied that he was fully aware
of the urgencies of political matters, but that in his plays
essences, not existence, came first. In *The Madwoman of*

Chaillot he definitely takes sides. Preoccupation with material gain is dehumanizing. Poetry, imagination, and love of others can bind hearts together. Giraudoux is on the side of the joy of life, a positive affirmation of man's need to overcome despair and of the possibility of doing so.

It is a welcome note in the contemporary theatre. The same expressionistic style in which the characters transcend psychological reality to demonstrate social or universal truth was displayed in another remarkable play, *The Visit,* but whereas Duerrenmatt concludes with the ultimate weakness of man and his submission to evil, Giraudoux sees happiness in man's recognition of his minor role in an order of vaster proportions. To him, the theatre was a means of achieving religious majesty and ceremonial awe in the face of petty absurdity. He wrote:[2]

> There is no theatre which is not prophecy. Not this false divination which gives names and dates, but true prophecy, that which reveals to men these surprising truths: that the living must live, that the living must die, that autumn must follow summer, spring follow winter, that there are four elements, that there is happiness, that there are innumerable miseries, that life is a reality, that it is a dream, that man lives in peace, that man lives on blood; in short, those things they will never know.

These thoughts are not over-profound, but there is the poet's prophecy in Giraudoux. His form transcends his meaning, but the form is a combination of music, wit, language, and style, which gives to the diminished theatre a sense of greatness, and the prophecy is of the inaccessible that may become the attainable tomorrow.

Jean-Paul Sartre: the Theatre of Ideas—"Every man must find out his own way."

Since the death of Camus and Giraudoux, Sartre has been the unquestioned dean of the French theatre, the rare example of the philosopher turned playwright. Before 1943,

he had won his reputation as novelist, essayist, and polemi-
cist. Like most French writers of distinction, he was drawn
to the theatre because he found it a direct medium in which
to portray his insight into man's condition on earth. Sartre's
political activities, his communist associations, his repeated
cry that the writer cannot stand alone but must be actively
engaged in the solution of world problems, endeared him to
those to whom art is a weapon in the class struggle. His
plays, however, are a consistent definition of existentialism;
in them, he is not the ardent pamphleteer but the artist
with a specific point of view, and he consciously works to
give it form. Sartre has matured as a playwright, and well
understands that in the theatre the poet and not the poli-
tician commands respect.

His first play, *Les Mouches* (*The Flies*), produced during the last year of the Occupation, was directed by Charles
Dullin, a member of the Cartel. It was followed a year later
by *Huis Clos* (*No Exit*). These two plays reveal new poten-
tialities in the theatre of ideas, much in the manner of Shaw,
but whereas Shaw was the master of comedy proffering socialism in a witty debate of inverted epigrams, Sartre is the
serious high priest of existentialism.

The Flies is a retelling of the Orestes legend. The plot
is as well known to a French audience as it was to the
Greeks, and they delight in hearing it again with permis-
sible variations. Sartre's play was received enthusiastically as
a hidden reference to the German overlords and an attack
on imposed authority. The implications are there, but Sartre
was using history to project a universal concept of responsibility. Orestes returns to Corinth after an absence of sixteen years, to find Clytemnestra married to Aegisthus and
in tyrannical control of Corinth. Electra, the rightful heiress,
sits in rags at the palace entrance, full of hate. The city is
cursed with the plague, injustice and corruption thrive,
and a huge swarm of vile-smelling flies hovers over all as
the avenging Furies. Orestes has come back to find roots, the

wanderer in search of his homeland. When he slays his mother, he does so of his own free will. The Gods have failed him, and so he creates his own morality and accepts responsibility for his act. In doing so, he takes on the guilt of all men, and as a consequence separation from them. Exile and loneliness are his reward.

The core of the play is the debate between Orestes and Zeus, between man and God. Orestes, now that he has created his own freedom, spurns Zeus, who had made him free to serve God better. Orestes is devastating in his blasphemy:[3]

ORESTES: You were my excuse for being alive, for you had put me in the world to fulfill your purpose . . . And then you forsook me.

ZEUS: I forsook you? How?

ORESTES: Yesterday, when I was with Electra, I felt at one with Nature, this Nature of your making. It sang the praises of the Good—your Good . . . Suddenly, out of the blue, freedom crashed down on me and swept me off my feet. Nature sprang back, my youth went with the wind, and I knew myself alone, utterly alone in the midst of this well-meaning little universe of yours . . .

ZEUS: What of it? . . . Remember, Orestes, you once were of my flock, you fed in my pastures among my sheep. Your vaunted freedom isolates you from the fold; it means exile . . . Come back. I am forgetfulness, I am peace.

ORESTES: Foreign to myself—I know it. Outside nature, against nature, without excuse, beyond remedy, except what remedy I find within myself. But I shall not return under your law; I am doomed to have no other law but mine. Nor shall I come back to nature, the nature you found good; in it are a thousand beaten paths all leading up to you—but I must blaze my trail. For I, Zeus, am a man, and every man must find out his own way. Nature abhors man, and you too, god of gods, abhor mankind.

Orestes refuses to deny the Corinthians the right to despair, and adds, "They're free; and human life begins on the far side of despair." He urges Electra to go with him.

She asks, "Where?" And his answer is, "I don't know. Towards ourselves." She prefers to remain in Corinth, for she is still tied to Zeus, and Orestes goes into exile, pursued by the Furies, who fling themselves after him. But behind him is a city cleansed of guilt and fear.

Sartre is stating the reverse of the Christian concept of redemption through martyrdom. Man has been one with Nature, but that relationship has been dissolved. Through conscious will, the individual creates anew his own existence. He must act, even if in doing so he separates himself from all men and is exiled to solitude—an exile of freedom. The worst crime is not to act. The sickness of the world is the mute acceptance of authority, the evasion of choice. The meaning in terms of the Occupation was apparent, but Sartre, long after the defeat of Germany, continued to explore other interpretations of the same theme.

No Exit is more compact in structure, a continuous debate. Three people arrive in Hell, an Empire room with mirrors and no exit. They are condemned to spend eternity together. Each tries to work out a solution with one of the others, but there is no way for all three to achieve happiness. The play is in one act, modeled on Strindberg's *Miss Julie,* but here there is no intermission; the characters have to be on stage all the time since they cannot leave. The structure is the clever well-made play, with Hell as the drawing room. The three characters are facets of one action —the agony of man. They await the hangman, but none comes. One says, "They're economizing in personnel. Each one of us is the hangman for the other two." The three are a compendium of human crime: violence, adultery, Lesbianism, army desertion, murder. Garcin, a pacifist journalist, was shot attempting to avoid military duty. Inez, a post office employee, seduced her cousin's wife and drove the husband to an accidental death. Estelle married for money, killed her child, and goaded her adulterous lover to take his own life. Not a pleasant lot, but they become absorbing characters in their meaningful debate to find out the reasons for punishment. Garcin questions the judgment of a whole life by one cowardly action, and says, "A man is what he wills himself to be," protesting that he had no time to "do his deeds." Inez replies, "One always dies too soon—or too late. And yet one's whole life is complete at that moment . . . You are—your life, and nothing else." When Inez breaks up his love scene with Estelle, Garcin laughs, "There's no need for red-hot pokers. Hell is—other people." As they remain locked within the room, the final line is, "Let's go"—the same as in *Waiting for Godot*, when Vladimir and Estragon do not move. The group in *No Exit* can go nowhere but within the Hell of their failure; the two tramps can go nowhere at all, for life is perpetual waiting.

The Sartre characters are humans in the realm beyond despair. The weakness of the play dramatically is the lack of a protagonist. The characters are the reverse of the Holy Trinity, but the three never become one. The play is a brilliant discussion of Sartre's own version of existentialism, and a consideration of the philosophical background is essential to understand his later plays. Kierkegaard had initiated the revolt against purely positivistic systems by declaring that truth is within man himself. This truth determines his actions, whether they be rational or not. The unique quality of man is that he is the only animal who is self-conscious; that is, conscious of his own self. He alone is consciously aware of existence. Kierkegaard used the ethical implications of the nonrational world as proof of the necessity of God. Sartre believes the opposite, and he has become unacceptable to the orthodox followers of Heidegger, Karl Jaspers, and Martin Buber. He is closer to Neitzsche's "God does not exist," for since man creates his own existence, there is no need for a supernatural being. All agree that the trouble stems from Descartes, who in his dualism of mind and matter divorced the qualitative world

of everyday pleasures of sense and sound from the quanti-
tative world of physical objectivity. The mensurable world
that now dominates our lives has ignored human warmth
and feelings. Science has fashioned weapons of power, but
no comparable science has investigated loneliness and political fears. Human and spiritual questions remain ignored.
The duality has left man rootless. The existentialist begins
with a return to man and his freedom. Sartre has said, "Man
is condemned to be free"; exercising freedom may bring on
the exile of Orestes, but man achieves his essence by accepting responsibility. This is the basis of Sartre's dramas. Man's
conscience, by rigorous discipline, exercises choice. The
choice not to act is Garcin's cowardice. He would now use
Estelle and Inez to mirror the reflection of himself as hero,
but they and the added mirrors on the wall give back only
his posturing. Hell is the opposite of existence. Man can
no longer create his destiny. The necessity to have others
assert one's personality is negation. This is the meaning of
Garcin's cry, "Hell is—other people."

In *Les Sequestrés d'Altona* (*The Condemned of Altona*), Sartre deals with the problem of German war guilt.
It is too long in development of theme, and too discursive,
but it is a drama of towering proportions. Wealthy Von
Gerlach is an industrial magnate in the booming postwar
German economy. He is dying of throat cancer, and like
Gorky's Yegor Bulitchev, is a commanding figure who symbolizes a past that is crumbling. He forces his younger son
to take over the shipbuilding empire. Franz, the older son,
had been the father's hope, but he locked himself in his
room at the end of the war and has remained there, taking
on himself the guilt of a nation. In revulsion at Nazi methods, Franz had once hidden a rabbi in the house, but his
father, to save him, informed the authorities. Franz then
exiled himself to the Front and sought death in reckless
cruelty, but he became a war hero instead. Now, secluded
or sequestered (the title of the play) from the world in silent

expiation, he refuses to see his father, but a prosperous Germany makes redemption senseless. He is reconciled with his father at the end and they die in a double suicide.

The theme is daring, a reminder to Germany of its crimes, which have been too quickly forgotten. Franz is the conscience of those who have failed to assume responsibility, and yet his is a personal act, one man's recognition of necessity, for only through the individual can meaning be restored to the world. The crimes of Hitler are the springboard for an intricate display of existentialist exercises. Franz buries himself away from the world and uses his madness to avoid responsibility, but the results of one's acts cannot be sloughed off. They pursue the doer relentlessly; they are the Flies that buzz around until the consequences of action are fulfilled. People who do not act out of fear of being alone commit a worse crime in not making the initial effort for freedom. Franz is alone, he has acted, and now he addresses posterity. He records on tape his message to the world:

> . . . you who were, who will be, and who are—I have been! I have been! I, Franz von Gerlach, here in this room, have taken the century on my shoulders and have said, "I will answer for it."

Those who hear him may be only a race of crabs, the symbol of a future in which a bomb turns off all the lights. There may be no more centuries after this one, yet even Franz, whose name may be a symbol for France, has deep compassion for those who will come after him. His ravings are heard on the recording machine as the curtain comes down:

> Beautiful children, you who are born of us, our pain has brought you forth. This century is a woman in labor. Will you condemn your mother?

Franz's justification is an agonizing and self-pitying cry. He refuses to face the consequences of his guilt. His death cannot expiate a race. Each individual must find his own solutions, and he cannot rely on the laws of God. Sartre wrote an entire play to demonstrate His nonexistence, *The Devil and the Good Lord*. It is his most elaborate work, a continuation of the Orestes debate transferred from the Greeks to the Renaissance.

THE DEVIL AND THE GOOD LORD

The form is traditional. Sartre was more concerned with content than with innovations in structure. The play is in the romantic tradition of Goethe and the Shakespearean histories. The protagonist is Goetz, inviting a comparison with *Goetz von Berlichingen,* but the themes are distinct. Goethe was writing an apostrophe to freedom; Sartre, a declaration of freedom from God. The time is that of the Peasants' Revolt during the Lutheran Reformation in Germany. Goetz, the military leader, is cruel, vindictive, and lusting for power. He besieges the town of Worms in revolt against the Archbishop, slaughters the people, kills the clergy, turns on his legitimate brother, mocks the churchmen and bankers whose only thought is wealth, and stands alone in control. His debate is with two contrapuntal figures: Heinrich, a defrocked priest who would sacrifice the people to save the Church, and Nasti, leader of the peasants, who would eliminate the Church to make a heaven on earth. Goetz alternates between the two, but he decides that since God alone can create Good, he will create evil, all that is left to man. To Heinrich, he says:[4]

> Since the day of my birth, I have only seen the world through the keyhole; it's a fine little egg, neatly packed, where everyone fits the place God has assigned to him. But I give you my word we are not inside that world. We are outcasts! Reject this world that rejects you. Turn to Evil. You will see how lighthearted you will feel.

But he tires of Evil. It has become too commonplace, and he makes a wager in the Faustian manner that for one year he will devote himself to Good. He gives the land to the peasants, erects a model community, The City of the Sun, and takes himself off to the desert for prayer and contemplation. On his holy pilgrimage he blesses the deformed, but quite dishonorably carves his own stigmata on his body. He forsakes his mistress for Hilda, a holy woman, who would give him her eyes to see his soul, "which he can no longer see for it is under his nose." Before the year is up, the City of the Sun is sacked by the lords and bishops, who regard its existence as a threat to their power, and the people are massacred when they practice nonviolence at the behest of Goetz, the new Christ. He faces Heinrich in the final debate, the most sacrilegious scene in contemporary drama. Good and Evil have both failed. Goetz begins by saying, "Half of myself is your accomplice against the other half. Search me to the depths of my being, since it is my being that is on trial," but he confesses his own doubts:

Accuse me of detesting the poor and exploiting their gratitude to enslave them. . . . Listen, priest: I had betrayed everyone, including my own brother, but my appetite for betrayal was not yet assuaged; so, one night, before the ramparts of Worms, I thought up a way to betray Evil, that's the whole story. Only Evil doesn't let itself be betrayed quite so easily; it wasn't Good that jumped out of the dice-box; it was a worse Evil. What does it matter anyway? Monster or saint, I didn't give a damn, I wanted to be inhuman.

He demands to talk to God directly, while the Devil stands at the side of Heinrich. Silence is the only reply. Goetz shouts, "Why does He refuse to manifest Himself to me" when He manifested Himself to the ass of the prophet, and the priest says, "God doesn't give a damn . . . for man is nothing." It is the moment of resolution; Goetz knows why God has not answered—"Silence is God. Absence is God. God is the loneliness of man. There was no one but myself; I alone decided on Evil; and I alone invented Good. It was

I who cheated, I who worked miracles, I who accused myself today, I alone who can absolve myself; I, man. If God exists, man is nothing; if man exists" . . . The priest would run away, but Goetz holds him with his final outburst, "Heinrich, I am going to tell you a colossal joke: God does not exist."

He kills the priest and rejoins Nasti, no longer as Christ on earth, but as the leader who knows that on earth Good and Evil are inseparable, and that to become good he will agree to be bad. The kingdom of man begins, now that he can create his own existence. He says to Nasti:

> I shall make them hate me, because I know no other way of loving them. I shall give them orders, since I have no other way of obeying. I shall remain alone with this empty sky over my head, since I have no other way of being among men. There is this war to fight, and I will fight it.

Goetz will be responsible only to his conscience, freed from any outside interference. He has discovered the infinity of man in his finiteness. In the absence of God's justice, he will stand alone, and like Franz in *The Condemned of Altona* pass judgment on history.

Sartre's answers may shock a conventional world, but he does not submit to despair. He is a moralist with a positive approach. Man's choice determines his destiny. Such decisions are the essence of dramatic conflict, and in debating the issues Sartre has extended the limits of the theatre. To him, literature should be "a perpetual affirmation of human freedom," and writers, like their characters, must assume responsibility, be committed to a "positive theory of liberation," and condemn violence and oppression in all forms. If they talk of "changes in postage stamps rather than why millions of Jews were massacred by the Nazis, their silence is revelatory." He insists that the writer "give his thoughts without respite, day in, day out, to the problem of ends and means; or again, to the problem of the relationship of ethics and politics."[5]

It is significant that in today's apathy, the religious theatre has had a major renaissance, from the piety of Montherlant, the return to grace of Graham Greene, the chosen martyrs of Eliot, to the existentialist atheism of Sartre.

Albert Camus—"The maximum danger implies the maximum hope."

The sudden death of Albert Camus in an automobile accident at the age of forty-six, three years after he had won the Nobel Prize for literature, was a major loss to France and to the contemporary theatre. He had written but five plays, in addition to his novels, collections of essays, and adaptations for the stage, but under the reorganization of André Malraux, he was given his own theatre where as director and producer he would have had full freedom to experiment. He had long hoped for such an opportunity, and once wrote that the theatre was "one of the places in the world where [he was] happiest."

Camus belongs to the theatre of ideas, but unlike Sartre, he was never convinced of certainty, and his doubt made him all the more human. His ideas were few, but in coming to them he had eliminated many others in order to explore those few more exhaustively. In *Noces*, he said:

> It takes ten years to have an idea all one's own— about which one can speak. Naturally, it's a little discouraging.

Though he was not an existentialist, he was close to Sartre in affirming a universe without God, but he did not erect a philosophical system of ethical values. He was content to say that "man's responsibility is to do nothing to increase suffering." His own anguish, which is the central theme of his plays, is the fear that we may have failed to do that which would spare another human being. Men must act, and Camus, like Sartre, believed in the "committed" writer, but only because inaction may fail to prevent or lessen the misery of others. We cannot rely on chance.[6]

> The time of irresponsible artists is over. We shall regret it for our little moments of bliss. But we shall be able to admit that this ordeal contributes meanwhile to our chances of authenticity . . . The freedom of art is not worth much when its only purpose is to assure the artist's comfort.

He sought a positive affirmation of life even if it lay only in the freedom to search for that affirmation. In his essays on rebellion, he wrote:

> . . . I am tired of criticism, of disparagement, of spitefulness—in short, of nihilism. It is essential to condemn what must be condemned, but swiftly and firmly. On the other hand, one should praise at length what still deserves to be praised. After all, that is why I am an artist, because even the work that negates still affirms something and does homage to the wretched and magnificent life that is ours.

It is the most succinct reply to Ionesco and Genet.

Camus was born in Algeria, the son of an agricultural worker, and knew poverty and the struggle to gain a university education. Never completely at home in Europe, he always longed for the sun and the sea of the African coast. He formed his own theatre group in Algiers, mostly with students and workers, and wrote his first play, *Caligula,* for them, but it was not produced until years later in Paris. His fame was the result of his novels, *The Stranger* and *The Plague,* and a book of essays, *The Myth of Sisyphus,* in which occurs the oft-quoted phrase, "There is only one really serious philosophical problem—suicide." His essays contain more serenity, hopefulness, and resolution than the plays, which, with their moments of doubt, the thinking out of human problems, the action prior to resolution, are pessimistic. They deal with loneliness, with crime that is accidental and fatal, with "groping in the dark . . . dreaming of justice," yet contributing to injustice. Above all, to Camus—as to many—the source of anxiety is the absence of any real reason for living, a problem covered over by habit and sentiment. The symbol of dislocation and futility is Sisyphus rolling his rock up the mountain and having it roll down just as he reaches the top, but Camus respected man and found "help in hope," and in preserving those few values "without which a world, even transformed, is not worth living in."

Le Malentendu (*The Misunderstanding*), written while Camus was living in the mountains of central France as a member of the Resistance, was his first produced play. The scene is an inn in Bohemia, run by Martha and her mother. To save money to escape from their barren, dismal surroundings, they kill the occasional guest who arrives, dispose of his body, and rob him of his funds. The son, Jan, returns after a long absence and expects to be recognized without giving his name. Instead, he is murdered. This is the misunderstanding. Aware of what they have done, mother and sister commit suicide. It is a gloomy play in which the inner conflicts are insufficiently visualized. Camus, like others of the theatre of ideas, is less concerned with psychological motivation than with philosophical implications. He called his play "a work of easy access," but the access is choked by the emphasis on the verbal; yet, paradoxically, the theme is the absurdity of relationships that depend on words. The failure of Jan to say the right word leads to his death. Camus tells in one of his essays of a visit to Prague. A stranger dies alone in his hotel room, while the narrator next door, aware that something wrong is taking place, studies a shaving cream advertisement. Leaving things to chance, through inaction permitting the accidental to happen, may lead to another's death and our own failure to lessen human misery. When Jan is alone in his room at the inn, he says:[7]

> The evenings are depressing for a lonely man . . .
> and I know what it is. It's fear, fear of the eternal loneli-
> ness, fear that there is no answer.

The play is also the story of the son's return—"He came unto his own and his own received him not." All the characters are lost in their private solitude, and though they may be of the same blood, there is no recognition. Their lives touch but do not communicate.

The Old Man, who is the servant and accomplice of Martha and her mother, moves silently throughout the action. When, in the final scene, Jan's widow calls upon God for help, the Old Man enters and says, "No"—his only word in the play. Camus wrote that the Old Man could not have helped if he had wanted to, for pain is solitary. But there is an implication of the distance between man and God, of the lack of any explanation for ugliness and brutality.

Les Justes (*The Assassins*), which deals with the murder of the Russian Archduke by a band of terrorists, is a discussion of ends and means, of the relationship between ethics and politics. Camus said that he admired the assassins because "they understood the limits of action," and that there is no good or just action that does not recognize those limits. Our world today is run by men "who go beyond those limits and kill others without dying themselves . . . Justice serves as an alibi throughout the world for the assassins of justice." In the most dramatic scene, the Grand Duchess comes to the prison cell to interview her husband's murderer, the one who threw the bomb. She offers him the grace of God and the forgiveness of man. He angrily rejects both. He must accept death, for otherwise he would not have had the right to take a life, and would not have recognized the limits of his action. Is murder ever justified, even if done to restore justice and better all humanity? It is the question raised by the Resistance fighters and by Brecht in *Die Mass-nahme* (*The Expedient*) and by Sartre in *Les Mains Sales* (*Dirty Hands*).

L'Etat de Siège (*State of Siege*) is the weakest of the plays. It is a treatise about the effects on men of being closed within a sick society. Despite the production by Barrault, it won little acclaim. The plague is more skillfully treated in the novel. The best of Camus' dramatic work is *Caligula,* the first play he wrote, and one of the finest examples of the theatre of ideas.

CALIGULA

Caligula, Emperor of Rome, is overwhelmed by the death of Drusilla, his sister and mistress. He goes off to the wilderness to be alone with his grief, and when he returns he has discovered a new truth: that "men die; and they are not happy." He will no longer be content with the usual and the commonplace. He will find happiness even if he has to destroy the world to do so, for he alone has the power to be free. He begins with truth as he sees it, tearing away the outward appearance of lies and deception that have become rooted in all government and seeped through to all of life. He kills and murders and destroys, reveling in the sensuous release that he believes is happiness. For he, the Emperor, is "the unpunished murderer" in a world of scorn and hatred, but his happiness is illusory and his freedom brings loneliness and the anguish of being a man. He has shed tears of love, but now he weeps because "the world's all wrong." He says:

> I knew that men felt anguish, but I didn't know what that word anguish meant. Like everyone else, I fancied it was a sickness of the mind—no more. But no, it's my body that's in pain . . . but worst of all this queer taste in my mouth. Not blood, or death, or fever, but a mixture of all three. I've only to move my tongue and the world goes black, and everyone looks . . . horrible. How hard, how cruel it is, this process of becoming a man!

His loneliness is deceptive. One is never alone. There is always the future and the past, and those we have killed are always with us. But they are no great trouble. It's those we have loved, those who loved us and whom we did not love; regrets, desires, bitterness, and sweetness, whores and gods, the celestial gang! Always, always with us! . . . If only in this loneliness . . . I could know, but for a moment, real solitude, real silence, the throbbing stillness of a tree.

He casts out love to go beyond love. He will love the moon and attain the impossible. In mounting fury, he plays before the mirror the image of himself, and in the final scene, strangles his faithful mistress Caesonia, so that he may achieve beyond love "the glorious isolation of man." He has searched for the impossible "at the confines of the world, in the secret places of his heart" and knows that his freedom has led to nothing. He smashes the mirror and exclaims, "Soon, I shall attain the emptiness beyond all understanding." The young poet Scipio and the old cynic Cherea, the disinterested minds who love him for his madness, are the ones who destroy him. As the conspirators plunge their daggers into his body, Caligula cries, "I'm still alive."

Camus condemns the Emperor's absolute nihilism. No man can save himself alone. Caligula refuses to escape the absurdities of life by accepting the accessible refuge of God's unknowable justice, and rejects faith in another life that may transcend this one. He would make the impossible attainable here on earth, change the order of the universe, cause laughter from pain, beauty from ugliness, and he observes his power in a mirror for he alone is witness of his deeds. He fails because he chose a way without humanity. The result is isolation and hate, and he smashes the mirror that reflects his failure. But he lives on after death, since his was the supreme effort of the passion for the impossible, which Camus stated is as "valid a subject for drama as adultery or avarice."

Sartre had Goetz in *The Devil and the Good Lord* turn to evil as the only creative act left to man. Caligula turns to evil to imitate the gods. His error lies in negating man. In his preface to the play, Camus wrote that "one cannot destroy everything without destroying oneself . . . Caligula is a superior suicide . . . Unfaithful to mankind through fidelity to himself, Caligula accepts death because he has understood that no one can save himself all alone and that one cannot be free at the expense of others." in this sense, *Caligula* is a modern morality play, a debate on the nature of man. Though the conclusion seemingly is nothingness and a return to what had existed before, the Emperor's rebellion exposes the emptiness of an ill-considered nihilism, a rebuke to the facile writing of despair. Camus could offer little in the way of positive answers, and he rejected the glib assumptions of indifference to life. During the Resistance he had said that, though this world has no superior meaning, "I know that something in it has meaning. It is man, because man is the sole being to insist on having a meaning." He accepted no systematic concepts either of totalitarianism or existentialism—the end may not justify the means. However, his outlook was not one of fear but of devotion to the task of serving human dignity by "means which are honorable in the midst of history which is not honorable." And he added, "I should not want to change eras, for I know and respect the greatness of this one. Moreover, I have always thought the maximum danger implied the maximum hope."[8]

11. The Epic Theatre—Bertolt Brecht

THE GOOD WOMAN OF SETZUAN

AFTER THE FIRST WORLD WAR the poet was compelled to respond to an age in disequilibrium. He sought refuge in what was comfortable and tangible—the past, or the Church, or pure form; or he made a resigned confession of confusion and indifference and sang of the lost generation in self-pity; or he attacked what still remained standing, as though, having abandoned belief, he would have none possess it. Transitional groups, each proclaiming its eternal perfection—cubism, futurism, surrealism, constructivism—had their moment of glory, their disciples, their manifestoes. The age was unhinged, but beneath the surface there were discernible trends that presaged the major battle for the future.

Realism Under Attack—"Back to the eternal . . ."

Particularly vulnerable was the realistic theatre, only recently triumphant. Fathered by Zola and perfected by Ibsen, psychological realism had invested the theatre with a concern for social issues and psychological truth. With Chekhov and Shaw, the romantic and neoclassical adherents suffered a further severe setback. But they were far from routed. They were merely biding their time, awaiting a more favorable moment to reassert themselves. That opportunity came with the empty hunger of the postwar period. Ibsen himself had set the example by deserting realism for forays into the unreal and the unknowable, and there had always been Strindberg and Maeterlinck and Yeats. Now, the desire to forget the unpleasant memories of war reinforced the argument that the theatre could never be life itself, nor should it aspire to be since it is always arranged and artificial. The only honest realism would be a recorded reproduction of the speech and actions of daily life, undramatic and dull. Otherwise, it was merely another form of make-believe. The words of Evreinov were hauled out and repeated. In 1905, he had declared that if verisimilitude was the goal in the theatre, then antique tables should be used on the set when called for, painted flats should give way to the scene of action, actors should speak the language of the nationality represented, and the fourth wall should be closed, sealing off the audience! The demand grew for the theatre as a refuge of "the lost sense of myth," a place to "forget the incidental and cast memory once more back to the eternal."

Epic Theatre Joins the Fight—"We have to go elsewhere . . ."

These claims had been heard before, but realism now found its own allies in open opposition. Writers interested in political issues claimed that a revolutionary situation demanded a revolutionary theatre; that what was needed was a more selective and scientific realism; that the superstitions of the temple should be replaced by the facts of the forum. The most intense battleground, where the struggle, raw and violent, reflected all facets of the Western world, was the Germany of the Weimar Republic.

The defeat of the Kaiser's armies left a nation dedicated to science and its own superiority, a rich soil for competitive values. Communism and National Socialism fought for eventual control. In the theatre, within a few years of each other, Friedrich Wolf presented *The Sailors of Cattaro,* a lyric apostrophe to the mutinous sailors of the Austrian navy and their martyrdom for freedom, whereas Hanns Johst dedicated his play *Schlageter* to Adolph Hitler, a play in which occur the lines later attributed to Göring,

"When I hear 'Kultur,' I loosen the safety catch on my revolver."

Bertolt Brecht summed up the general attitude by saying, "The drama from Diderot to Ibsen is one completed epoch, and now we have to go elsewhere not only because of the exhaustion in techniques but changes in society and man."[1] The result was Epic Theatre. Its rapid rise in Germany before Hitler came to power occasioned the most searching re-examination of dramatic values.

The Meaning of Epic

The name "Epic" is most unfortunate, for it evokes irrelevant connotations. The word is derived from the Aristotelian division of literature into three fields: epic, lyric, and dramatic. Epic Theatre was intended to be essentially narrative, to relate events, using the theatre as a more effective presentation medium. It was thus from the beginning a combination of the dramatic and the narrative. Brecht, also one of the most distinguished contemporary German poets, combines the lyric as well, thus merging all three elements. To limit Brecht's theatre to the word "Epic" is fairly meaningless. He realized the inadequacy of the word and tried frequently to change it, his final suggestion being "the dialectic" theatre, but to no avail; the misnomer had become too deeply ingrained. But the term does serve to distinguish the form from the romantic or the realistic, and some day Epic Theatre may fittingly be known as the Brechtian theatre.

The purpose of Epic was to present historical fact in such a way that the audience would be compelled to act as tribunal and judge events. It was theatre as education. This concept of theatre, however, was not original with Brecht and his followers. From its very beginnings, the theatre had, as an immediate didactic purpose, the transmission of the cultural heritage and a knowledge of the practical arts. The dance, ritual, or ceremonial chant, performed in common or by selected experts, were visual and oral education at its most direct and primitive level. But Epic Theatre is distinct in its techniques and procedures and its function at a particular moment in history.

The Forerunners

Many contemporary experiments paved the way for Epic Theatre, particularly the revival of Georg Büchner, who had died in 1837 at the age of twenty-four, and been completely forgotten in the heyday of the romantics' *Sturm und Drang*. He was now unearthed and played all over Germany, exerting a strong influence on the rebels in the theatre, for in his two better-known plays—*Wozzec,* set to music by Alban Berg, and *Dantons Tod* (*The Death of Danton*), elaborately performed by Max Reinhardt—Büchner, a representative of Young Germany, broke with conventions of form and meaning, used effective sequences of short, instructive scenes, and employed a powerful new-minted language.

The rise of Expressionism, following the dream plays of Strindberg, likewise broke long-held tradition in the theatre. In prewar Germany, it was evidenced in the varied work of Walter Hasenclever and the spectral abstractions of Franz Wedekind. In 1920 appeared the plays of Georg Kaiser, whose *Gas I* and *Gas II* were precise, intellectual, constructivist antiwar documents. The stage was filled with weird, superrealistic industrial plants, and the background consisting of distorted production charts spattered with red ink. In the same year came Lion Feuchtwanger's *Thomas Wendt,* in which a poet becomes a revolutionary leader, which had an immediate influence on Brecht's early work. This was followed by the explosive lyrical outburst of Ernst Toller, whose expressionistic plays were a continued demonstration of the need for a more humane and peaceful world.

These forerunners contributed to the form of the Epic

Theatre, but the audience was supplied by the trade union movement. Organized labor had for years conducted an intensive educational program of which one aspect was a form of *commedia dell'arte*. Union members, with but a few lines of prepared script, would pose as casual spectators at bread lines, in crowds waiting for the bus, in gatherings of people anywhere, and would point up the need for action on specific social issues. More formal short pieces and skits were presented at regular union meetings. Out of such beginnings rose the labor theatre, pioneered in 1919 by Karlheinz Martin and his "Die Tribune" theatre, but the most spectacular work was achieved by Erwin Piscator.

"Piscatoring" a Play

After earlier successes in Königsberg, Piscator was appointed theatre director for the *Volksbühne,* the trade union educational center, but he was in constant disagreement with the old-line leadership, which insisted on giving the workers only the classics of the past, on the ground that the theatre's slogan was "culture for the masses," and culture meant the literary heritage. Piscator wanted the theatre to take an active role in affecting vital social decisions of the day. In 1924, he had written, "Not man's relation to himself, nor his relation to God, but his relation to society, is the main issue."[2] His opportunity came in 1927 when he broke with the Volksbühne and took over the old and distinguished Theatre-am-Nollendorfplatz.

The opening night of *The Good Soldier Schweik* was a landmark in theatre history. Piscator's reputation for the unusual made attendance an intellectual requirement for the regular first-nighters, and so top hats and dress suits mixed with the torn shorts and ragged sweaters of the workers. The play was an adaptation of the Czech novel by Jaroslav Hašek, depicting the experiences of a peasant soldier caught in the inefficient stupidities of war. Brecht was called in to collaborate on the script. He was deeply impressed by the character of Schweik and later did his own complete version. The simple peasant exposes the absurdity of the world, not by defiance but by cheerfully complying with the letter of every order.

Piscator transformed the old picture-frame theatre drastically. Short, rapid scenes rose out of the orchestra, flowed in from the wings and aisles; placards, signs, graphs, and posters pointed out what was happening on stage; motion pictures flashed on the screen to interrupt the action and supply more background information, and a treadmill ground away, taking Schweik to different scenes of battle. The success of the production is debatable, but Piscator had no doubts. War had been presented without hysterical overtones, factually, scientifically. In any case, the production was a technician's holiday.

So violent grew the debate between the advocates of simple staging and the proponents of Epic Theatre that the name Piscator became identified with mechanical excesses. In his review of Brecht's *Galileo* in 1948, George Jean Nathan, the mellowed iconoclast, uses "piscator" as a disparaging verb:[3]

> And if such a play which should properly be staged in a more or less conventional manner offers an opportunity to piscator it almost out of recognition with lantern slides, loud speakers, off-stage juke boxes, and topsy-turvy scenery, they grow delirious with delight.

The Man Brecht

The man most closely associated with the Epic Theatre is Bertolt Brecht, poet, playwright, and theoretician. He was born in Bavaria in 1898, studied to be a doctor, and served in the medical corps in the First World War. He had already established his reputation as a poet, for at the age of twenty-two, he won the honored Kleist prize for his first play, *Drums in the Night*.

The first period of Brecht's work stems from the disillusionment and despair and wild experimentalism of post-war Germany. He felt close to Rimbaud and Villon, the lonely, lost, bitter, and anarchic poet, often attacking accepted institutions to provoke scandal, often groping in a wild and savage outburst for new symbols to express a confused belligerence. Jazz rhythms, American gangsters, prize-fighters, combine in a defiant and often romantic self-pity. *In the Jungle of Cities* is an example of this obscure, tantalizing, and brutal morality whose form precedes by twenty years the work of Ionesco and Adamov. The best play of this period is *The Three-Penny Opera,* with sprightly music by the serious composer Kurt Weill. Like most of Brecht's work, it is based on someone else's play, this time *The Beggar's Opera* of John Gay. It is a travesty on the world of business, with acid comments on love, money, success, parental relations, and the law twisted into apparently inoffensive lyrics. Brecht's most popular play, it delighted a war-weary Germany and ran for four hundred performances at Piscator's Schiffbauerdamm Theatre, and was repeated throughout Europe. Other collaborations with Weill, such as *The Rise and Fall of the City of Mahagonny,* wherein money alone is the test of survival, established Brecht as a leader of the young iconoclasts.

His second period is mostly devoted to the *"Lehrstücke"* or learning pieces. He had come under the influence of Marxism, and with Hanns Eisler as composer, he wrote such plays as *Die Massnahme* (translated as *The Expedient* or *The Disciplinary Measure*), in which the theatre is arranged like a courtroom and the judges sit with the audience, to determine whether four communist organizers are justified when expediency demands the murder of a young revolutionary who has failed in his mission. The plays of this period are outright propaganda, the least dramatic of Brecht's prolific output. Such crude political lessons as those contained in *Saint Joan of the Stockyards* and *Round Heads and Peak Heads* are naïve, untheatrical simplifications. They appeal to a partisan audience.

The final period of Brecht's work encompasses his best plays and his more mature conception of Epic Theatre as historical realism. *Mother Courage, The Good Woman of Setzuan,* and *The Caucasian Chalk Circle* are less thunderous, more implicitly political, and more artistically formed. By the time he was forced to leave Germany in 1934, Brecht was recognized as the outstanding playwright of the German theatre. He lived in Denmark, Finland, and the United States during his exile, and after the war, returned to Switzerland, then cautiously and as an Austrian citizen to East Berlin. The Soviet sector gave him complete charge of his own theatre, plentiful funds, adequate time for rehearsals, and a permanent company. Out of this long-awaited opportunity came the Berliner Ensemble, a superbly coordinated troupe devoted almost exclusively to the production of Brecht's work. He died in 1956, a few days before the triumphal appearance of his company in London.

It is questionable whether Brecht's reputation would have grown so amazingly in the past decade had he not had the opportunity to work with a theatre able to execute his ideas. In the United States there is much discussion on the Brechtian theatre, but it is largely confined to literary circles. *The Good Woman of Setzuan* has been selected for detailed analysis here, not only because it is available in English, but because it represents the controlled rather than the excessive claims of the Epic Theatre.

THE GOOD WOMAN OF SETZUAN

PROLOGUE—*"Only the gods can help us . . . "*

The setting and characters are Chinese, for Brecht was deeply impressed by the simplicity and symbolic shorthand of the Oriental theatre. The Chinese artist has always excelled in saying much with little—a few words, a few

strokes—and moreover, the actor is never emotionally involved in his role. He stands apart and projects his interpretation. Setzuan has been touched by the Western world
and is not completely removed from European problems,
and so costumes and sets can be of two civilizations with a
suggestion of each; the moral of the play is more dispassion-
ately emphasized by removing it from the large industrial
cities of the Occident.

Changes in time and place throughout the play are
indicated by projections, light effects, display cards, or simply
by telling the audience directly.

The Prologue opens with Wang, the water-seller, intro-
ducing himself in a masterpiece of irreverent irony:[4]

WANG: I sell water here in the city of Setzuan. It's a difficult
business. When water is scarce, I have to go a long way to
find any. And when it is plentiful, I have no income. But
in our province, there is nothing unusual about poverty.
It is generally said that only the gods can still help us . . .

Wang has heard from a cattle-buyer that the gods are coming, and he is on the lookout for them. A succession of
people passes by.

WANG: It can't be those people over there, they are coming
from work. Their shoulders are crushed from all the carrying they do . . . But look at those three! They're well fed,
show no sign of having any occupation, and have dust on
their shoes, which means they have come from far away. They
must be the gods.

Wang prostrates himself before the visitors, who ask him to
find them a lodging for the night. He scurries about, knock-
ing at every door, pleading with every passer-by, but no one
will take the gods in! Only the prostitute Shen Te offers her
humble abode. The gods leave the next morning, pleased
that they have found one good person, for that is their mission here on earth. Even the water-seller had failed them,
for when he offered them a drink they discovered his cup
had a false bottom. Shen Te, despite the gods' assurance, is

not so sure of herself, and cries out after them, "How can I be good when everything is so expensive?" The gods, though they "mustn't meddle with economics," decide that Shen Te would have a better chance if "she were a little richer." They therefore pay her handsomely for the night's stay, even though, considering her profession, "such an action could be misinterpreted."

THE BODY OF THE PLAY—*"Change human nature or . . . the world?"*

The rest of the play, ten scenes and an epilogue, is the story of Shen Te, now that she has money. Seven of the scenes have a brief companion interlude; in five of these, the gods return to see how their charge is faring, and in two of them Shen Te speaks to the audience about her newly acquired problems. She purchases a tobacco store and becomes one of the propertied class. The poor take advantage of her goodness and exploit her mercilessly, sleeping in her quarters and robbing her of her stock. She is overcharged by the former owners, cheated by the carpenter, gouged with an exorbitant rent, and is unable to pay her bills, but she continues to be generous and good. Her charity is her ruin, and so she invents a cousin, Shui Ta, who only the audience knows is Shen Te herself with a mask. If she is to survive, this other side of her character must also find expression. Since she must face the world with goodness, her mask is her ruthless opposite, her non-goodness. Shui Ta expels the poor family living in the store, reduces the tradesmen's bills, refuses rice to the hungry, and finally arranges for Shen Te's marriage to the wealthy baker.

All would have gone well if romance had not come into the picture. But Shen Te, who reappears when all is arranged by the fictitious cousin, falls in love with a young pilot, Yang Sun, whom she meets as he is about to commit suicide by hanging himself.

In the interlude, Wang reports to the gods that Shen

Te remains good and is known as "the Angel of the Suburbs," but that her cousin, a "highly respectable businessman," is hard and cruel, and responsible for all the evil
acts, at which the gods, perplexed, ask, "What does business have to do with an honest and dignified life?"

Yang Sun, as the betrothed, makes his financial demands
on Shui Ta, who rejects them, but Shen Te capitulates,
and reports to the audience:

> I couldn't resist his voice and his caresses. The bad
> things he said to Shui Ta didn't teach Shen Te anything.
> Sinking into his arms, I thought: the gods wanted me to be
> good to myself too.

If Yang Sun, her lover, takes her money, she will no longer
be able to aid others, but she is compelled to give aid, for
everywhere she finds misery and cowardice. When Wang's
hand is crushed by the barber, no one dares to testify to the
police. Shen Te sings angrily:

> Unhappy men!
> Your brother is assaulted and you shut your eyes!
> He is hit and cries aloud and you are silent?
> The beast prowls, chooses his victim, and you say:
> He's spared us because we do not show displeasure.
> What sort of city is this? What sort of people are you?
> When injustice is done, there should be revolt . . .

She does not go through with the marriage but returns to
her store. When she discovers that she is pregnant she is very
happy, and sings and dances with her future son. Then
Wang, the water-seller, enters with a homeless waif who
needs her aid, and she sings, "A bit of tomorrow is asking
for a today!" Horrified at the sight of the hungry child
searching for food in the garbage, she rebukes the audience
again. However, the thought that her own son may face
a similar fate proves decisive. She will no longer be good.
She will abandon her selflessness. She will think only of herself and her son:

Having seen this, from now on, I divorce myself from
  everybody! . . .
I will be good to you, and a tigress, a wild beast,
To all others . . .

Romantic love distorts objectivity. Brecht underscores its
possessive nature. It arouses Shen Te's self-protective and
antisocial instincts. Once again she calls upon Shui Ta. He
ousts the poor, becomes a big manufacturer, the Tobacco
Tycoon, exploits his workers with enforced speed-up and
starvation wages, and hires the opportunist Yang Sun as his
factory manager.

Shen Te is soon to have her child. Shui Ta's waistline
expands. One day, Yang Sun hears a woman's sobs in the
rear of the office and accuses Shui Ta of keeping his cousin
imprisoned. The police are called, and Shui Ta is summoned
to court to account for the disappearance of Shen Te.

The final scene is the trial. The gods are the judges.
The poor testify in behalf of the goodness of Shen Te. The
rich testify in behalf of the respectability of Shui Ta. The
crowd shouts out, demanding to know why their friend and
benefactor, Shen Te, had to go away. Shui Ta cries, "Because you would have torn her to shreds!" He asks for the
court to be cleared, and alone with the gods, confesses all.
He is Shen Te. The two are one and the same person:

Your former injunction to be good and yet to live
Tore me like lightning in halves . . .
When I was unjust, I walked mightily and ate good
  meat . . .
And yet I wished to be an Angel to the Suburbs . . .

To be good means the loss of all she possesses; to be selfish
and crush others means providing for her son's future. She
is caught in a moral dilemma. Will the gods please help her
out? But they themselves are confused. They rise upward on
a pink cloud to the accompaniment of soft music, blithely
saying:

You can do it. Just be good and everything will turn out well!

The scene concludes:

SHEN TE: But I need my cousin!

FIRST GOD: Not too often!

SHEN TE: At least once a week!

FIRST GOD: Once a month. That's enough!

Shen Te stretches out her arms in desperation as the gods disappear upward, smiling and waving and singing.

To make sure the lesson of the play is clear, an actor appears to deliver the Epilogue:

. . . We're disappointed too. With consternation
We see the curtain closed, the plot unended.
In your opinion then, what's to be done?
Change human nature or . . . the world? Well? Which?
Believe in bigger, better gods, or . . . none?
How can we mortals be both good and rich?
There must, there must be some end that would fit.
Ladies and gentlemen, help us look for it!

Epic Morality—"Terrible is the temptation of goodness . . ."

In *The Good Woman of Setzuan*, as in all Brecht plays, the moral is direct. To be good means to lose the little one has. The conflict between business ethics and Christian morality is irreconcilable. The gods are of no help; rather, they are partly to blame, for it is they who first give Shen Te her money. And even the gods admit the ambivalence of sin—the cousin is necessary, if only once a month, like going to church on Sundays to atone for sins on the other six days. All the gods can do is repeat platitudes: Just be good and all will turn out well. However, the remedy lies not in the lap of the gods but in the hands of men. There is only one recourse—to change the morality. But to do so requires changing the world.

Existing social relations have corrupted even the poor, who are as omnivorous, out of necessity, as the rich. Yet Brecht rejects any doctrine of original sin. Man is essentially good, not from any divine blessing but from the compulsion of mutual existence. Brecht voices his optimism in the ironical, "Terrible is the temptation of goodness."[5]

The theatre is the courtroom of concentrated reality. Thus, Brecht uses a trial scene in many of his plays, for it contains all the elements of theatre and avoids the illogical presumptions of realism. In *The Caucasian Chalk Circle,* Judge Adzak rules which mother shall have the child, the one who gave it birth, or the one who mothered and loved it; in *The Trial of Lucullus,* a radio play, all those whom the Roman general oppressed during his life sit in judgment on his fate after death; in *The Expedient,* the audience itself is to decide whether the taking of a man's life is politically acceptable if the end justifies the means. Epic plays are thus the morality plays of a scientific age wherein decisions should be made coldly and logically. "Truth Is Concrete" is the slogan Brecht kept on his desk wherever he traveled. The script is the accumulation of evidence, a classroom demonstration. In *The Private Life of the Master Race,* a scene such as that between "The Two Bakers," here given in its entirety, is notable for its compactness, its exposition of the inner weakness of the Nazi boast, its dispassionate presentation. From off stage, the rolling panzer is heard. A voice sings out:

> Hungry as locusts we come
> devouring the food of whole countries in a week
> for we had received cannons instead of butter
> and with our daily bread we had so long mixed bran.

The lights go up on a prison yard where men are walking around in a circle. A huge placard indicates time and place —Landsberg, 1936, a historical throwback to the early days of Hitler. The panzer is in motion in the present, the ad-

vancing conquest, but the supermen are like corpses reliving what put them where they now are. Each time the
circle comes front, the two bakers speak to each other. Silence, the movement of the prisoners in the circle, then the
whispered words:[6]

FIRST: You're a baker, too, newcomer?

SECOND: Yes, are you?

FIRST: Yes, what did they get you for?

SECOND: Look out!
  (*The circle revolves once*)
  Because I didn't put bran and potatoes in the bread. And
  you? How long have you been here?

FIRST: Two years.

SECOND: And why are you here? Look out!
  (*The circle revolves again*)

FIRST: Because I did put bran in the bread. Two years ago that
  was still a crime.

SECOND: Look out!
  (*Dim out. The panzer is heard*)

Brecht's earlier work, though much more free, contains
this element of demonstration. In *The Three-Penny Opera,*
he attempts an absurdly farcical *Peer Gynt.* The original
play of John Gay was an attack on grand opera, its non-
sensical folderol and its pompous, aristocratic heroes. In
Brecht's version, MacHeath, the highwayman, and his associates in crime are not the enemy but the archetype of
accepted morality. The only objection to MacHeath is that
he is too openly what others would conceal. He is the perfect
example of the middle class, and when the Police Captain
comes to the wedding, two friends are publicly reunited: the
representative of the law, and the one who can best use it
to his advantage. In the end, MacHeath is not hanged but
raised to the ranks of the nobility and given an income of

ten thousand pounds a year by the Queen. The spirit of the middle class is incorporated into the peerage.

Ibsen would rededicate bourgeois morality to high resolve. Brecht would replace it entirely. The closing lines of *The Caucasian Chalk Circle* announce:

> . . . what there is shall go to those who are good for it,
> Thus, the children to the motherly, that they prosper,
> The carts to good drivers, that they are well driven,
> And the valley to the waterers, that it bring forth fruit.

The Epic Playwright—"Images informative of the world . . ."

The conventional playwright with a nineteenth-century romantic heritage regards himself as the creator of the world. Alone with his characters, he moulds his universe. According to the Epic philosophy, this is an indication of the author's absorption with himself. The writer cannot create the world; he can only give "images informative of the world";[7] he is an observer of events, and his task is to portray a character in his external relations. The goal to achieve is distance from one's characters, not identification with them—abstract form as in mathematics, with lyric fervor in presentation. This is the supreme achievement of the modern scientific world—the mathematician and the poet, discipline and beauty.

Any playwright, claimed Brecht, can arouse the emotions of the audience with the usual suspense and hysteria, climax and crisis, techniques which are deterrents to thinking. Often the writer who is concerned with "the age itself" becomes so involved with the personal drama that he is sidetracked into "pathetic overtones." Clifford Odets' *Golden Boy,* in which the artist sells himself as a prizefighter—the creative force transformed into animal destruction when society puts a price on human beings—is watered down to melodramatic intrigue: Joe and Lorna die in a suicide crack-up. And the father-son relation so dominates Arthur Miller that the social probing of the *Death of a Salesman* is obscured.

To Brecht, the conventional form—division into acts, suspense, plot development—is inadequate to express historical fact. Its emotional demands destroy objectivity. Epic prefers scenes, each complete in itself, each a poem, a portrait, a contribution to the totality of life, so that the play becomes a series of narrations. The rigid, neoclassical mold with its veneration of the three unities, as well as the open Shakespearean canvas, gives way to a succession of episodes. Epic thus claims to be more realistic than the realistic theatre, since it is akin to living itself and deals with contemporary fact. As Piscator said:[8]

> No longer the individual with his private, personal destiny, but the age itself . . . is the heroic factor of the new dramaturgy.

Epic Production—"Drama too can use footnotes."

Should this approach be criticized as didactic, Brecht would reply that didacticism was precisely his aim, and accuse the critic of unconsciously identifying education with boredom. To Brecht, education can be a most satisfying experience, provided that the playwright uses his art and skill to take advantage of the rich medium of the theatre. Production challenges the ingenuity of director and technical staff, not to create mood nor heighten emotional participation, but to enhance the learning process. "Complex seeing" as well as hearing "must be practiced"[9] so that evidence is offered not linearly but in interacting layers, through multiple sense appeals. Cheated of emotional excitement, the audience is more alert mentally.

Epic plays are scored for music, light, sound, and pictorial devices—breaking the usual theatre limitations of time and space. The technician, calling on the full resources of the modern physical plant, plays an important role in the presentation. Like epic poetry, Epic Theatre is cinematic rather than stage-bound. Posters, charts, slogans, graphs, slides, or projections can alter locale; a screen can be lowered so that a motion picture provides past history or future possibility; a treadmill can carry Schweik cross-country; a song can supply philosophical comment—a sort of living montage, a series of abstractions to fortify the specific, a "literarization" of the theatre. In Brecht's words, "The drama too can use footnotes."[10]

Traditionalists are naturally aghast at Epic's reliance on the mechanical:[11]

> . . . plays which would be relatively more acceptable if staged honestly and simply are made ridiculous by staging and directing them as if they were the progeny of stereopticon machines, radios, choirs, Greek burlesque shows, and the warden and matron of an institution for the mentally unbalanced.

Brecht would answer that there are too many dark corners in the temple, too many devices that obscure, and that once the audience is accustomed to montage techniques, the result is not to distract, but to intensify—the newspaper come alive. The eye and ear are trained to assist the reasoned verdict of the brain.

For Epic staging, the usual picture-frame theatre is outmoded. Walter Gropius, among others, designed a model that contained a revolving acting area, a belt that moves around the auditorium, and walls on which motion pictures are projected. In Moscow, Okhlopkov staged *Mother* (not the Brecht version) using a central platform in the middle of the hall, broad ramps leading away from it in four directions, and a balcony circling the walls, on all of which the action took place, sometimes simultaneously. The only thing lacking was revolving seats for the spectators so that they could rotate properly with the events.

The production problems of the Epic Theatre are comparatively simple compared to those of retraining the actor, mainly because of the human factor. Actors only recently weaned from the exhibitionist histrionics, sweeping gestures, and voice virtuousity of the romantic school have become ardent disciples of the introspective, psychologically developed portraitures of the realistic method. Brecht had to retrain the Stanislavsky "method" actor.

According to Epic, for an actor to think he can relive another's life is pure deception. What happens is that the actor becomes so emotionally attached to a role that he is unable to interpret it or to make his own comment. The Stanislavsky actor strives to enter into the hearts of the spectators, to achieve empathy or *Einfühlung*. Brecht advocates distance or *Verfremdung,* an objective "two-way traffic between actor and audience" in which the aim is to enter into the minds of the spectators. The actor absorbed with "psychological truth" is too distracted to be aware of "social truth."

Epic Theatre claims not to be concerned with mounting emotional tension. The actor should, much as in the high comedy of Molière, stand aside from the character and evoke a dispassionate laughter. The audience does not identify itself with M. Jourdain or Orgon. The Epic actor should avoid "naturalism and stylization" and all mannerisms. He should make an effort to unpeel the layers of traditional acting and reveal the elemental simplicity of real people on stage. Effect is obtained not by the use of suspense nor the build-up for the big scene, but by the accumulation of evidence, much in the manner of Dreiser's *American Tragedy,* or the Soviet film *Potemkin.* The worship of the individual's little soul has warped insight.

To the actor this is a most annoying problem, and also theoretical nonsense. He is bound to revolt. Proud of his avoidance of romantic clichés, he has sought "inner truth" and discovered that his own ego suffered little in the process. A sensitive actor insists he can adjust to any demands. Epic ignores personal pretensions and headline mentality. Thus, in 1935 when the Federal Theatre Project offered *Triple-A Plowed Under,* its first Living Newspaper, an American example of Epic Theatre, the actors refused to go ahead with rehearsals. They claimed the play was not a drama, that it lacked plot development, and that it gave them no opportunity to build character. It took all the persuasiveness of Hallie Flanagan, the director of the Project, and her associates to win their reluctant consent to stay on until opening night, after which, if the production failed to win audience and critical approval, the entire project would be dropped. To the amazement of the cast, *Triple-A* proved to be a major success and made a permanent contribution to American theatre.

Prior to this incident, the Theatre Union had its own peculiar difficulties with Brecht during the production of *Mother,* the adaptation of the Gorky novel. The play was a failure, as had been *The Three-Penny Opera* two years before. The actors and directors wanted increased suspense and psychological development. Brecht wanted straight narration. The result was neither one nor the other, neither Brecht nor Ibsen. Brecht saw in the story of Pelageya Vlassova, the mother, a lesson in education, but the character is too warm, too human, to lend itself to cold objectivity. Even in the Berliner Ensemble production of *Mother Courage,* Helene Weigel, Brecht's widow and leader of the company, stirs the audience with a magnificently human portraiture of a woman torn between love of her children and devotion to profit, contrary to Brecht's aim. He rewrote the play several times to make the central character a symbol of greed untouched by the wastefulness of war, but to no avail. She remained a mother symbol, and audiences responded sympathetically.

Charles Laughton performed *Galileo* to a mixed and bewildered reception. Laughton, who had worked with Brecht, was hailed for his expansive humanity. But Brecht wanted a weak character unable to maintain the truth under pressure, a demonstration of how society withholds scientific knowledge. Audiences, however, have always leaned to the Laughton interpretation and been touched by the suffering of Galileo.

The Claims of Epic

The work of Ionesco, Beckett, and Genet, like that of Brecht, rejects the conventional techniques, but whereas the "theatre of the absurd" denies communication, Epic develops on all levels the fullness of communication. There is no doubt that Brecht's plays make stirring theatre. The Berliner Ensemble is the proof. Every tour of the company to Western Europe has been a succession of triumphs, and critics who journeyed to East Berlin returned with unstinted praise. Few productions in translation have been equally successful, for the sharp irony, the biting wit, and above all the poetry, are lost. Brecht, like Büchner and the young poets, rejected the heavier classic German and hammered out a violent metaphor and modern rhythms, which are a delight to the ear but not captured in translation. Brecht has been a powerful influence in the reshaping of German lyric poetry.

As for his theatre, Brecht did not regard it as merely an addition to existing techniques. He would have it displace all drama. Although demonstration and evidence can be stirring, and the theatre is broad enough to welcome an additional technique to capture an audience, the sweeping generalizations of Epic Theatre leave it vulnerable to attack. It has been criticized for neglecting character development in favor of preachment, for ignoring the role of the individual in history, for dramatizing issues rather than people, for mechanizing the theatre, and for reducing it to political partisanship.

The overuse of technical devices is the easiest criticism to answer. All theatre creates effect with whatever means are available. Lights, costumes, props, sets, and sound instruments are tools in the scientific kit, and have always been used to greater or less extent, even though poetry and insight may need none of them. The theatre of suggestion is often more powerful than that of calculated detail, and yet Epic would entirely replace mystery with clinical precision. Technical display can overwhelm meaning, but this is a production problem to be determined by the degree to which it is needed. With the Berliner Ensemble, it becomes co-ordinated mastery of judicious timing and totality of effect. With others, technical display may become an awkward interference.

The political use of theatre is Epic's Achilles' heel. All significant plays express a point of view, and in making decisions the protagonist chooses between moral alternatives that ultimately have political repercussions. Man's actions affect the welfare of the state, but this is politics in its broadest sense. Epic is narrowly partisan. It has been fashionable in the United States to admire Brecht as a playwright and to discount his politics. This is wishful tolerance, divorcing form from content, or accepting either when palatable, a reaction made possible by the confusion in Brecht's theory. He would have Marxism and Epic techniques wedded in indissoluble unity, but no form will respond to such dictation. The rapid scenes, episodic interludes, songs, asides and direct address to the audience, the taut language, the ironic wit, are all interrelated with meaning, but the specific meaning is the choice of the playwright. The form, perhaps the only new form to arise in this century, is available to all regardless of political alignment. Others have used comparable techniques to express an opposing point of view or a more personal and imaginative philosophy. Brecht superimposed a content. When as in the "Lehrstücke," this is insular and restricted, so is the drama. When, as in *Mother Courage* and *The Good Woman of Setzuan*, the content is general, common to all mankind, it has the sweep of humanity. Brecht's most successful plays are those in which he violates aspects of his own theory.

Epic has also been accused of minimizing the role of the hero. Brecht's characters do not attain tragic dimension, for none is more than a pawn in a schematic deployment of facts. Objective narrative demonstration eliminates the extravagance of a Lear or an Oedipus. Epic also exposes the absurdity of social relationships and removes the dignity of personal courage. Such was Brecht's design. Galileo is not intended to be a heroic figure. His dishonesty leads to self-preservation and a goose for dinner. He sells a telescope to the Venetians, claiming it as his own invention when he has in reality copied it from the Dutch. Even though he still believes that the earth is not the center of the universe, he publicly recants. Brecht's "distance" is belied by Galileo. There is much of Brecht himself in the character. He too repeatedly connived to achieve what he considered worthy ends. He accepted return to East Berlin when he was presented the theatre he had always dreamed of, but he arranged for his works to be published in West Germany so that he would have ample funds for travel abroad. Almost as though Galileo were a personal confession, Brecht would have the audience condemn the protagonist as a traitor to the future of mankind, but he inwardly admires Galileo's ultimate success. Heroics end in martyrdom, but also in the loss of the opportunity to write more plays. When Andrea, Galileo's disciple, bitterly denounces his master by saying, "Pity the country that has no heroes," Galileo retorts, "Pity the country that is in need of heroes."

Such thinking runs counter to communist doctrine and to the official demands of socialist realism. The hero is honored as an element in ultimate victory; even his death is optimistic, for it presages the success of socialism. The Soviet world had an embarrassing hero in Brecht. He was coddled as a prestige figure for international exhibit, but inner pressures were applied to win him to complete conformity. His work suffered as a result, and he wrote little after his return to Berlin. He was awarded the Stalin Peace Prize in 1955, but his plays had few performances in Moscow. His greatest acclaim was won in Western Europe.

It is a common phenomenon of contemporary theatre that playwrights accompany their work with elaborate essays on the nature of drama. Such is the case with Camus, Ionesco, Sartre, T. S. Eliot, and Arthur Miller, as it was with Pirandello, Strindberg, and Shaw before them. Brecht is no exception. He wrote a great deal on the nature of drama, but like all revolutionaries he overstates his case. Epic is a precocious child guilty of exaggeration. Though Brecht violated his theory in practice, he held his theatre together by the strength of his own personality. Whether a successor can be found, only time will determine.

Similar movements have risen independently elsewhere. In the United States, Epic Theatre was used by such varied institutions as the International Ladies' Garment Workers Union and the United States Army. The Garment Workers opened their own theatre in 1937 and presented soon thereafter *Pins and Needles,* a musical review, which offered events of the day from the workers' point of view. It was fresh and original and invigorating, not only to its own union members but to the regular Broadway public as well. At March Field, California, during the Second World War, a group of professional artists, actors, and directors working with the Engineer Camouflage School of Aviation noted that their fellow soldiers fell asleep when given instruction. So they devised an educational show using song and dance, movable sets, clever satire, and good-natured tomfoolery that not only had the soldiers sitting up and taking notice, but toured the western states as a dramatic hit!

The operettas of Marc Blitzstein, some of the work of Paul Green and Thornton Wilder, Odets' *Waiting for Lefty,* and Irwin Shaw's *Bury the Dead* are in the Epic manner. The outstanding example is the Living Newspaper of the

Federal Theatre Project. In England, W. H. Auden and
Christopher Isherwood were milder followers of Epic in
their earlier, more cynical period. But Epic has made its
deepest inroads in radio, television, and motion pictures,
particularly in the documentary field.

Epic may have to soften with maturity and merge with
existent forms, as it has already in the plays of Duerrenmatt, Frisch, Tennessee Williams, and the recent work of
John Osborne and Robert Bolt. It has broken new ground,
and is the most discussed movement in contemporary theatre. The modern age needs new forms. As John Gassner
has well said, we are living on tired handouts from the
nineteenth century. Epic is a bold and often brash innova-
tion, but it has occasioned a refreshing upheaval and been
another effort to go beyond Ibsen.

12. The Folklore Theatre
—García Lorca

BLOOD WEDDING

LIKE CHEKHOV AND CAMUS, García Lorca wrote few plays,
and yet he ranks as one of the major figures of the contemporary theatre, and is the only Spanish playwright since
Calderón to achieve international recognition. Camus and
Chekhov wrote four major works for the theatre; Lorca
wrote only three tragedies, but they are enough to indicate
a distinct form and meaning that arose out of the particu-

lar nature of Spain. Lorca became the poet of the people, the welcomed cry against a pagan-Catholic order too proud to confess its anguish. His sharp images of nature reflect the violence and vitality of passions held back by the law of caste and order. Today his works are performed everywhere and his poetry is read avidly, particularly by the young. However, though his appeal is universal, he is intensely provincial.

One should know Spain to appreciate Lorca. His plays are produced as well in London and New York as in Madrid and Buenos Aires, but the audience is different. In other countries, Lorca has been adopted by the experimental groups with aesthetic pretensions. In Spain, his work runs deep into the life of the audience, which, through the poet's eyes, sees itself on stage. His plays are based on gypsy lore, but the conscience of an entire nation is bared. No playwright of our time has been more completely accepted by his own people; quotations from his poems are part of the language, and his idiom has been integrated into their lives. Spain, though of ancient blood and indomitable pride, is a poor country with a peasant economy, caught in the mire of outworn tradition and an unwillingness to brave the new. Drought, disease, and earthquake plague those who struggle with the soil to maintain a marginal existence. Political fervor has dwindled into apathy and indifference, a tendency to remain content with past glories.

During the Renaissance, Spain was a formidable power. Her armies were the resplendent Defenders of the Faith, and of the sources of revenue that made Madrid the most lavish court of Europe. Her empire stretched from the Mediterranean to the North Sea and across to the Pacific Ocean, and her theatre rose in equal magnificence. Among those who clustered in the *siglo de oro* were Ruiz de Alarcón, the first important playwright born in the New World; Cervantes, with his gay, satiric interludes; the incredible Lope de Vega, "monster of Nature," who wrote

more than two thousand plays; and Calderón, who sensed
the illusory quality of a brilliance too intense to be permanent. The dream faded fast, and then Spain slumbered for
three centuries.

The awakening occurred with the "Generation of '98,"
the writers and philosophers who sought to express the defeat, the spiritual solace, and the aesthetic sterility. They
became obsessed by the soul of Spain and the dark recesses
of the nation's myth, as did Unamuno, or by the bitterness
and despair and the bleakness of the future, as if their tense,
impatient yearning toward change were caught in a mystical resignation to God's will. The simplicity of a life untouched by modern urban complexities permitted exploration in depth of man's relation to both God and nature,
and of the ever-present contradiction of the soil—the kinship with death and the passionate love of life. The lone
poet to give it form and enduring beauty was Federico
García Lorca.

Death in the Afternoon—"because you have died for-ever . . ."

So much a legend has he become that the exact date
of his birth, like Shakespeare's, is unknown. He himself
preferred to say that he was born at the end of the century.
His family was sufficiently wealthy to send him to the University of Granada to study law, but his interests were in
the arts. He painted well, studied music with De Falla, and
was an actor and director, besides being a poet. A childhood disease left him with a slight limp throughout his
life, which may have contributed to his retiring nature and
companionship with women. When he moved to Madrid
and came under the influence of the "Generation of '98,"
he wrote his first gypsy ballads. These, sung to guitar accompaniment, are his most popular works. But he refused
to be labeled as the poet of the Andalusian gypsy, and

reached for new forms; for a time he attempted with words what Salvador Dali was creating on canvas.

Lorca came to New York in 1929 to study at Columbia University, but he was terrified and estranged by the asphalt city with its coldness and inhumanity, and its steel towers where mechanical people dwelt—all the details of life so foreign to his loved world of the gypsies. His book of poems about New York is a savage indictment of the loss of contact with nature, expressed in a burst of surrealist images. He did admire Walt Whitman, to whom he addressed a special ode, and also Harlem, where he was to be found every night singing his songs to his own guitar accompaniment. Finally he rushed off to Cuba, where he felt free again.

On his return to Spain, Fernando de los Ríos, the Minister of Education, Lorca's lifelong friend, put him in charge of a mobile theatre unit, La Barraca, which toured the country presenting the classical plays of Lope de Vega and Calderón. For this group Lorca wrote his first plays, which reveal a new style, more personal, less surrealistic, and delightfully comic. His tragedies were written later. When the war broke out, he returned to his own Granada for a brief vacation, and there at the age of thirty-seven he fell among the first victims of Franco's firing squad. He had never engaged in active politics, but his associations with the Republic were sufficient for a group of Falangistas to bury him in an unknown grave. The lines he wrote for his friend, the bullfighter Sánchez Mejías, will apply to García Lorca himself:[1]

Because you have died forever,
like all the dead of the Earth . . .
You courted death and the kiss of her mouth.
The sadness that was part of your courageous joy . . .
It will take a long time, if not forever, to give birth to
An Andalusian so bright, so rich in adventure.

Lorca's gypsy ballads were sung everywhere. They are taut, broken rhythms, with elemental metaphors springing out of the earth—the horse, the stream, the knife, the colors of the leaves—placed in startling contexts to give them a repeated symbolism of life and death. Man and nature are one.

> The point of the knife
>   enters the heart
> like the edge of the plow
>   in virgin soil.

Or:

> The cry
>   of the guitar
> breaks the edges
>   of the dawn.

The moon, the olive trees, the colors of the changing landscape, become charged with emotional intensity:

> Black the horse, full the moon
>   And olives in my saddle pack.
> Across the plain, through the wind
>   Black my horse, red the moon.
> Death looks out upon me
>   From the towers of Cordoba.

The forces beyond the horizon lie hidden in the soil:

> The cock
>   with his beak
> digs for the dawn.

To describe the gypsy maiden waiting for her lover, whom she knows will be killed by the dreaded Civil Guard, he uses green as the warmth of life in contrast to the icy cold of moon and silver:

> Green flesh, hair that is green
>   and eyes of cold silver—
> An icicle of the moon
>   Imprisons her above the water.

Though his short poems have become traditional and are known even to the illiterate peasant, his long "Lament for Ignacio Sánchez Mejías" is his most loved work. What Unamuno called "the tragic sense of life" is centered around the goring of the torero at "five o'clock in the afternoon." From an essentially Spanish institution, he evoked his most powerful cry against the inevitable, the moment of truth that becomes Death's easy victory.

These metaphors are elements of Lorca's plays, which are extended ballads, dramatized in movement rather than in song. Lorca turned to the theatre because, as he said in a talk to the actors who were performing *Yerma* in 1935 in Madrid:

> The theatre is a school of tears and laughter, and a free forum where men can expose outworn or ambiguous morality, and where with living examples can be shown the external laws of man's heart and feelings.

The Early Plays—"He will love you with the infinite love of the dead . . ."

For his own troupe, and for easier performance with a traveling company, Lorca wrote puppet plays such as *Don Cristóbal,* an impudent travesty that was played frequently at the front lines of the Loyalist forces. In his period away from folk lyrics, he experimented with a surrealistic drama, *And So Pass Five Years,* a series of disconnected images of the subconscious. The first of his plays to achieve wide popularity were the comedies *The Shoemaker's Prodigious Wife* and *The Love of Don Perlimplín for Belissa in the Garden,* stylized parodies of Spanish honor. These are obviously contrived and border on the precious, but in skillful hands they are highly theatrical. In *Don Perlimplín* an old man is married to a young wife, the age-old theme of Spanish comedy, but with Lorca the burlesque has a tender humanity. The scene is a large bed in which Don Perlimplín lies with gilded horns. He is surrounded by five balconies, from which extend five ladders with a man's hat on top of each. He knows he cannot satisfy his wife nor ever possess her, but he loves her sufficiently to disguise himself in a red cape and stroll through the garden at night. She sees the phantom figure as a gallant lover, and dreams of imagined happiness in his arms. When Belissa tells her husband of her idealized affair, old Perlimplín asks, "Do you really love him?" And when she answers in the affirmative, he says:

> I don't want him ever to leave you . . . and to make sure that he will be completely yours, it would be best to pierce his heart with this dagger . . . so that once dead, you will be able to caress him in your bed . . . without the fear that he will ever leave you, for he will love you with the infinite love of the dead . . .

He runs out to the garden. Belissa waits, fearful that her knight may be harmed. The man in the red cape enters, bleeding, with the dagger in his heart, and says:

> Your husband just killed me because he knew I loved you as no one else could.

He removes the cape, and Belissa realizes that Don Perlimplín and her lover are the same person. His love is so selfless that he has created the image by which she can discover love. His is the ideal in fancy, which can never be realized physically, and he gives his life so that she will learn the meaning of love.

These plays are of minor significance. Lorca achieved greatness with the tragedies.

BLOOD WEDDING

All three, *Blood Wedding, Yerma,* and *The House of Bernarda Alba,* are aspects of a central theme: the conflict between the law of honor and the law of the passions. They are intense lyrical dramas of sex in which woman, who should be fruitful, remains unfulfilled. The worship of virginity to preserve the right of inheritance, the code of moral conduct to insure the continuity of life, is in violent opposition to the natural flow of the emotions, but the code is preserved. The rotting past weighs down the living, and the women are left alone among the dead, or go mad with frustration, "dried up forever." Out of the tragedy of women is implicit the story of Spain herself.

In *Blood Wedding,* the first three scenes are components of one situation—the contractual marriage arrangements, suppressed love, and the blood feud of two families. The second act is the serenade to the bride and the wedding feast. The last act is the pursuit in the forest and the mourning of the dead. The form is a musical orchestration of changing rhythms, folk songs, and lamentations, a verse drama in which there is no concern with psychological motivation but with pagan forces in a primitive pageant of revolt, vengeance, and death.

Of all the characters, only Leonardo has a specific individualized name, for his is the passion that is the propulsive force. The others are abstractions: the Mother, the Bride, and—in the expressionistic fantasy of the forest scene—the Moon and Death. Lorca thus employs as did the creator of the dream play, Strindberg, before him, a touch of reality to make the fantasy more real. Leonardo's intensely personal self holds the abstract quality of the others close to the earth.

The Mother is convention, the code of honor, the strength of the land, the embodiment of the preservation of the family blood. Hers is the tragedy, for she senses the doom in the initial scene as she sends her remaining son to the fields to cut the grapes.[2]

Cursed be all knives and the scoundrel who invented them.

The metaphors of the poems are now incorporated into the dramas, where they become integrated with the lives of the characters and essential elements in the theme. The knife to cut the grapes will also cut down the young men, and the Mother's premonition of death rises to the living image of the moon. Throughout the play, concrete objects are used as symbols of death, which as Lorca once said are known to all, for in "Spain the dead are more alive, dead, than in any other place in the world; their profile cuts like the edge of a barber's knife." He even enumerated the everyday objects that, to others, sound like obscure images but to the Spaniard carry associations of "the frozen air of departure from this life": the beards of shepherds, the full face of the moon, the fly, "the cutting outline of eaves and bay windows," and water which the horse will not drink but which is the giver of life.

The play opens with a staccato exchange between mother and son, simple one-word rhythms, as he leaves for work in the vineyard—here land is in need of water—dry lands which the father "would have covered with trees," as he would have covered her with sons had he lived longer. From the land that needs to be made fertile, they turn to talk of the girl he would like to marry. The themes are interrelated, for marriage means children and sons to work the fields. Women, like the earth, must give life, and sex in the traditional code of the Church is for procreation, not pleasure or passion. The Mother is the earth—violent, lusty, tender, strong, but no longer fertile, for a knife has taken her husband. She is the preserver of life from whom life has been taken.

> I looked at your father and when they killed him, I looked at the wall in front of me. One woman with one man, and that's all.

The son must carry on, and she will be content with "six grandchildren." She agrees to arrange the marriage, even though the girl had once been in love with Leonardo Félix, whose family is responsible for the death of her men. Leonardo has been married for two years and has a child "and another one coming." Like Shakespeare in *Romeo and Juliet,* Lorca contrasts the power of love which springs from passion and brooks no obstacle, and the contractual marriage, which is planned to unite two families. Paris is worthy and honorable, but he seeks the hand of Juliet by discussion with old Capulet. The Bridegroom likewise pursues the established pattern of order. But Leonardo, like Romeo, is unrestrained—individual love that knows no barriers—and acts impulsively and takes the consequences. Juliet knows that "it is too rash, too unadvised, too sudden, too like the lightning." This is the common theme of all great tragedy, Greek as well as Shakespearean—the rash act that brings down the world of reason and crushes the transgressor. With Lorca, the form is a folk ballad of symbolic beauty and surging emotion.

The rest of the play is the working out of what has been announced in the opening scene. In Leonardo's home, his Wife and Mother-in-Law sing a lullaby to the child. Like so many cradle songs, it is filled with cruelty and premonition of disaster, but it is one of Lorca's finest lyrics with its repeated images of the stream, the flies, the horse with the bleeding hooves and frozen mane, "and deep in his eyes a silvery dagger." Relations between Leonardo and the women in his home are strained, for they know he rides at night to see his former love. The Wife is the symbol of patient suffering that must be endured for the sake of her son. The code makes the man the master; woman's role is to obey and be faithful. Leonardo tries to hold back his anger when he learns of the marriage, but it is too powerful and he races out of the house in a violent outburst as the lullaby resumes.

The nuptial contract is discussed by the Mother and the Bride's Father. The sex theme is carried over into the joining together of two farms. The Father says, "How beautiful it is to bring things together." The Bride is quiet, subdued, and gives her consent with full awareness of her duties—"a man, some children, and a wall two yards thick for everything else." When she is alone with the Servant, she hears Leonardo's horse on the plains and her repressed love rises to torment her. The cold marriage is played against the unmanageable fire of man for woman. The Bridegroom has been proper and respectful, the parents have followed the ancient customs, the Bride has attempted obedience—but the sound of the horse's hoofs beats like an ill omen against this wall of conformity.

The second act opens with the Bride dressing for the wedding. She is determined to love her betrothed. Then Leonardo arrives in advance of the other guests, and tells her:

> To burn with desire and keep quiet about it is the greatest punishment we can bring on ourselves . . . When things get that deep inside you there isn't anybody can change them.

The dry rivers now run swollen and fast, and the Bride trembles with excitement as she replies:

> I can't listen to your voice . . . It pulls me along and I know I am drowning—but I go on down.

The villagers interrupt with a serenade, and with dance and music and flowers escort the couple to the church. Leonardo is left alone with his Wife. She recalls her own wedding day when she left her home "shining with a star's glow." She can endure no more humiliation. She orders Leonardo to accompany her to the ceremony.

The banquet after the wedding is another opportunity for song and dance and gaiety. The Mother and Father look forward with hope for future "hands to chastise and dominate the soil." Her father boasts that his daughter "is wide-hipped" and well able to bear children. Leonardo stalks in the background. Unable to bear the thought that another man will possess the Bride that night, he runs off with her. The Bridegroom's Mother, who had thoughts only of preserving her son, knows now that there will be no children, that her only son will die, but she rallies all to kill "quickly and well," for though it is the end of the family line, its honor must be maintained. "The hour of blood has struck again!"

The scene in the forest is a feast of death. The action moves beyond the home into nature itself, in an expressionistic fantasy of specters, symbols come alive, and the reality of the young lovers pursued by the Bridegroom. The Woodcutters who chop down life, shadows in the dark, gloat over the impending meeting of the young men and the desecration of the bridal bed. The Moon appears, a young Woodcutter with a white face, and calls for red blood to "spurt over the mountains" of her chest, and offers to aid Death, the Beggar Woman, with her fullness "to light up the waistcoat and open the buttons; the knives will know the path after that." Leonardo and the Bride, exhausted from the pursuit, halt in the darkness of the woods. The Bride is filled with regret and shame:

> What lamenting, what fire
> Sweeps upward through my head!
> What glass splinters are stuck in my tongue!

Their mutual recriminations serve to arouse their love, and in a sensuous embrace they transform their violence into a recognition that they are joined forever. The Bride says:

> Nails of moonlight have fused
> my waist and your chains.

They run off. The Moon appears to light up the forest. Two violins are heard in the distance, then two shrieks, but the sounds are cut short, and the Beggar Woman "opens her cape and stands in the center of the stage like a great bird with immense wings," as she welcomes the bodies of two young men.

The final scene is the funeral dirge. Only women are left, for that is all that remains of life. In black against the

white walls, they mourn the dead. The Bridegroom's Mother
is resolute and strong, facing death with pride, without
wailing, now that her son "is a fading voice beyond the
mountains." All that is left for woman is to water the graves,
"the bed that shelters them and rocks them in the sky."
The Bride returns to weep alongside the Mother. In wild
fury, the Mother leaps upon her and shouts, "Where is my
son's good name, now?" Herein lies the peculiarly Spanish
flavor of Lorca's play. The Mother's husband and sons have
been wiped out. Vengeance and hatred have spilled her
family's blood, and she is all alone. Yet her main concern
is with the honor of her family. The Bride is conscious of
her guilt. She had meant to respect her vow, but the Bridegroom was "a little boy of cold water," whereas Leonardo
was "a dark river, choked with brush." She tells the Mother,
"Your son was my destiny . . . but the other one's arm
dragged me along like the pull of the sea." And she adds
that she is still a virgin, that not "a single man has ever
seen the whiteness of my breasts." Leonardo's wife joins the
mourners, and as the bodies are carried to the village, the
Mother and the Bride lead the chorus with a lament to
death.

The Bride:

> . . . fish without scales, without river,
> so that on their appointed day, between two
> and three, with this knife,
> two men are left stiff,
> with their lips turning yellow.

The Mother closes the play with:

> And it barely fits the hand
> but it slides in clean
> through the astonished flesh
> and stops there, at the place
> where trembles enmeshed
> the dark root of a scream.

The emphasis on virginity and the Bride's willingness to undergo an ordeal by fire as a test of her purity are remnants of the feudal code and the law of the Church, deeply imbedded in the people of Spain. The Bride has been swept away by an uncontrollable desire. She has denied her wedded husband the right to make her fertile, but she has not been violated by another man. Her purity remains with her body, destined to wither unfulfilled. Adultery is beyond law and destroys all continuity of land possession by casting doubt on rightful heirs. Lorca is not treating of social reform nor recommended change, but of emotions choked by a persistent morality, and he held his theme within those limits.

The play, like folk ballads, is a pageant of life stripped to its bare essentials. The real and the symbolic merge in concrete images, then blur into vague and imperceptible shadows. Analysis injures its vitality, for as a whole the play leaves the impression of the cry of the earth for ripeness and fecundity. Tradition and honor and the imposed morality crush the outpouring of life that is secretly admired but outwardly condemned. All that is left of the struggle between passion and reserve is a chorus of wailing women. The stark ballet of the forest scene is a dance of death, but whereas Strindberg employed expressionist techniques to emulate the flow of dreams, and O'Casey as well as Ernst Toller and Georg Kaiser to visualize social forces, Lorca uses them to portray a primitive battle for survival.

Yerma is another aspect of the same problem, an entire play devoted to a woman's anguished need for motherhood, which her husband fails to supply, not that he is impotent, but that he enjoys her physically without wanting children. She has never been told of the pleasures of sex. All she feels is that her body is ready, but it remains empty. A woman without children is useless, a dishonor to her man. He works the earth and it bears fruit, but she too is of the earth and does not bear. She looks at pregnant women long-

ingly and dreams with tenderness of her own child who
will not be. In gathering clouds of hatred, she visits the
Pagan Woman to find in ancient superstitions a cure for
sterility. She rejects the advances of another man who rouses
her emotionally, for she is dutiful to the code of honor.
Mad with frustration and longing, she sings to her body:

> But you must come, sweet love, my baby,
> because water gives salt, the earth fruit,
> and our wombs guard tender infants,
> as a cloud is sweet with rain.

Spurned by other women, rejected by herself, she goes on
a pilgrimage to a sanctuary in the mountains. Her husband
seeks her out, and tells her that life can be sweet without
children, that they can enjoy their bodies in peace. She
loathes the thought of his wanting her as he sometimes
wants "a pigeon to eat." She will be barren forever. She
cannot endure sex without maternity. Her disordered mind
has received the final blow. With the pilgrims' chorus in
the distance, she chokes her husband to death, and says:

> My body dry forever! . . . I've killed my son. I myself
> have killed my son.

If *Blood Wedding* is a ballad of vengeance, *Yerma* is a ballad of fecundity, full of magic and tribal ritual, and the
burning fire of a woman quenched by ignorance and obedience to order.

In *The House of Bernarda Alba,* the last of the trilogy,
there are only women, from the old crazed grandmother to
the young and sensuous Adela. Bernarda Alba, proud of her
blood, holds her five daughters locked within the house
after the death of her second husband, to mourn for eight
years. She looks down upon the villagers as beneath her
family, none of the men worthy of marrying her daughters.
She is the upholder of the past, the morality of the clan.
Face in the eyes of the world and honor of the name are
above any concession to the starved emotional life of the

women. The daughters writhe in revolt, terrified by the mother but secretly longing for release. Even Angustias, betrothed to the handsome Pepe Romano, can only talk to him briefly through the barred windows. She is able to get married, even though she is unattractive and almost forty, for she has the largest dowry. The girls never go out, never see a man save in the distance, merely sit and sew and seethe with longing. Adela, the youngest, is in love with Pepe and knows that he wants her. Martirio, crippled and sensitive, spies on Adela, whose clandestine talks with Pepe arouse her virginal desires to envy and hatred. The grandmother represents what they will become, and in her ravings, tells them:

> I want fields and houses, open houses where the women lie in bed with their little children, and the men sit outside in their chairs. Pepe Romano is a giant. All of you love him. But he will devour you, because you are grains of wheat. No, not grains of wheat, but frogs without tongues.

Adela steals away to meet Pepe in the open fields. Martirio surprises her when she returns, and arouses the household. Adela faces her mother and says, "There'll be an end to prison voices here," and proud of her "triumphant body," breaks Bernarda Alba's cane in two. "No one but Pepe commands me!" Seizing a gun, the mother rushes out, and a shot is heard. When she returns she declares, "That does away with Pepe el Romano." Adela, thinking he is dead, hangs herself. Pepe has raced off on his horse, but will return no more. To Bernarda Alba, the code she has guarded all her life cannot be broken. She announces that Adela "died a virgin. Tell them, so that at dawn the bells will ring twice." The anguished Martirio utters the thoughts of all the girls when she says, "A thousand times happier she who had him." So too with Spain, holding back the new life, boasting of her pride, sunk in the misery of death.

Bernarda Alba is the most realistic of the three tragedies and therefore the most comprehensible. Its form is the developed situation of the well-made play, and the characters are more psychologically realized. The images center around the house, doors, windows, walls that hold out the world beyond and keep the women cloistered from life. The theme is the same in all three plays—darkness and love, sex and frustration, passion and death. Women bear the tragedy, for they are the bearers of life, and are left alone to mourn in silent suffering the renewal of their fate and the emptiness of their bodies. The cycle repeats, for Lorca's plays are a tribal theatre of primitive power, ancient in form but shaped by a sophisticated modern mind.

The plays of Lorca are among the few successful efforts in the contemporary theatre to integrate poetry and ideas and action. Lorca is of the people, his imagery being woven into dramas that rise out of a communion of feeling. Benavente, his contemporary, the popular writer of the comedy of manners, added Spanish situations to European forms, but he remained provincial. Lorca created a form out of the meaning of Spain, and belongs to the world.

13. The Revolt of the Irrational
—Beckett, Ionesco, Genet

WAITING FOR GODOT
THE CHAIRS
THE BALCONY

THE EXPERIMENTAL THEATRE of the 60s is characterized by a revolt of the irrational and the most devastating attack on traditional forms. An unexampled frenzy of sensationalism, shock, nudity, and obscenity transformed the proscenium theatre of middle-class entertainment into raucous scurrying of actors running up and down the aisles, twisting nude bodies on bare scaffolding, chanting and grunting in ritual ecstasy, shouting for liberation in reenactments of tribal orgies and group therapy, performing self-lacerating grotesqueries that invaded lofts, basements, and converted churches.

Hair, a high-decibel hippie tribal rock musical which originated in Greenwich Village in New York, became a box office hit in major cities of the world. *Oh! Calcutta!,* a pornographic revue, conceived by the distinguished literary critic Kenneth Tynan, exploited the breakdown of sex taboos and captured popular acclaim in its worship of sensual titillation.

The guerrilla attack on established form was not confined to the theatre. In painting, sculpture, music, and dance, the rebellion became the mainstream. Claes Oldenburg's plastic lipstick adorned the Yale University quadrangle. Robert Rauschenberg conducts a painting with

259

twenty Bell Telephone technicians in a multimedia extrav-
aganza. Jean Tinguely creates kinetic sculpture that dis-
integrates when set into motion, while his associate, Nicki
St. Phalle, constructs huge female plaster-of-paris figures
that the spectator enters through the various body orifices
and at each internal organ experiences a new happening.

To playwrights like Beckett, Ionesco, Genet, Adamov,
Vauthier, Schehadé, Arrabal, and Ghelderode, the realistic
theatre was false, anachronistic, dishonest, partial and destructive, concerned with the private neuroses of domesticated man. In an age where science seeks to control the
universe and all life can be destroyed by the push of a
button, the individual, they believed, was insignificant, his
writhings inconsequential. And if the theatre reflects its
age, then a century of rushing toward annihilation should
have a theatre equally as mad. They therefore write non-
plays of "none-sense" in which dramatic structure like civilization itself is shattered and out of the debris arises a di
Chirico nightmare of mushroom clouds and shadows behind
the ruins of the temple.

Man is alone, lost in a world in which God has
deserted him; science and reason are illusory; nature has
reaped its revenge, and the individual is trapped in the
contemplation of his own image. The only certainty is
death, and that is but the final act of absurdity. Communication is no longer possible, for even language has died.
New symbols alone can express the total madness.

The response to contemporary conditions is a revolt
against the Cartesian order of the universe as the sole de-
terminant of the knowable, the instrument by which to
understand man and the forces that surround him. According to Descartes's dualism, that which can be measured or
scientifically observed is real. That which is nonmeasurable
—feelings, emotions, qualities—are subjective and divorced
from the domain of the rational, which alone can reveal
the laws of nature. Objective reality responding to causal

relationships provided insight into a coherent, logical universe. Knowledge is cumulative and history an onward progression. For all phenomena, there exists a rational explanation. The theory worked and satisfactorily answered the questions which had split the rigidly structured medieval world of faith, obedience, and honor. By the twentieth century, modern science, using logic and causality, had mastered the physical forces of the universe and created a technological age of air conditioners, instant communication, computerized production, saturation bombing, and long range missiles with atomic warheads. The Great Chain of Being was replaced by the mechanical laws of nature. Reason replaced God and guided the destinies of man and the world with purposeful determination.

For the first time in the history of man, it seemed possible to eliminate hunger and misery. The quality of life became a new preoccupation. Everything before the present era could be called prehuman history. But the agonizing truth remained that man and social organization were little prepared for the generation, management, and control of technology. Reason had gotten out of hand and produced an irrational world of wars, poverty, racial hatred, deterioration of the environment, and national self-interest. Instead of liberating man, science and technology had imposed dehumanizing restrictions upon him. Man knew little more about himself, his purpose on earth, and the mystery of life than he had in the Middle Ages. As William Barrett states in *Irrational Man:*

> Science stripped nature of its human forms and presented man with a universe that was neutral, alien, in its vastness and force, to his human purposes. Religion, before this phase set in, had been a structure that encompassed man's life, providing him with a system of images and symbols by which he could express his own aspirations toward psychic wholeness. With the loss of this containing framework man became not only a dispossessed but a fragmentary being.[1]

As a result, in the midst of material wealth and vast production capability, man feels himself estranged from God, from nature, and from his own self. Reason had presumed to answer all questions in life, but it had ignored the spiritual aspects of man which cannot be understood by the scientific method and objective empiricism alone. Unanswered questions left a sense of the absurdity and contingency of human life, and the collapse of the well-built logical structure. Yeats put it as follows: "Things fall apart; the center cannot hold. Mere anarchy is loosed upon the world."

Down with Reason was the new battle cry. Writers and thinkers wished to return to what had been ignored: emotions, feelings, and appetites over which reason has no control. Descartes's reliance on what could be measured and objectively analyzed had eliminated the subjective elements of man—his instincts, experiences, and passions, the response of the senses, the intensity of love and hate, of beauty and pain. If the rational explanation of existence had failed, the irrational could do no worse.

In contemporary art, the first concept to be discarded was the traditional use of rational forms. To quote William Barrett again, "The modern artist sees man not as the rational animal in the sense handed down to the west by the Greeks, but . . . at the limits of reason, one comes face to face with the meaningless; and the artist today shows us the absurdity, the inexplicable, the meaningless in our daily life."[2] In the theatre, all phases of the revolt of the irrational have one common aim, rejection of the realistic drama of plot, action, crisis, and individual characters psychologically developed. Realism was regarded as the art form of a scientific age, for it presumes a time-space sequence that is logical and coherent and characters that are definitely knowable.

Some contemporary playwrights have sought a different logic to replace the one that no longer functions. Jean-Paul Sartre, with rigorous intellectual discipline, negates all past values and finally says No to God himself. Condemned to be free, man creates his own history on the other side of despair. He is not bound by a fixed human nature, but creates his own human nature with every act he makes. Orestes in *The Flies* murders his mother not because tradition demands it but because he has willed it himself, knowingly. In his debate with Zeus, Orestes rejects the Establishment and chooses his own self-imposed destiny of loneliness, exile, and freedom to choose.

Bertolt Brecht, likewise, sees human nature as an ever-changing interrelationship between man and society. But whereas Sartre would have man reconstitute himself within the present framework, Brecht would change the social order completely. Mother Courage is consumed by greed because the society which surrounds her has equated all human values in terms of money. A new Reign of Reason in which property values give way to human values can alter society and man.

Jerzy Grotowski would eliminate conventional feelings and customs to transcend experience by returning to tribal roots and commonly felt ecstasy. His theatre eliminates traditional plot and character analysis to concentrate on terrifying ritual reenactment of suffering, penance, and redemption. The actor is transformed into an instrument of physical flexibility, working in collective interplay to return the theatre to its origins as religious communion. Jean Genet turns the world of Reason upside down to construct a separate order in which Evil is the highest Good and Crime the purest of emotional experiences. His outcasts impose on criminality a beauty of its own: crime becomes the final condemnation of accepted practices.

Few playwrights, however, have opted for a positive alternative to existing chaos. Happenings, multimedia, nonverbal theatre, theatre of the streets, sex, and nudity, all spring from the same roots, a return to the irrational to seek meaning where Reason failed. Faith in a logical continuum gives way to a search for the incoherent, the discontinuous, the random disorder, the fragmented aspects of life. Much of it is extreme, exaggerated, outrageously lacking in discipline, but behind the fury lies a search for illumination, for insight, for positive goals.

The theatre is our pact with the Furies, our necessary self-revelation, for as André Malraux has said, "The greatest mystery is not that we have been flung at random between the fusion of the earth and the galaxy of the stars, but that in this prison we can fashion images of ourselves sufficiently powerful to deny our nothingness."

Foremost among the playwrights who have fashioned such images are Beckett and Ionesco, but they are preceded by some of the most significant playwrights of the century. August Strindberg, a wild, restless, sensitive genius, found realism too limited to express the deeper mystery of man. In his dream plays, he sought to present on stage the illogic of the subconscious, the hidden truth in the disconnectedness of fantasy. He wished to give dramatic shape to what had been formless. He was the first to explore a new set of symbols, a new language to express the inconceivable, the impossible, the imaginary, the irrational.

Luigi Pirandello joined the fight with an attack on the very nature of reality itself, mocking the arrogance of logic in presuming to discover truth. Realism sought to pigeonhole a person with a single adjective, but to Pirandello, truth and character were endlessly relative, endlessly unknowable: "one can never penetrate another's identity when beneath the assumed self lies another self equally indistinct." Pirandello broke with the proscenium theatre's rigid separation of actor and spectator, had action take place in many areas simultaneously: actors moved on stage, in the auditorium, and in the lobby, as well as up and down the aisles. Life was being reenacted as it was, yet framed by all the artifice of self-conscious theatricality.

Although he predates Pirandello, Alfred Jarry had

fallen into oblivion until the present decade when his *Ubu Roi,* a kaleidoscopic, grotesque fantasy of surrealistic figures, flaunted its four-letter words at every rational sequence of events and became the apostolic model of irreverence and unrelated images. Jarry himself set the pattern for today's rebels when he declared "every man is capable of showing his contempt for the cruelty and stupidity of the universe by making his own life a poem of incoherence and absurdity." He followed his precept and died young in filth and poverty, a victim of drugs. Today, years after his death, he is enshrined as the Chancellor of the College of "Pataphysicians," a select coterie of iconoclasts of whom Ionesco is Dean of Admissions. Their philosophy is cryptically defined in the phrase, "the science of the particular, of the laws governing exception," which means that every event is a law unto itself, or that there is no law. Twenty years after *Ubu Roi* during the chaos of the First World War, Guillaume Apollinaire followed Jarry with *Les Mamelles de Tiresias,* a surrealistic composite of phallic symbols and gruesome laughter.

The most important book on the revolt of the irrational is Antonin Artaud's *The Theatre and Its Double,* in which the phrase "the Theatre of Cruelty" was coined. Artaud was a visionary but not a very capable director. *The Cenci* was his only production. It took Grotowski, two decades later, to work out Artaud's dreams into practical theatre. Artaud condemned realistic theatre as "the closed egoistic, personal art." He called for a Theatre of Cruelty to one's nerve ends, not the cruelty of violence and sadism, but the cruelty that induces trance, that affects the organism by physical means beyond control. He advocated a return to a theatre of poetic images, audience shock, and a communion of the spirit. Although overeager disciples have transformed each of his causal phrases into a positive dogma, almost every aspect of the present revolt stems from Artaud. He is the high priest to Jarry's Holy Ghost. His apocalyptic revelations are tersely recorded in pronouncements such as: "All our ideas about life must be revised in a period when nothing any longer adheres to life; it is this painful cleavage which is responsible for the revenge of things."[3]

The break from realism occurred in all the arts. Joyce and Kafka had led the way in literature as had Kandinsky and Mondrian in painting. The writer or artist working alone can respond immediately to social and technological change. The theatre which is a collective art requiring the cooperation of many individuals moves more slowly but provides a greater impact through a multiple sense appeal and communion with live audiences. In the process of dissolution of past belief, of profanation of the old, and demystification of what was, the theatre of the irrational provides a living experience that cuts deeply, particularly when barbed with the laughter of insolence.

Were such theatrical experiences localized in the dim quarters of the Left Bank, they would occasion nothing more earthshaking than ceremonial visits by curious intellectuals, but in the last decade these plays have been honored as the new academy and performed in the commercial houses of the West End and Broadway and repeatedly seen on television. A consideration of Samuel Beckett's *Waiting for Godot,* the outstanding work of the theatre of the "absurd," offers detailed insight into the nature of the movement.

WAITING FOR GODOT

Samuel Beckett—"It's never the same pus from one second to the next."

The sequence is extremely simple, as starkly naked as the set. Two tramps, Vladimir and Estragon, are waiting on a lonely road for Godot. Only a barren tree is visible on the empty plateau. They argue, take off their shoes, button their flies, discuss philosophy, embrace, attempt suicide, eat a carrot. Two other characters appear, Pozzo and Lucky, master and slave. Lucky, burdened down with a heavy bag, a folding stool, a picnic basket, and a greatcoat, has a long rope tied around his neck. All four characters wear bowlers. Pozzo pulls the rope and snaps his whip. Lucky falls, gets up, does nothing until ordered to. When Pozzo commands him to think, he goes into a long verbal outburst, with his hat on, incoherent fragments of medieval scholarship and modern science. He is silenced only when all fall on him. Pozzo eats, tosses the chicken bones to Estragon, sprays his throat, discusses his pipe, the weather, time. Then the two go off, leaving Vladimir and Estragon alone, waiting for Godot. A boy appears to tell them that Godot will come tomorrow.

The second act takes place the next day. The only change in the scene is a few leaves that have sprouted on the tree. Nothing is finite. All is continuous with blurred edges, the shadows of existence. Time is elastic. It may be the next day, or any day, or another season, for waiting is all of life without beginning or end and the days matter little. As Estragon says, "There's no lack of void." They go through the same burlesque antics and comedy routines with hats and shoes, carrots and trousers and suicide. Pozzo and Lucky return. The rope is shorter now, the two tied together more closely, for Pozzo is blind. They leave, and the tramps go on waiting for Godot.

The play lends itself to innumerable interpretations. Beckett, unlike most contemporary playwrights, has refused to discuss the definition of his symbols. Perhaps he prefers the purposefully vague so that every member of the audience will supply his own meaning. Since no certainty exists, art cannot impose one. The play is unquestionably a morality play in which not faith but doubt binds man to God, if Godot stands for God—or a little God more intimate and clownish, like Pierrot for Pierre, or a combination of God and Charlot (the French for Charlie Chaplin). Names, like time, are elastic. Vladimir and Estragon are so called only in the listed cast of characters. Are they the split aspects of Everyman, reason and the senses, which would desert each other yet are bound together, or are they the divided world of East and West? In the play, these two characters use their childish nicknames of Didi and Gogo, two-syllable names with double repetition of vowel and consonant, but they are also referred to as Adam and Monsieur Albert. Pozzo becomes Bozzo or Gozzo, whose mother had the clap, or perhaps Godot, who passes by unrecognized, for he is evil and we seek the unknown, the unseen, the ineffable. Even Godot is called Godet, Godin. Neither man nor God completely possesses his own name; each may have many names like Shiva or Dionysus. Only Lucky remains so. Is he lucky because of his fixed and known relationship as slave? In any case, religious references run throughout the play: "hope deferred," "tree of life," "ye fools and blind," Christ and the two thieves. And the action is a series of separations and unions, of pilgrimage and appointment. Gogo and Didi twice attempt suicide; first they have no rope, and then the rope breaks, but there is hope that tomorrow they may have a stronger rope. At least there will be the sexual excitement that accompanies hanging, for "where the desire cometh, it is a tree of life." The tree becomes the Cross for their self-imposed crucifixion.

The movement of the play consists of conflict between the two pairs of characters and the conflict within each pair, intensified by successive symbols of duality. One couple is always on the move, the other stays and waits; one is tied together by necessity, the other by a rope. Pozzo and Lucky have distinct duties: one serves, the other consumes; the dominated and the dominating. They are closer to the real world, and undergo change. At the end they are tied closer together, the dumb leading the blind. Of Gogo and Didi, Didi is more rational, more compassionate; Gogo, more animal, more abused. He eats and sleeps and his shoes hurt. They are married to each other. Perhaps that is why there are no female characters—there is no need of birth and the continuity of the race if all is empty nothingness. For them, there is no change other than the festering of the sore and the leaves on the tree, the slim hope always deferred. Didi hopes for change, and Gogo answers, "It's never the same pus from one second to the next." For them there is no age, no time, their animal and intellectual longings competing with their spiritual salvation in the waiting for a Godot who will never come, whom they will never know, but for whom they must go on waiting. The parable is a bitter comment on existence. "What are we doing here?" asks Vladimir. "Are we needed?" They at least can find something to give them the impression that they do exist, and they can pass beyond "the danger of ever thinking any more."

The most ludicrous scene occurs when the two pairs meet for the second time. They all fall on the ground in a tangle of interweaving arms, heads, and legs, and lie there —the absurdly comic plight of helpless man, and only Pozzo, the blind, makes an effort to rise. They do get up, clumsily, bumping into each other, none too much alive and all close to death, for birth and life and death are inseparable and merge when there is no time. Pozzo cries out, "One day we were born, one day we shall die, the same day, the same second . . . they give birth astride of a grave." And Vladimir echoes his words with, "Astride of a grave and difficult birth. Down in the hole, lingeringly, the gravedigger puts on the forceps." And like the final scene of Sartre's No Exit, the play ends with the words of Vladimir, "Shall we go?" Estragon pulls up his trousers and says, "Let's go."[2] They do not move. For we are caught in the going and the coming and the getting nowhere, and though there is only suffering and little hope, man can go on waiting, not with the dignity of the hero but with the pathetic submission of the tramp.

The architecture of the play is austerely classical, observing all the unities and balancing both halves with geometrical precision. The language varies from common vulgarity to lyric beauty, and the varying rhythms and pauses are skillfully orchestrated. Scenes start up, die off, and reappear later, but Beckett has an excellent sense of the theatrical, using all the devices of vaudeville and popular comedy to keep nonaction and waiting constantly alive.

Like many of the writers of the "absurd" living in Paris, Beckett is not a Frenchman. He is an Irishman who writes in French and translates his own work into English. His novels, *Murphy, Molloy, Malone Dies, The Unnamable, Stories and Texts for Nothing* and *Watt* are recognized classics, following in the tradition of Joyce with whom he worked closely in Paris. Of his other plays, mostly short pieces, none has the vigor and power of *Waiting for Godot.*

The title of *Endgame* (1957) comes from the third and final part of a chess game, but the reference is vague, save as it relates to the overall theme of waiting for the end, which characterizes all of Beckett's work. Nagg and Nell, the two old people, live in ash cans and remove the covers at specific intervals to show their heads and speak. Their son, Hamm, paralyzed, blind and, confined to a wheelchair, is attended by Clov, his servant. Clov is constantly threatening to leave but never does, in contrast to Godot who is constantly expected to arrive. Hamm waits for death which likewise never comes. The room is barren, isolated, mysterious—the indeterminate womb symbol—as the ash cans are wombs within the womb for the older folk. The Hamm-Clov relationship is that of master-slave, the divided self, raising again the inevitable question in Beckett's work of the elusiveness of being. The play intersperses the dialogue with long periods of mime, abrupt silences, innumerable pauses, surprising shifts in subject matter, and moments of broad farce and vaudeville antics that emphasize the play's underlying tension—the pain of existence, the inadequacy of reason in the absurd and perhaps final game in man's existence on earth.

Happy Days has two long acts with only two characters: Winnie, about fifty, and Willie, about sixty. Winnie is buried up to her waist in a mound in an expanse of scorched grass. She does all the talking, except for a few grunts from Willie, probably the longest monologue in the theatre. She plays with objects as a substitute for action, an array of articles that she pulls from a big black bag—toothbrush, toothpaste, mirror, handkerchief, spectacles, and a revolver. In the second act, she is even less mobile. She has sunk a little deeper into the mound, and only her neck and face are visible. With her hands imprisoned, her only props are her facial gestures and tonal variations. Willie is hidden behind the elevation and appears spasmodically on all fours. Yet despite her hapless condition, Winnie exclaims, "Oh, this is a happy day!"—the most ironic comment on man's unawareness of his own absurdity. In production, the play is a tour de force for an actress who remains immobile from the waist up.

In *Krapp's Last Tape,* a filthy old man in his dingy cluttered room relives his past with his tape recorder, gleefully recalling a moment of youthful romance and questioning a life without purpose. *Play,* a short piece, has three nameless characters, a man and two women, who are confined in death urns up to their necks, as Winnie was confined in her sand heap. They are bathed in sepulchral dimness while a spotlight focuses on the one who speaks, often shifting back and forth for half sentences or parts of words. In the first half, the characters recall fragments of a dull life. The second half takes place after death and the conversation is equally dull and inconclusive.

Act Without Words is a mime for one player, with sounds, props, gestures. It is an example of minimal art, of nonverbal theatre reduced to absolute simplicity. Doubt and emptiness are expressed through acted symbols. Beckett sounds the final note of futility, Descartes's order is reduced to empty repetition.

Eugene Ionesco—"Choose the reality . . . that's best for you."

Eugene Ionesco, a Romanian by birth, who lives in Paris and writes in French, is, together with Samuel Beckett, the recognized leader of the theatre of negation. Ionesco has been closer to the theatre and has written many plays. Unlike Beckett, he has gone into detailed explanations of his work. Since *The Bald Soprano* was first presented in the Théâtre des Noctambules on the Left Bank with only three people in the audience, his popularity has grown so enormously that *Rhinoceros* was performed with a simultaneous gala opening in Basel and Paris, following the world premiere in Germany. Austria, Sweden, England, and the United States saw the play soon after, with leading directors and actors anxious to be associated with the production. In contrast to the lonely Paris opening of *The Bald Soprano*, *Rhinoceros* was received at the Théâtre de France with a capacity audience, including André Malraux, Minister of Cultural Affairs, and members of the diplomatic corps. Jean Louis Barrault played the role of Berenger; in London, Laurence Olivier played it. Thus, in ten years, a neglected *avant-garde* writer has become the sought-after prize of the commercial theatre.

Rhinoceros, however, is not pure Ionesco. It has a recognizable plot in developed climactic sequence, and its language is relatively understandable. French critics in alarm accused Ionesco of deserting experimentalism and succumbing to the theatre he had so vigorously condemned. He replied, "They accused me of being incomprehensible, now they accuse me of being too clear."

Though he has written other full-length plays, such as *The Killer*, Ionesco's innovations are more carefully worked out in the shorter pieces—*The Bald Soprano, The Lesson, The Chairs,* and *Jacques.* He is like Beckett in rejecting established theatre conventions, but he differs in method. Both agree that since the world is absurd, its representation should be equally absurd. Science and reason, arising out of the Renaissance, have in four centuries distorted reality, confining it to demonstrable logic and eliminating the vaster areas of fancy, imagination, dreams. Artaud had called for a theatre that translates life into universal forms, and evokes hidden, primitivistic images. To Ionesco, mind has been free in only one direction, with the result that man is bereft of faith and freedom in others. Realism, which dominates the theatre:[3]

> falls short of reality . . . It does not take into account our basic truths and our fundamental obsessions: love, death, astonishment. It presents man in a reduced and strange perspective. Truth is in our dreams, in the imagination.

The middle-class world has become a victim of the rational universe decreed by the eighteenth century. Everything is confined to the narrow scope of proof by the laws of logic. Ibsen wanted to infuse that world with spiritual vitality. Ionesco would eliminate it entirely. But a choice of other realities is also possible. In *Rhinoceros,* before she joins the herd and becomes a rhinoceros herself, Daisy says to Berenger:

> There are many realities. Choose the one that's best for you. Escape into the world of the imagination.

This is the basis of Ionesco's departure. Science gave order to the world, but falsified it by eliminating all that does not flow from its own premises. Strindberg had sought

to go beyond material existence—to discover the nature of
man in the freedom of dreams, the absurdity of the subconscious, the flow of the imagination—but he was the mad
poet. Ionesco, coldly and with his own laws of logic, exposes
the absurdity of common-sense logic. He recently stated in
Premières Mondiales that he was pleased to have his plays
performed by young people because the young, "in their un-
reason, reason rightly as opposed to the unreasonable rea-
soning of their elders."[4]

In *The Killer,* the final scene is a gruesome example of
how logic can destroy. Berenger, alone with the killer, tries
to convince him that murder is wrong and useless. It is a
long monologue, for the killer only laughs in reply. But
Berenger becomes engaged in a debate with his own mind.
He gives reasons pro and con, and finds that if there is no
reason to kill, there is also no logical reason not to kill. Lost
and in panic before the killer's menacing silence, he struggles for reasons beyond logic:[5]

> Maybe you're wrong, maybe wrong does not exist,
> maybe it's we who are wrong to want to exist.

Failing to understand the mysterious, he loses power
over himself, drops his pistol, and is a victim of the killer's
knife. He was unable to reach the unspoken mind of his
foe, unprepared for understanding beyond reason. In effect,
his reliance on logic destroys him.

Ionesco's technique flows from his concepts. Since he is
opposed to realism, all the elements of the traditional play
are discarded. Plot, logical sequence, development of crises,
use of time and space, give way to a juxtaposition of images
often violent and contradictory. The world of sense is turned
inside out, and a rhythm of *non sequiturs* replaces the expected. A plot or story is unnecessary; Ionesco has remarked
that the entire history of the theatre from the Greeks to the
present day is a series of detective stories: "There's a riddle
and it's solved in the final scene." All stories usually depend

on time sequence. Events happen as a result of what has gone before. Thus, to eliminate plot, Ionesco eliminates time in order to master it. If possible, he would do away with action, at least by individuals, and have no characters. In realism, passion and sex are predominant, but to Ionesco, marriage and love belong to the nonrational world. They are powers beyond scientific analysis, and suppressed by the rational, are distorted into bickering. Theoretically, a play should then have no characters, no plot, no action, no time element, but since the ideal is not possible in our present theatre, compromises have to be made. In his longer plays, Ionesco violates most of his own theories.

His preferred dramatic device, excellently worked out in such pieces as *The Lesson* and *The Chairs,* is a single metaphor, a dramatic conceit expanded with ingenious use of language. Words become the most powerful instrument to replace action and plot. They are used not as thoughts of the characters, but as weapons to shock and startle, to hold attention, to explore ideas, to play one against the other, to become—through manipulation—the demonstration of the absurd. Words are so important that they can bring characters to life as they do in *The Chairs,* or destroy life as in *The Lesson.* Seemingly significant remarks are followed by completely extraneous, ribald nonsense, outright vulgarisms, or irrelevant phrases, as in a vaudeville act. Above all, Ionesco uses the cliché, the platitude, and gives it startling freshness by using it out of context, twisting it to remove the dead weight of non-communication. Since language is the system of symbols used to express the world of sense, it too must be made absurd if it is to have new vitality. The clearest explanation is given by Ionesco himself, in commenting on the origin of *The Bald Soprano:*[6]

. . . it is by the automatism of his language that the inherent conformism of the bourgeois is betrayed . . . The Smiths and the Martins have forgotten how to talk because they have forgotten the meaning of emotion, because they are devoid of passions; they have forgotten how to be, and therefore they can become anyone, anything, for since they *are* not themselves, they are nothing but other people, they belong to an impersonal world, they are interchangeable.

The staging of the plays is of utmost importance; because the language is so essential, the staging must give physical movement to the verbal gymnastics, act out the flow of irrelevance, and establish the rhythm of drama. Yet with all their reliance on language, both Ionesco and Beckett have written plays without words, to emphasize the uselessness of verbal communication. In *Act Without Words* by Beckett and *The New Tenant* by Ionesco, the metaphor is worked out in mime. The imagery flows from the use of nonverbal objects to underline the meaning.

The Bald Soprano, the first and most hilarious of the anti-plays, is a travesty of domestic life and the middle class. Mr. and Mrs. Smith, an English couple who have been married for many years, are seated in the living room after dinner. She knits as he reads a newspaper. The actors play it with mechanical precision like marionettes, without emotions but with varying speech patterns. They review their life in nonsense words; the remarks of one have no relation to what the other has said. Ionesco thought of them as mechanical toys, so meaningless that they could be taken apart and put together in the wrong order with no differing results. The clock strikes seventeen, and Mrs. Smith announces it is nine o'clock. The opening note is the technique of the unexpected, the reverse of the normal, the device of farce. But behind it lies the implication that time is of no importance, for whatever the hour, their lives are equally routine and their conversation equally dull. They talk of Bobby Watson, who has just died, and of his wife, who is also named Bobby Watson. "Do you know her?" asks Mrs. Smith, and he answers:[7]

She has regular features and yet one cannot say that she is pretty. She is too big and stout. Her features are not regular but still one can say that she is very pretty. She is a little too small and too thin.

We discover that the children, the aunt, and the uncle are also all called Bobby Watson. Seemingly pure nonsense, yet again an indication that all the middle class are exactly alike and could have the same name. Ionesco may have taken the idea from a note by Giraudoux in which he says of Americans:

They come to France to study the architecture of happiness in the hearts of French women, and go racing back to Minneapolis to plant it in the hearts of gigantic girls usually called Watson.

With Ionesco, regardless of sex or physical appearance, they are all Bobby Watson, since fundamentally their existence is identical. Mr. and Mrs. Martin come in and are attracted to each other. They discover that they live on the same street in the same house, sleep in the same bed, and have the same child. Mr. Martin ends this interlude in a flat, monotonous voice, saying:

Then, dear lady, I believe there can be no doubt about it, we have seen each other before and you are my own wife . . . Elizabeth. I have found you again.

Ionesco is mocking the melodrama and the usual love scenes of recognition, but he is also parodying the failure of love, the emptiness of marriage, wherein husband and wife are unable to know each other. Love belongs to the world beyond reason, and it has never been understood by the Smiths and the Martins, with their reasoned conformity that has suppressed love and rendered it sterile. The Fire Chief comes in unexpectedly, joins in the conversation, talks to his sweetheart, the maid, and when he leaves, the two couples engage in a rapid exchange of clichés, the cocktail conversation, until they wind up saying pure nonsense syllables. The curtain rises again to show the Smiths—or if a director chooses, the Martins—in the same position, carrying on the same conversation as when the play started. Such is the continuing emptiness, the sameness of the world around us when "things cling to life." Ionesco describes the people in *The Bald Soprano* as those who:[8]

> have no hunger, no conscious desires, they are bored stiff. But people who are unconsciously alienated don't even know they are bored.

The Lesson, which followed, differs in that it has more plot development. The entire play is the lesson of a young girl who comes to the Professor's house. She is studying for the "total doctorate" even though she cannot subtract three from four, but she can give answers to the most complicated multiplication, for she has memorized all the answers to all possible multiplications. The Professor lectures on philology. The pupil is reduced to moanings about her toothache, and finally the Professor murders her. The body is removed, and the maid then answers the bell as the next pupil arrives to undergo the same treatment. Most of the play consists of long harangues by the Professor in his frustrated efforts to impart knowledge. Ionesco is obviously satirizing education, society's means of communication, which is absurd. The Professor is logically clear with simple arithmetic, but when he delves into comparative linguistics, he himself—the person in charge of teaching communication—becomes unintelligible. The mounting frustrations of pupil and teacher result in the girl's physical pain and the murder, both of which have sexual overtones, since sex itself is a form of communication of life, and all communication is a frustrating absurdity.

The other plays of Ionesco are variations on this theme.

THE CHAIRS

Ionesco calls this play a "tragic farce," another example of his juxtaposition of opposites. The place is a circular room atop a tower, surrounded by water, a setting for the wasted, isolated, mediocre lives of the Old Man, aged ninety-five, and the Old Woman, aged ninety-four, who are the only characters until the entrance of the Orator at the end. The opening lines are about the "bad smell from stagnant water," the world around them. The Old Woman wants to watch the boats in the sunlight and is told that it is night-time. They review their past; childhood scenes merge with the present and the future. The Old Woman cradles her man in her lap, the return to the womb, and they play games, like imitating the months, the visual form of nonsense. The Old Man's words when he refers to Paris may even suggest Ionesco's prediction that the world is threatened with atomic annihilation. "It was the city of light"—he uses the past tense—"but it has been extinguished for four hundred thousand years . . . Nothing remains of it except a song."[9]

OLD WOMAN: What song?

OLD MAN: A lullaby, an allegory. "Paris will always be Paris."

As they tell their past, the syncopated speech changes to a slow, dreamy rhythm. Words vanish into multiple meanings. The Old Man sits in her lap and wets, moaning: "I'm all spoiled . . . my career is spilled." Platitudes of success flow in and around their tale of failure. Many guests have been invited to hear the final message of the Old Man, his vindication. The couple speak to them as they arrive, arrange seats for them, interrupt conversations. The stage becomes full of chairs, until finally the Emperor enters. All the guests are imaginary and invisible, but idle chatter, flirtations, arguments with all of them, and the Old Man's hopes make them real. The scene rises to the animation of a ballet with the placing of the chairs, the music of doorbells, the sounds of the boats—all leading up to the great message of freedom from the misunderstood intellectual. So full of people is the imagined stage that the Old Man and Woman get lost in the crowd, and when the Old Man finds her, he says: "I am not myself. I am another. I am the one in the other"—an echo of Rimbaud's concept of the division of self, but here used also to show the sameness of all. The Old Man seeks certainty and truth in the midst of the absurd. Now that the Emperor is present, the Old Man can at last have the Orator deliver his message. His life "has been filled to overflowing." He will not have lived in vain. His words will be revealed to the world. Conscious that all has been arranged, or unable to undo the complications of their own plans, the Old Man and Woman leap out of the window to their death in the water below as the Orator moves to the dais. He, who is real, stands before the non-existent assemblage and delivers to posterity the great message:

> He faces the rows of empty chairs; he makes the invisible crowd understand that he is deaf and dumb . . . he coughs, groans, utters the gutteral sounds of a mute, "He, mme, mm, mm. Ju, gou, hou, hou. Heu, heu, gu, gou, gueue."

Unable to speak, he writes on the blackboard: ANGEL-FOOD; then mutters more unintelligible sounds, erases what he has written, and replaces it with ADIEU.

The futility of life and the inability to communicate have rarely been dramatized so graphically. Ionesco wrote:[10]

> In *The Chairs,* I have tried to deal with the themes that obsess me; with emptiness, with frustration, with this world, at once fleeting and crushing, with despair and death. The characters I have used are not fully conscious of their spiritual rootlessness, but they feel it instinctively and emotionally.

In the longer plays Ionesco found it difficult to sustain

interest purely with variations of metaphor, and he resorted to more of the usual plot development. Both *The Killer* and *Rhinoceros* are expanded single conceits, amazing examples of the author's ingenuity. Berenger is the protagonist in both plays, not that he is the same person, for names are of little meaning and one can serve for many. In *The Killer,* he represents good in a fearsome, nightmarish struggle with evil. In the City of Radiance where all is seeming perfection, a mysterious Killer takes the lives of many people and cannot be apprehended. When Berenger tracks him down, he is too uncertain as to the nature of evil to destroy his foe.

Rhinoceros, the most widely known play, is Ionesco's attack on conformity. When all have deserted Berenger and turned to beasts, he stands alone, not completely defiant, and would become a rhinoceros too, but he cannot. He must remain human in a dehumanized world, for there is something within him that persists in retaining what is left of man's dignity. The play was presumably an anti-Nazi document, but Ionesco refuses to be engaged in political action. For this he has been severely attacked. Sartre wrote:[11]

> It is absolutely impossible to derive any meaning from Ionesco's play except that a great misfortune, a great peril of annihilation menaces the world and that, good heavens, the danger of contagion is very grave . . . And why is there one man who resists? At least we could learn why, but no, we learn not even that. He resists because he is there. He resists because he is *Ionesco:* he represents Ionesco, he says I resist, and there he remains in the midst of the rhinoceroses, the only one to defend man without our being very sure if it might not be better to be a rhinoceros. Nothing has been proved to the contrary.

Ionesco answered that he is interested in life beyond the political, as in the Radiant City, where politics has achieved Utopia, but evil persists. In advice to young people of the theatre, he said:[12]

Philosophers are assimilating and going beyond ideologies which try to limit man to his historical context. Once they get past historical determinism, they rediscover "trans-history," the permanence of fundamental human realities. The theatre often lags behind ideas. It should not do so again.

Both plays are replete with Ionesco's themes. Intellectual pettiness and pretense, trade unionism, bureaucracy, love, sex, and logic are brought under fire. Neither play is heroic. They are pictures of man pathetically alone in a world devoid of meaning, surrounded by verbal barrages that splatter aimlessly around him.

Three full-length plays indicated a growing mastery of theatrical form. In *Pedestrian of the Air,* Berenger again appears as he did in *The Killer* and *Rhinoceros.* This time he is a French writer who has retired to England because, as he says, "I am paralyzed because I know I am going to die and I want to be cured of death." On a beautiful Sunday morning when people are idly strolling in the countryside, among them The Bald Soprano who did not appear in Ionesco's first play, an old Englishman dressed in garish white with an upside-down pipe floats in, walking on the air, and vanishes. Berenger recognizes him as an apparition from the "antiworld," a world one senses in "the reflection of a castle in the water, in the tricks of a juggler, or in the refracting rays of the sun." Filled with joy, Berenger, to the amazement of all, hops about, then remains aloft in the air and finally flies out into the "antiworld." His wife and daughter remain with their fears, death symbols, and ghostly figures, until Berenger returns crawling and exhausted to tell of visions of a world in flames, a terrifying place of cruelty and pain on the edge of an immense void. The final scene contains an explosion of fireworks, a Mardi Gras celebration, and the only line of hope, "Perhaps the flames will be extinguished."

In *Exit the King* Berenger is now a king who is dying.

His first wife, Queen Margaret, practical and resigned, prepares him to meet death gracefully as all men must, sooner or later. The second wife, Queen Marie, young and vibrant, wants him to go on living and loving, to defy death by transcending life. "Escape from definitions and you will breathe again." Berenger I, as king, believes he is beyond even the law of death and cries to countless thousands before him, "Teach me how humanity is to accept death and die." With acid wit and surrealistic fantasy, Ionesco, having shown the absurdity of life, now offers the equal absurdity of death.

Hunger and Thirst is far superior to the other two plays and a major dramatic achievement. In Ionesco's own words, it is "the story of Jean, a man who leaves his home— where he might discover a spiritual joy he fails to see within himself—to seek an improbable happiness, a key to the mysteries of life. He will not succeed in piercing the wall of knowledge; he finds only a world of anguish and distress."[15] In the first episode, "The Flight," Jean is at home with his wife and child. They live in a dark dungeon, dank and moldy, the upholstered furniture shabby and torn. The wife finds it beautiful, for here is the man she loves and the child she has borne. Jean is restless, not knowing why, but searching for sun and flowers and mountains to climb. The wife is everyday necessity, the reality of compromise. Jean is fancy, searching for reality to replace the one he detests. He runs away disappearing like an apparition; his wife searches for him everywhere, in the closet, under the couch, shouting, like Ibsen's Solveig that her husband will always live in her heart and her love. Episode Two has been changed several times by Ionesco. It was intended to recount Jean's pilgrimage and his arrival at the Wall of Knowledge which opens to prepare for the final magnificent scene, "The Black Masses of the Good Inn," in which, surrounded by hooded friars, Jean is given food and drink and recites the tale of his travels over the past fifteen years. He is inarticulate, having found no meaning, no beauty, no insight to communicate. He is the eternal pilgrim—not the poet in quest of the unknowable but an insensitive mediocrity on the go. He is the opposite of the knight errant, a bourgeois pedestrian of the air. When he wants to pay his bill, the Brother Superior detains him and has reenacted a play in which two men in cages are offered food and drink if they will deny their beliefs. Being men of principles and ideals, they refuse. When their suffering is unbearable, one says there is a God, and the other denies His existence, the opposite of beliefs they had previously held. Both are given food and drink. Jean remains to pay his debt, which consists of waiting on tables for eternity. His wife and daughter appear in the background, still offering love as Jean rushes back and forth serving tables. Nothing is real but the need to satisfy hunger and thirst.

Both Beckett and Ionesco herald the end of the conventional theatre. The difficulty in understanding their plays results from their complete departure from all that has been traditional, and their effort to pioneer a new tradition, discarding the myths of the past and, as the poet should, evolving new myths. Contradictory as their work is, it is so because they themselves are involved in contradictions. Though they revolt against the rational world, they attempt to achieve the rigor and beauty of mathematics in rationalizing the irrational. To their credit lies the thoroughness with which they annihilate realism and introduce to the theatre the vast expanse of the impossible. Both are amazingly gifted in wit, mastery of language, knowledge of theatre, and ability to project freshness of vision. Freedom of speech acquires an internal meaning, for words are loosed from previous connotations. Though their laughter is acidic, it is man laughing at his own vacuity. Both face the same dramatic problem. Resignation to disaster and the description of its approach may be made terrifyingly comic, but if the characters lack the conscious will to resist, drama can register only the lost Paradise, a death-in-life, and man reduced to silence. The only hero of Ionesco's plays is Ionesco himself.

Jean Genet—"I beg of you, evil, and I beg you standing upright, impregnate my people."

Genet does not truly belong to the theatre of the "absurd." He creates a new Reason in which Evil establishes its own order with the purity of religious ecstasy. Beckett and Ionesco present comic images of loneliness to emphasize the tragedy of man. But Genet glories in the triumph of evil with the religious intensity of a convert and the delirious delight of a criminal.

Sartre, his enthusiastic admirer, wrote glowingly of Genet's plays, "Good is only an illusion. Evil is a Nothingness which arises upon the ruins of Good."

Strindberg, the source of the theatre of despair, felt surrounded by hate and corruption, but he did strive to discover a return to spiritual purity. Genet wallows in emptiness with sadistic pleasure, and exploits the horror of vice to give it prestige.

He hailed Genet as the greatest of the "black magicians," a worthy heir to Villon, Sade, Rimbaud, and Baudelaire. Genet's characters are all angry outcasts from society because definition has made them so. The poet, also an outcast, is identical with the criminal, alone able to create a new beauty, uncontaminated by social decree.

In his preface to *The Maids*, Genet blasted the triviality of the conventional theatre, and following the dream of Antonin Artaud, called for a theatre of communion, ceremony, and awe arising from outside society, because those within are too weak from its decay to create beauty, the beauty that has "the power of a poem, that is, of a crime." Genet is the poet-criminal. No writer has more intimately known perversion, drug addiction, smuggling, thievery, and the inside of the jails of Europe. Born illigitimately and reared by a peasant family, he was sent to a reformatory at the age of ten for stealing. His first work, *Our Lady of the Flowers*, was written in jail. In 1948, he was sentenced to life imprisonment as a repeated offender, and was released only after an appeal to the President of the French Republic by a group of writers, including Cocteau, Sartre, Camus, and Claudel.

From Pirandello he took the unknowability of appearance and reality, and transformed them into merging polarities in which characters are born "in the sleeping imagination" of the master, "low, hypocritical, disagreeable, and mean because their employers dream them that way." On stage are phantoms created by "the minds of decent people" in the audience, and their rebellion is in imagining that:[13]

> they are becoming the Master who imagines them . . .
> They are disturbing only in that they are dreams who
> dream of swallowing up their dreamer.

The Maids, which was directed by Jouvet in Paris in 1947, has three female characters who, Genet indicated, should be played by adolescent boys, presumably to achieve another level of unreality. The two maids, reduced to servility and silence, play the role of the Mistress, putting on her clothes in her absence. The two become distinct and also interchangeable with the Mistress. Out of love and hate, as well as the need to establish an existence of their own, the maids plan to murder the Mistress. The plot fails. One takes poison and the other awaits her fate orgiastically. It is a play of extended and almost unendurable horror, relieved by the fact that the personal anguish of the characters is never fully real. In their games the maids become the Mistress, and act out their own dream of being accepted by society. Their dream world fuses with the real world.

They unconsciously portray the fears of those accepted by society—fears that the servile will rise up and destroy them. What survives is hate.

In *Deathwatch,* three young criminals are in a prison cell. Green Eyes, who is chained by the feet, has committed murder, and so he is the leader—symbolizing the hierarchy of crime in the closed world of the damned. They revel in their tales of legendary heroes of evil. They are drawn to one another, even sexually, and alternately repelled. The hate finally rises into the strangling of the youngest, as the others reach a radiance of self-glorification. Out of this concentrated hell is evoked an obscene beauty of emotional freedom, possible only to those who are released from convention.

The two plays that followed develop the same theme more fully in a wider structure of demonic fantasy. In his foreword to *The Blacks,* Genet wrote:

> One evening an actor asked me to write a play for an all-black cast. But what exactly is a black? First of all, what's his color?

The play is a Black Mass in which Negroes, on several levels physically and intellectually, act out the myths of the race, the image the whites have of them, and their image of the world of the whites. The play within a play is a barbaric ritual of hate. In his first play, the outcasts were two maids; in his second, three criminals; now, the entire race. The Queen's Court of the ruling whites is played on the upper level by Negro actors in masks. In life they are cooks, maids, prostitutes. On the lower level, around a catafalque, is reenacted the murder of a white woman by a Negro. Simultaneously, reports are brought in of the execution of a black by the whites. The rest of the play is an exploration of the inner nature of the Negro, his pretense, his posturing, his psyche, his rebellion—acting out for a white audience what is expected and feared. If an audience should be all black, Genet asked that "a white person . . . be invited every evening" for whom the actors would play.[14]

> But what if no white person accepted? Then let white masks be distributed to the black spectators as they enter the theatre. And if the blacks refuse, then let a dummy be used.

The result is illusory. When the sheet over the catafalque is removed, two empty chairs are revealed. There is no murdered white woman. The Queen's Court of pretended whites is ceremoniously led to annihilation, grovelling abjectly. The purity of the Negro is hate. Genet discounts the world of integration or social improvement. In a polarized world, the antithesis triumphs. Those outside society, like Genet himself, dominate in fantasy or reality, not out of love but out of purer elemental drives against an exhausted myth imposed upon them.

The Balcony confines the world to a house of prostitution; again a portrayal of shadows within shadows, of shifting levels of appearance and reality. The Balcony is a brothel, run by Irma, wherein petty men are made bigger than life through reenacting their fantasies. The clients impersonate their suppressed desires—to be a bishop, a general, a judge, a masochist defiling the Virgin. The brothel is the concentrated center of depravity, where men obtain momentary release in their dream world for a fee. Outside, a revolution is taking place. The gunfire increases in intensity as destruction in the real world threatens the House of Illusions. Chantal, who formerly worked for Irma, becomes the goddess of the people, the prostitute-saint. Roger, her lover and the leader of the revolt, will take over the city and destroy The Balcony. All the heads of government have disappeared. The clients who acted out their dreams now assume in real life the characters they imitated. Irma becomes the Queen, the symbol of order, to destroy Chantal, the symbol of freedom. Accompanied by the false Judge, General, and Bishop, she defeats the revolution. The Chief of Police, her accomplice and partner, lord of earthly power and vice, becomes the new Hero. The only obstacle in his path to perfection is his failure to have someone impersonate him— the proof that he belongs to the legendary myths of the people. In the final ironic touch, Roger, the revolutionary, enters the brothel to act the role of the Chief of Police. He ends by castrating himself. The symbolism implies that the revolution and the society it would overthrow are variations of the same sham and hypocrisy. A revolution from within the established order cannot effect change. Only evil, from without, deserves to triumph.

Each character sees a double who turns and mocks him. Each lie wears a mask, and men await its fall to return to reality, which is unendurable. The enjoyment of the heroic self remains a repeated but temporary vision that men prefer to pay for in private, while publicly they submit to servility. Genet's highly fantastic ceremonies are uncompromising desecrations, the destruction of all myths in order to elevate the criminal to sainthood. In *The Blacks*, Archibald addresses the audience, saying:

> . . . in order that you be assured that there is no danger of such a drama worming its way into your precious lives, we shall even have the decency, a decency learned from you, to make communication impossible. We shall increase the distance that separates us, a distance that is basic, by our pomp, our manners, our insolence.

The Screens, Genet's most ambitious and complex play, was written in 1961 at the height of the Algerian crisis but not presented in Paris for fear of public reprisals. Jean-

Louis Barrault finally presented it in 1967 despite vitriolic cries that the play was anti-French and outrageously obscene. Peter Brook was so fascinated by the play that he spent two years rehearsing actors of the Royal Shakespeare Company but never got beyond presenting a few scenes in an evening devoted to the Theatre of Cruelty. The play is a spectacle in seventeen scenes played on multiple levels shifting between appearance and reality, the rebellious living and the settled dead. Saïd, the anti-Hero, the non-Self, is the incarnation of total evil. He lives in filth, marries Leila, the ugliest woman in the world, commits every known crime, including betrayal, the highest achievement of courageous will. In one scene, the old Kadidja, blesses Saïd and Leila for "You realized that in evil lay the only hope. Evil, Wonderful evil, you who remain when all goes to pot, miraculous evil, you're going to help us. I beg of you, evil, and I beg you standing upright, impregnate my people."[18] In the interlocking, interweaving scenes there are moments of poetic grandeur, others wildly surrealistic as the one in which Madani is transmuted into the Mouth of the murdered rebel leader Si Slimane, others perversely scatological like the one in which the Arabs paint their atrocities on moving screens. As with all of Genet, the play defies the destructive forces embodied in the present Good; it is a fantasy of theatrical shock, the ultimate expression of the Theatre of Cruelty.

14. Duerrenmatt, Frisch and the German Theatre—The Brecht Influence

THE VISIT OF THE OLD LADY
ANDORRA
MARAT/SADE

THE SEMINAL FORCE of Bertolt Brecht effected a comprehensive revolution in all aspects of contemporary theatre. The tight, well constructed form of psychological realism, the theatre of illusion, gave way to theatrical theatre, a return to the open episodic far-flung Shakespearean canvas. Placards, films, posters, projections, and songs were employed in a multimedia presentation of historical evidence, aimed at transforming the theatre into an educational forum to change political convictions.

Fundamental to Brecht's vision is the conception of human nature as not fixed but constantly changing, a result of interrelation with environmental factors. Man is neither basically evil (as in the Middle Ages) nor naturally good (as in the Age of Reason) but a product of specific and endlessly changing social conditioning. Freedom is limited by necessity, but man can alter that necessity and himself by creating a more favorable, rational structure in which to live. Brecht evolved a unity of form and content based on the principles of the Marxist dialectic which to him was the essential framework for political drama. This unity was admirably achieved by the Berliner Ensemble. The form, however, was so attractive as a break from realistic theatre that many playwrights—John Osborne in *Luther,* Robert Bolt in *A Man for All Seasons*—employed it to express different political preferences. Gunther Grass applied the epic structure to attack Brecht's role during the workers' uprising in East Berlin in the play *The Plebeians Rehearse the Uprising.* The form became divorced from the content Brecht intended. Other playwrights leaned toward overt political propaganda and documentary presentation, ignoring the magic of fantasy and the power of language, as Heinar Kipphardt with *In the Matter of J. Robert Oppenheimer* and Peter Weiss in *The Investigation.* The most completely realized achievement of the Brechtian aesthetic rivaling that of Brecht himself is seen in the work of the Swiss playwrights, Max Frisch and Friedrich Duerrenmatt.

When Brecht left the United States, he stopped in Zurich before accepting the offer to work in East Berlin. His plays were revived at the Schauspielhaus with great success, and he became the center of intellectual ferment, which influenced his decision to return to practical theatre. In turn, he supplied the impetus which catapulted the Swiss theatre into international recognition.

Duerrenmatt—"The world made me into a whore, now I make the world into a brothel."

Friedrich Duerrenmatt has to his credit a substantial body of work: full-length plays, radio scripts, and serious detective stories. His first play, *It Is Written* (1946) contains the basic elements of his later mature style: grotesque comic situations, a Boschlike reliance on the bizarre and the demonic, a romantic sweep, caustic irony, irreverent parody, absence of the normal time-space relationship, and the persistent theme of moral corruption and death. The story, a man's search for God, takes place at the time of the Anabaptist massacre in Münster, and deals with John of Leyden, the fanatic leader whose vanity and abuse of power led to total disintegration. *The Blind Man* followed two years later and then the first of the major plays, *Romulus the Great,* written in 1949 and revised in 1957. It has the conventional division into acts and a sequential story line.

Romulus, the last of the Roman Emperors, an inversion of the mythical founder of the city, is more interested in chickens than affairs of state. Rome, to him, has lived by violence and deserves to die by violence. He is surrounded by pretense, an outmoded code of honor, and an effete civilization and threatened by an invasion of the Goths under Odoaker. Caesar Rupf, a wealthy pants manufacturer, offers to buy out the Emperor or Odoaker in return for the Emperor's daughter and a contract for trousers. In the final act, all have fled the palace except Romulus, who calmly awaits the entrance of the conqueror, prepared to die as the sacrifice for his country's failure. Odoaker turns out to be a man of culture, a student of history, an admirer of Roman civilization, and an equally dedicated chicken fancier. He fears his coldly insensitive nephew, the youthful Theodoric, a Hitler prototype, who will assassinate him and lead the Teutons to greater military victories. Odoaker came to surrender to save the glory of Rome, while Romulus pleads for his own death and the end of Rome.

The confrontation has a Shavian tone in its wit and its unexpected surprise ending. Odoaker is proclaimed King of Italy, and Romulus, after receiving the homage of the Teutons, retires on a government pension to his chicken farm. Romulus declares, "My dear Odoaker, I wanted to play fate and you wanted to avoid yours. Now it is our fate to be shipwrecked politicians. . . . I wanted to see the end of Rome because I feared its past, you wanted the end of Germania because you shuddered at its future. We were ruled by two ghosts, for we have no power over what was, nor over what will be. We have only power over the present. But we did not take it into consideration and now we both

founder. . . . Let us bear our bitter lot and try and give the
world a few years of peace which history will of course
skip for lack of spectacular feats of heroism, but they will
be among the happiest years this confused world has ever
lived through."[1] With its mordant satire and burlesque
overtones, the play is a tragic comment on the impotence
of man's will to alter destiny. Duerrenmatt wrote, "If
Romulus sits in judgement over the world in Act Three, the
world sits in judgement over him in Act Four. . . . His
tragedy lies in the comedy of his end; instead of a sacrificial
death he has earned for himself retirement. But then—and
this alone is what makes him great—he has the wisdom
and the insight to accept his fate."[2]

 The Marriage of Mr. Mississippi (1952) is a return to
extravagent stage techniques in a complicated political melodrama. *An Angel Comes to Babylon* (1953) takes place in
Heaven and Babylon and gets somewhat out of hand in its
overinvolved and confusing metaphors. The Angel brings
Kurrubi, a diaphanous creature of selfless love, to be offered
to the lowest man on earth, who turns out to be Akki,
a marvelous creation of Duerrenmatt's, comparable to
Brecht's Azdak, who represents common sense and sensitivity, the unconventional free man.

THE VISIT OF THE OLD LADY

 The Visit of the Old Lady is Duerrenmatt's best-known
work and one of the finest plays of the century. In the
United States, Alfred Lunt and Lynn Fontanne toured the
country after a long Broadway run in the play but, unfortunately, used Maurice Valency's adaptation, which softens
the bite, eliminates most of the choral counterpoint, and
makes Madame Zachanassian into a rather pleasant female
instead of a mechanical plastic dehumanized product of
cosmetic surgery. The tremendous power of *The Visit* comes
from its reenactment as ritual of the deepest and most dis-

concerting suspicions of modern man: that not only do justice and democracy have a price, but that their sale is justified as a morally righteous act to preserve justice and democracy. Terrifying in its tragi-comic destruction of basic human values, it has the massive proportions of Greek tragedy, and vindicates Brecht's ideal of historical realism and political message as dramatic art. Money is God, and the experience is purifying in its imitation on stage of man's impending disaster.

The town of Güllen boasts of its democratic heritage but is suffering from the plague—unemployment, poverty, stagnation. In act one, Clara Wascher (she who washes clean) now Madame Zachanassian, a multibillionaire, arrives as the only hope, "except for God," but "He doesn't pay off." She owns Armenian Oil, Western Railways, the Wagonworks, the Golden Eagle Pencil Factory, and the Hong Kong red-light district. With her full entourage—two blind eunuchs, a future eighth husband, a black panther, and an empty coffin—she returns to the place of her birth, from which she had been driven out as a prostitute after her affair with Alfred Ill,* now a local shopkeeper. At a ceremonial banquet, she offers a billion dollars in return for justice. She restages her trial, but all the original witnesses are in her employ. For reparations, she asks for the life of Ill. In the name of humanity, the Burgomaster declares that justice cannot be bought.

Act Two portrays the effects of the visit. Factories are working, money is available, people buy on credit, and everyone is in debt. The town's attitude toward Alfred begins to change. He who had been revered as the future Burgomaster, the salvation of the city, is now regarded as the guilty one, the sacrificial victim needed to cleanse the city.

---

* In Maurice Valency's adaptation of the play, the name Alfred Ill is changed to Anton Schill. In his later translation of the play, James L. Rosenthal returns to the original Alfred Ill.

Act Three is the death of the antihero. Alfred is murdered by the entire community in a ritualistic ceremony in which all participate. As Madame Zachanassian leaves with her coffin now filled, and ready to be placed in a beautiful mausoleum on the Isle of Capri, the villagers burst into a choric ode of rising religious intensity, hailing her as "the bringer of blessings! the giver of Good." The old lady drops the check for a billion at the feet of the mayor and boards the train as all the worshipers at the temple of money chant in unison to their new goddess, "Long live her goodness."

Brecht had once said about contemporary playwrights, "The reason money is not the subject of the plays is that too often it is the object." Duerrenmatt, who is also a painter, boasted that he was painting "a truly capitalist art by incorporating bank notes into his canvases."[3] This way, he claimed, "they are sure to have an intrinsic value." *The Visit* is a sardonic morality play in which the marketplace is the modern temple debasing all human values but never overtly. The Mayor accepts the bequest of Madame Zachanassian, not for the love of money, but, he explains, in a highly stylized interchange with the community:[4]

THE MAYOR: Rather for the love of justice.

THE CROWD: But rather for the love of justice.

THE MAYOR: Out of the promptings of conscience.

THE CROWD: Out of the promptings of conscience.

THE MAYOR: We cannot live and suffer a criminal among us.

THE CROWD: We cannot live and suffer a criminal among us.

This choral response, modeled on Greek tragedy, indicates again Duerrenmatt's belief that the danger is not the atomic bomb but man himself. The theme is developed in *The Physicists* (1962), which deals with the social responsibility of nuclear scientists. The setting is a madhouse, the form that of a murder mystery. The three central characters are famous physicists. The first, Möbius, has discovered the Unitary Theory of Elementary Particles, which will give man greater control of nature than even atomic fission. He has retired to an insane asylum and assumed the role of a fool to avoid the consequences of his discovery. Two other scientists, one who pretends to be Newton, the other Einstein, represent world powers seeking to exploit Möbius's discovery for national superiority. Möbius convinces them to remain in the madhouse to prevent the world from becoming one, to wipe themselves "out of the memory of mankind or mankind will wipe itself out. To leave the world a faint chance of survival." As they engage in their final ceremonial libation, "to be mad but wise, prisoners but free, physicists but innocent," the efficient, deformed female scientist who runs the asylum discloses that she has already stolen Möbius's secret, put it to use, and now controls the world, which has become the victim of an "insane female barren psychiatrist."

Meteor (1965) concerns a Nobel Prize winner for literature who will not die, even after he is buried, for he is too full of life and love. He returns to earth to riddle the hypocrisy of the living with his corrosive wit and love of the truth. The trivial, the pretentious, and the tawdry have survived his death, and he comes back for another blast at human stupidity. In the end, he stands alone on the threshold of mortality, the complete individualist, the merciless seeker after truth, aghast at the realization that he still lives.

So too with Duerrenmatt, relentless seeker of truth, who despite his pessimism respects the basic courage of man. As Akki, the beggar, says in *The Angel Comes to Babylon:* "in front of us, sandstorms our faces scarring, high cliffs our freedom barring, and in the distance a land rising out of the dusk, full of new persecutions, new promise and songs of a new morning."

Max Frisch—"Repetition . . . that's all life is, repetition . . . that's the curse . . ."

Max Frisch, trained as an architect, turned to writing when he was in the Swiss army, stationed on the border at the time of Hitler's rise to power. Perhaps because they were outsiders who were never actively involved in the world events which surround them, Duerrenmatt and Frisch had a broader historical perspective than other European playwrights. Both deal with major world problems. Both are bitterly sardonic. But Frisch leans closer to Brecht's position that man never learns from history. *The Chinese Wall* is the *Mother Courage* of the age of the hydrogen bomb. Frisch has been a prolific writer. He has to his credit two novels, *Stiller* and *Homo Faber,* and many plays, *Santa Cruz* (1944), *When the War Was Over* (1949), *Count Oderland* (1951), *Don Juan or The Love of Geometry* (1953), and *Biography—A Game* (1967), but we shall be concerned here with his three most important works, *The Chinese Wall* (1955), *Biedermann and the Arsonists* (1959), and *Andorra* (1961).

The Chinese Wall, like most of his plays and Duerrenmatt's, has several versions. The original 1946 version, prompted by the dropping of the first atomic bomb at Hiroshima, was revised in 1955. The prologue and twenty-four scenes follow the structure of *The Good Woman of Seztuan.* The Contemporary, dressed in modern clothes, steps forward and announces that in the farce about to be performed he will play the role of an "intellectual."[5] He explains that the Chinese Wall before which he stands, now in disrepair and no longer serviceable, was designed by the glorious emperor Hwang-Ti as a defensive barrier against foreign invasion and an enduring tribute to preserve his mighty conquests. The scene is ancient China, the Emperor the symbol of tyrants of all ages. Most of the action takes place at a party to celebrate the completion of the Wall. Famous figures of history—Philip of Spain, Pontius Pilate, Napoleon, Christopher Columbus, Brutus, Cleopatra—as well as figures of the literary imagination—Romeo and Juliet, Don Juan, and L'Inconnue de la Seine—appear in a coalescence of time.

The Contemporary runs around trying to convince the historical figures that times have changed, that technology has altered the world, that the methods of the past no longer can succeed, that "whoever sits on a throne today holds the human race in his hand . . . a slight whim on the part of the man on the throne, a nervous breakdown, a touch of neurosis, a flame struck by his madness, a moment of impatience on account of indigestion and it's all over. Everything! a cloud of yellow or brown ashes boiling up towards the heavens in the shape of a mushroom, a dirty cauliflower and the rest is silence—radioactive silence."[6]

No one pays any attention to him. No one learns from history. Brutus wants to pursue his ideals, Cleopatra wants to "inspire great men," and Philip of Spain wants to continue the Inquisition. On a separate level, indicating the hollowness of political majesty, Hwang-Ti seeks an unknown Min Ko, the voice of the people, whose poems of protest are sung everywhere. Total victory for the Emperor means liquidating Min Ko. A mute peasant is brought forth and executed. The Contemporary knows the victim is innocent but is powerless to stop the Emperor. He uses reason, the lessons of history, the dictates of humanity, but is cowed by the Emperor's dagger. In the end, he and Mee Lan, the lovely Princess, are alone, defeated, weak and helpless. They have witnessed man's drive to self-destruction and are unable to alter events. Mee Lan says in the final words of the play, "I have come to understand you, and I love you. I, the arrogant, kneel before you, the scorned and despised, and I love you. And now it is you who are mute."[7] Frisch is devastatingly pessimistic, but the play is a beautiful pageant of color, wit and theatrical imagination depicting the ugly side of man. Although world war is inconceivable today, Frisch says, history will be repeated. The play is not a prediction but a warning.

Total destruction is the theme repeated in *Biedermann and the Arsonists* (1959), the most complex of Frisch's plays and the most terrifying in its depiction of the rise of totalitarian power through the unwilling complicity of all of us. Gottlieb Biedermann (the German equivalent for Babbitt, or Everyman, the solid bourgeois citizen with the ironic first name of "loved by God") is a successful manufacturer of hair tonic. He lives in his own home with a dutiful maid and a complying wife. He is ruthless in dealing with business associates but when the arsonists invite themselves into his home, he is unable to take a stand. He permits them to sleep in the attic, arranges an elaborate dinner for them, and, though he knows that they have brought in gasoline drums, fuses, and detonating caps, supplies them with matches. He fears opposing those who are in power. He relies on the pleasantries of conventional living to appease them. He will not recognize reality even when it is thrust in his face. He tries to save his own skin and not get involved, hoping that disaster will pass him by. If he is on their side, the arsonists will protect him. "If I report them to the police," he says, "I'll make enemies of them." His house goes up in flames and he winds up in Hell, still not having learned from experience. A chorus of impotent firemen stand guard, predict catastrophe, and do nothing about it. Frisch had written in his journal: "As long as people who desire Good, do not become evil, the evil have a splendid time of it." In Hell, still convinced of his innocence, still seeking to preserve his own skin, although it is already burnt to a crisp, Biedermann turns to his wife and asks if they have been saved. Hitler's rise to power followed the line of the arsonists—infiltration by getting a foot in the door of established institutions, reliance on the refusal of the middle class to act motivated by self-preservation. Once given an inch, the forces of destruction take over completely. Unlike most of Frisch's work, *Biedermann and the Arsonists* does have an impressive message—don't invite the enemy in for dinner and don't give him the matches. But Biedermann's world is already too inwardly corrupt— each man in trying to save himself brings down the world. As the chorus of firemen exclaim at the end:

> What all have foreseen
> From the outset
> and yet in the end it takes place,
> Is idiocy

ANDORRA

Andorra is the simplest and most direct of Frisch's works. Andri, a young man of twenty, has always considered himself a Jew and is so regarded in freedom-loving Andorra, a fictional community that has no relationship to the actual state of that name. He is in love with Barblin, the daughter of the village schoolteacher who has adopted him and who is not a Jew. Beyond the border, the Black Shirts are steadily advancing. With a Nazi takeover imminent, hidden prejudices rise to the surface, Those who liked Andri now find reasons for rejecting him. He is insulted in the local inn. A cabinetmaker puts obstacles in his way to bar him as an apprentice. The Doctor, the intellectual of Andorra, inadvertently lets slip derogatory comments about Jews. The Soldier rapes Barblin and beats up Andri, knowing the boy cannot rally public support. Lip service to individual liberties vanishes.

At the end of the first act, the boy's Mother appears.

She is not Jewish nor is his Father, who turns out to be the
man at whose home he is living. The Father had invented
the story of rescuing Andri from Jewish refugees to save
himself from public scandal and to protect his family life.
When the Priest welcomes Andri into the fold, the boy
rejects the invitation. He has lived all his life as a Jew and
he will remain a Jew, despite the protestations of the Priest,
his Father and Barblin. Twenty years of suffering cannot
be erased by a belated confession. Anti-Semitism is now
presented from an unexpected angle: prejudice has had no
basis in fact, the same theme Arthur Miller explored in
his early novel *Focus*. The people of Andorra are haunted
by spiritual nakedness and Andri remains a Jew because
their conscience demands it. The town is ready for the
Black Shirts to move in without opposition. The two most
completely developed scenes are those after the Occupation.
The Andorrans are lined up in the public square, made to
remove their shoes and parade masked before the Juden-
beschauer (the Jew Detector). A token offering is needed for
the village to avoid persecution and to display compliance.
The first to pass inspection is the Village Idiot, the others
follow in order of their willingness to submit. When Andri
appears, the Jew Detector sniffs him all over, examines his
feet, and declares him a Jew. The Father wildly shouts that
he is his own son. The villagers do not protest. Andri is
their salvation, a blood sacrifice to cowardice and human
degradation. The boy is led off to be executed. Barblin, now
mad, her hair shaved off, is on her knees, whitewashing the
asphalt of the public square. She caresses Andri's shoes, the
only objects still lying in the center of the stage. The Priest
says, "Her father hanged himself in the schoolroom. She is
looking for her father, she is looking for her hair, she is
looking for her brother." He tells Barblin that her hair will
grow again, and she replies, "like the grass out of the
graves."[9]

Out of her mental breakdown rises a bitter condemnation of all who shared in Andri's death and believed "it can't happen here." Each character—the miserable innkeeper, the churlish carpenter, the lecherous Soldier, the vain Doctor, and the Priest with his excess of ill-directed goodwill—has a chance to speak for himself. In T. S. Eliot's *Murder in the Cathedral,* the four assassins explain their motives after the deed. In *Andorra,* everyone who shares the collective guilt addresses the audience before the deed, pleading for understanding and exhorting the audience not to hold him responsible. In a parody of the Nuremberg trials the problem of anti-Semitism merges with the issue of war guilt. Self-pity and loss of dignity hide behind protestations of ignorance. Everyone sounds alike and all cease to be individuals. Only Andri and Barblin are worthy of specific names since they have faced life truthfully and have been willing to suffer the consequences of their deeds. The others have lost identity and are as interchangeable as the Watsons and the Smiths of Ionesco's *The Bald Soprano.*

The play unfolds on two levels: the story of Andri and Barblin, and the community's involvement with the Black Shirts, individual love, and man's responsibility for his fellow man. Neither can survive in an atmosphere of hate. Without shoes, man is pathetically naked and anonymous. Frisch uses the technique of the trial scene, so often the culmination point in Brecht's plays as well as in *The Visit of the Old Lady* and *Biography.* In Andorra the presentation of evidence is replaced by the public examination of the entire village by the Jew Detector. Black-uniformed soldiers with machine guns and expressionless faces ring the plaza as the Andorrans, huddled in one corner, remove their shoes and pass for certification before the dehumanized stare of the expert. The fact that Andri is not a Jew (or is he?), that he is young, capable of love, and thirsting for life makes his murder a grim rebuke to those who would make him over in the mold of their own preconceptions.

Frisch's insistence that man never learns from experience is balanced by the implication of his plays that we must learn from history if civilization is to survive. Like Bertolt Brecht, he is an artist transforming the theatre into a moment of awareness and a forum for judgment.

German Playwrights and the Documentary

Peter Weiss, the best known of the contemporary German writers, mainly because of the success of *Marat/Sade,* follows in the political footsteps of Bertolt Brecht, about whom he said, "Brecht never wrote for the sake of the dramatic event but rather to show how the world is and how to change it."[10] Weiss was born in Germany but fled when Hitler came to power and became a Swedish citizen, but he is close to the younger playwrights of West Germany— Heinar Kipphardt and Rolf Hochhuth—in his dedication to the theatre as an instrument of social change. They have eschewed experiments with fantasy, symbol, and abstract expressionism and seized upon Epic Theatre techniques as a method of reordering historical events. Their partisan political preoccupations and lesser artistic control of the medium ignored Brecht's admonition for entertainment with a message and reverted to straight factual documentation. In *The Investigation* and *In the Matter of J. Robert Oppenheimer* the playwright becomes an archivist, the dramatist turned editor, poring over court records, newspaper files, and tape-recorded testimony. It was the logical end of realism: a reliance on the horrifying and often unbearable testimony of fact.

During the Hitler regime there was little theatre of significance in Germany. The best minds had fled before the war, and, after the collapse of the Third Reich, the sense of despair and defeat left a nation stunned and inarticulate. It is ironic that the revival should have been occasioned by the Marxist impetus of Bertolt Brecht, but it took ten years after peace was restored before confidence and recognition of guilt as well as economic prosperity permitted a theatre of open discussion. The success of the Berliner Ensemble in East Berlin, and its international triumphs prompted intensive efforts in West Berlin to display a rival theatre of competitive excellence. But whereas Brecht set his sights on the future, his disciples in West Germany were trying to undo the past.

If history has a purpose and direction, the documentary becomes the logical method of unraveling cause-and-effect relationships. With the present German playwrights the effort is made to extend realism to its simplest original form, the dramatization of the headline. The upsurge of romanticism in the nineteenth century had protected middle-class audiences from a theatre of social concern. But the growth of technology, the rise of urban centers, and pressing social disintegration called for the presentation on stage of the raw aspects of existence, the lives of the neglected and misbegotten, the poverty-stricken, the outcast, prostitutes and beggars, criminals and derelicts. The German theatre proved fertile soil for the antiromantic movement from Hauptmann's *The Weavers* to Georg Kaiser's working-class dramas and agitprop *Lehrstucke* of Bertolt Brecht.

The question persists whether, apart from its social mission, recital of events constitutes an art form and whether the newspaper or camera cannot do a better job than the playwright. It is an academic question that clings to old criteria to judge a work of art. In arranging his material, the playwright selects, emphasizes, distorts, exaggerates, and imposes a point of view, transforming reality and rearranging history, giving form to the chaos of experience. When successful, it can be highly effective theatre.

In the days of the Depression in the United States the Federal Theatre Project initiated "The Living Newspaper," which evolved independently a dramatic technique similar to Brecht's, using multiple episodes, technical devices, pro-

jections, film interludes, and numerous blackouts. Such
scripts as "One Third of a Nation" (slum housing) "Power"
(the Tennessee Valley Authority and government-owned
electrical energy) "Spirochete" (venereal disease) broke with
traditional theatre practice and shocked a nation into realization of the need for social action. The point of view is
the determining element. Mere facts can be misleading and
misinterpreted or used to bolster one's own convictions.
What is essential, as Peter Weiss has said, is to "show the
society behind the images, the alternative to the stage disaster."[11] In a dislocated age, the documentary serves as a
reminder to the conscience of a people.

Peter Weiss—"and so we wrote into the declaration of the rights of man, the holy rights of property."

Peter Weiss's *The Investigation* (1965), which was
given simultaneous productions in sixteen German cities, is
a reenactment of the Auschwitz war-crimes trial. Almost no
action occurs as the accused and the accusers sit or stand in
ascending rows and tell what they have seen. The only
dramatic event is the confrontation of the victims and their
oppressors and the interruptions of opposing lawyers. The
accused plead either ignorance or inability to understand
any wrong that they may have committed. All the speeches
and statements are reports or extracts from trial records.
The facts pile up: the exact measurements of the gas ovens,
the quality of the ingredients of the poisons, the payments
received, the medical experiments attempted, the profitable
business the extermination camps offered to the chemical
giants of future German recovery, the callous, cynical, and
arrogant indifference of those involved and the calm emo-
tionless recital of the victims. No names are used. The word
Jew is rarely mentioned, for Weiss believed that "personal
experience and confrontations must be steeped in anonym-
ity." To him, the nine witnesses sum up what hundreds of

others expressed. The play ends with the final words of "Accused No. I," who says:

> All of us
> I want to make that very clear
> did nothing but our duty
> even when that duty was hard
> and even when it grieved us to do it.[12]

When Ingmar Bergman directed the play in Sweden, he kept intense lights on the audience as well as on the stage to eliminate the sense of isolation, to indicate that the problem persists, that it is not Auschwitz but all mankind. The individuals are symbols of a system that implicated others who never appeared in court.

The original script is overlong and was drastically cut for the New York production. The political climate and the sensitivity of audiences determined the play's effectiveness. Weiss is a man with a mission, using the theatre to illustrate problems and point out solutions. He said, "My plays do not have conventional lead roles. The lead roles are played by history and ideas." His next play, the *Song of the Lusitania Bogey,* is an indictment of the Portuguese suppression of the people of Angola and was intended as one of a series on oppressors and the oppressed, a sort of Divine Comedy in which Weiss would put the rich in Hell, the poor in Paradise, and "the intellectuals and artists who shirk their responsibilities in Purgatory." *The Lusitania Bogey* was a successful production of the Negro Ensemble Company in New York.

MARAT/SADE

Weiss achieved international fame with Peter Brook's production by the Royal Shakespeare Company of the amazingly entitled play *The Persecution and Assassination*

*of Marat as Performed by the Inmates of the Asylum of
Charenton Under the Direction of the Marquis de Sade*
(1964). More briefly known as *Marat/Sade,* the play was a
historical landmark in contemporary theatrical experience.
Konrad Swinarski directed the Berlin production; Ingmar
Bergman the one in Stockholm; Roger Planchon in Paris.
The Peter Brook version also became an internationally
distributed motion picture.

The action takes place in an insane asylum, the symbol
in so many contemporary plays of the retreat from the insanity of the world outside, the place where madness
evolves its own rationale. As the inmates and the attendants
undergo their daily routines, the central conflict is between
the Marquis de Sade, the black saint of personal pleasure,
and Marat, the dedicated martyr for social justice. The
device is a play within a play, a work that de Sade impro-
vises for the inmates to perform as a contribution to group
therapy. The language is in varied verse forms that shift
rhythms from long speeches to choral chants. The director
of the asylum (who is a spectator), the audience in the
theatre, and the institution employees represent different
levels of interrelated response to the debate of the principal
characters. To de Sade:

> Man is a destroyer
> but if he kills and takes no pleasure in it
> he is a machine
> He should destroy with passion
> like a man[13]

He decries the absence of pleasurable death, the presence of
murder that has become anonymous and cheap,

> which he could dole out to entire nations
> on a mathematical basis

> until the time comes
> for all life
> to be extinguished

Marat acts against nature's silence and contends:

> The important thing
> is to pull yourself up by your own hair
> to turn yourself inside out
> and see the whole world with fresh eyes

Marat, sick and dying, is attended by Simonne, who bathes him in vinegar and water, but his thoughts are on a better world, a world in which "the holy right of property" will no longer be written into the declaration of the rights of man. For de Sade, the only reality is imagination, "the world inside myself." In the stirring masochistic scene when Charlotte Corday whiplashes the naked back of de Sade, he chants his litany:

> To the withering of the individual man
> and a slow merging into uniformity

Marat is the selfless revolutionary; de Sade, the detached voyeur. Marat would change the world to glorify the individual; de Sade knows man dies unknown leaving little trace behind. The decision is made when the play is actually performed. The inmates transform the words they enact into a reality. In wild ecstasy, violent action, spinning and dancing, they move forward. De Sade laughs triumphantly as Jacques Roux, a former priest, exclaims,

> When will you learn to see
> When will you learn to take sides

The curtain comes down as the revolution threatens to engulf the world outside.

Weiss's preferences are clearly on the side of Marat.

He objected to Peter Brook's imposition of the techniques of Artaud's Theatre of Cruelty, which emphasized theatrical shock rather than political debate. He preferred the East German production, in which Marat is the hero and de Sade a representative of the doomed Western cult of the individual libertine. Peter Brook admits the play is "firmly on the side of a revolutionary change but it is painfully aware of all the elements in a violent human situation and it presents those to the audience in the form of a painful question" which leaves the responsibility of finding answers "back where it properly belongs"—with the audience.

Rolf Hochhuth—". . . to what extent can the fence-sitters be guilty?"

The impact of Rolf Hochhuth's documentary plays spread beyond the theatre and occasioned worldwide heated political controversy. In *The Deputy* (1963) he assailed the Vatican with the accusation that Pope Pius XII had placed expediency before principle in failing to speak out against Hitler's extermination of the Jews. In *Soldiers* (1967) he implied that Winston Churchill instigated the death of General Sikorski, head of the Polish Government in exile, to appease the Russians. In attacking two giants of contemporary history, Hochhuth was not seeking publicity but raising on the highest level the question of responsibility. If lesser men plead obedience to orders, what about those who are in a position to give orders? Churchill is forced to choose between public and private morality. The Pope is caught between investments and conscience. How shall the rest of mankind act, "to what extent can the fence-sitters be guilty?" is the question both plays raise. To Hochhuth if the individual can no longer be held responsible, then we have an alibi for all guilt "and that would mean the end of drama."[14]

For *Soldiers,* the British National Theatre refused to

grant permission for production despite the efforts of its artistic director, Laurence Olivier, and it had its premiere in West Berlin. If Brecht used the theatre as a courtroom in which the audience acts as jury, Hochhuth acts as judge and jury. *The Deputy* caused riots and demonstrations wherever it opened, even in New York, where the American Nazi Party picketed on the opening night.

Both plays are similar in structure. They contain numerous episodes, large casts, a battering metrical prose that rarely becomes poetry, and historical characters reciting passages from historical documents. Hochhuth is more the trial lawyer than the dramatist and his unnecessarily long scripts have been radically shortened for theatrical presentation.

In *The Deputy* Hochhuth added fictional material to fill out the meager historical facts. But every incident is accompanied with detailed explanation and source material. There is a slight effort to transmute events into imaginative symbols. It remains a documented tract that cuts the silence which the German people have maintained since what C. P. Snow called "the worst episode in human history."

The full script is in five acts and nine episodes and requires more than eight hours for production. It has been cut, rearranged and differently interpreted depending on the individual director and local political climate. Hochhuth's facts are unassailable, but his fictional embroidery make him vulnerable to charges of romanticizing character in the heroic style of Schiller to overemphasize a point. The action centers around Father Riccardo Fontana, a young Jesuit priest who becomes aware of Hitler's gas chambers and pins the Star of David on his cassock, and joins the Jews at Auschwitz when the Pope, the Vicar of Christ, refuses to speak out against genocide. To the Pope, he exclaims, "God shall not destroy His Church only because a Pope shrinks from His summons."[15] Most of the characters are cardboard figures and rarely convincing. The doctor in charge of the camps is a diabolical monster of evil, debating theology with the priest in fatigued cynicism, a mechanical Mephistopheles who acts, not out of orders from above, but with an arrogant belief in the historical need of Nazi experimentation. Kurt Gerstein, a member of the SS who gives his own life to save the victims of Hitler, simplistically represents the conscience of man.

The total effect of the play is overwhelming. It projects the theatre into active political commitment in defense of the spiritual mission of man. In calling the Pope to account, Hochhuth responded to Albert Camus's insistence that we "have a right to expect the most of those whose mission it is to represent the spirit."

Soldiers subtitled *An Obituary for Geneva* opens in Coventry in 1964, one hundred years after the signing of the first Geneva Convention. The Everyman figure (Group Captain Dorland is rehearsing "The Little London Theatre of the World," a reenactment of the few months in 1943 when Winston Churchill sanctioned the saturation bombing of German cities and eliminated General Sikorski to prevent Stalin from making a separate treaty with Hitler. The Prologue and Epilogue provide the play-within-a-play framework for Dorland's editorial comments and exorcism of his own guilt and the general conclusion that "history is the disproportion between intention and result." The action that follows is interrupted by a return to the rehearsal at Coventry. When Bishop Bell pleads for cessation of civilian bombing on humanitarian grounds, news of Sikorski's death is received, and the Bishop, seeing the Prime Minister deeply moved, comments that Sikorski was Churchill's friend. The Prime Minister replies, "Men may be linked in friendship. Nations are linked only by interest."

The two political themes—terror bombing and political assassination—do not mesh well, and long discussions are like political debates without action. Lord Cherwell, the atomic physicist who advocates victory at any cost, is the villain of the play. Churchill surprisingly grows in stature as a tragic figure, knowing his decisions affect the lives of millions but compelled to use immoral means for moral ends.

Heinar Kipphardt, who follows in the tradition of the theatre of fact, was a practicing psychiatrist before he became artistic director of the Deutsches Theatre in Berlin. *The General's Dog* and *Joel Brandt* established his reputation as a playwright in Germany, but his international reputation was achieved with *In the Matter of J. Robert Oppenheimer* which was first presented in 1964 at the Free People's Theatre in Berlin and given its American premiere at the Mark Taper Forum in Los Angeles.

The play deals with the events of April–May 1954 when physicist Dr. J. Robert Oppenheimer appeared before the Personnel Security Board of the Atomic Energy Commission for the purpose of determining his security status. The results are well known. Oppenheimer was declared a loyal American, but was not granted security clearance. He returned to Princeton as director of the Institute of Advanced Studies and did not participate in the development of the hydrogen bomb.

Kipphardt's play is a reenactment of the hearings. There is no plot in the usual sense and no suspense, but what almost amounts to a tape recording of the investigation. What results is not the story of Oppenheimer, the man, so much as a dramatization of questions that need to be asked. What is the moral responsibility of the scientist? Can the terrifying power of new weaponry be available to a society unfit to use it other than destructively? Is a scientist's loyalty to the nation or to mankind? Is the nation an outworn concept? The all-male cast debates the fundamental issues which still persist even though the events surrounding

Oppenheimer took place during the McCarthy period. Kipphardt's own sympathy obviously lies with Oppenheimer. Edward Teller, the atomic expert, is the villain of the piece,
but the play is less concerned with individuals than with
the historical questions raised by their confrontation.

The government's case against Oppenheimer is impressive. His first wife and his brother were members of the
Communist party. He himself liked to be called a "fellow
traveler." His genius was never questioned, but his naïve
saintliness rendered him a political danger. Does belief in
the principles of the Communist party presume disloyalty?
Is the political party in power alone capable of patriotism?
Oppenheimer felt that the Popular Front was the hope of
mankind. Yet despite his political leanings, he proceeded
to become the father of the A-bomb and the director of the
Los Alamos Project. Like many scientists, he never thought
that the power he had discovered would be unleashed. He
therefore opposed the development of the H-bomb on the
ground that the political organization of man was not ready
for it.

As in Peter Weiss's *The Investigation* and Max Frisch's
Andorra, Kipphardt has the principal characters step forward and address the audience in a self-explanatory confession while all others are frozen until the soliloquy is
finished.

The limitations of the documentary form are apparent.
History dramatized can be effective theatre, but too often
convinces the already convinced. Imagination and action,
symbol and poetry, can more effectively reach the hearts of
man, but the documentary writers have transformed the
German theatre into a vital force in contemporary political
life.

15. The English Theatre
—Osborne, Pinter, Shaffer

LOOK BACK IN ANGER
THE HOMECOMING
THE ROYAL HUNT OF THE SUN

MAY 1956, WHEN JOHN OSBORNE's *Look Back in Anger* was presented at the Royal Court Theatre, is generally regarded as the turning point in contemporary English drama. No date can precisely define a change in artistic direction. The revolt against a flaccid, polite, respectable drawing-room theatre was years in the making, but with the success of Osborne's play, the floodgates were opened for new voices, new techniques, and new audiences. George Devine with his young assistant, Tony Richardson, had already presented in April of that year Angus Wilson's *The Mulberry Bush*, a play excoriating public philanthropy and English liberalism. Joan Littlewood at her experimental Workshop had launched Brendan Behan's *The Quare Fellow,* and Bertolt Brecht's Berliner Ensemble had paid its first visit to London.

Since the retirement of George Bernard Shaw and Sean O'Casey, the theatre had belonged to Noel Coward and Terence Rattigan and plays filled with clever dialogue, witty innuendos and the neurotic problems of supersophisticated society. T. S. Eliot wrote infrequently and Graham Greene was rewriting dramas of lost souls recovering faith through present-day miracles. The Royal Court production of *Look Back in Anger* gave heart to a host of new play-

315

wrights—John Arden, Ann Jellicoe, N. F. Simpson, Arnold Wesker, Alun Owen, Peter Shaffer, Shelagh Delaney and John Mortimer—who put lower-class characters, rebellious youth, prostitutes and charwomen on stage, characters who spoke language that was hard, direct and, in many cases, regional. The movement was ill-defined and in need of a focus, but the energy it released revitalized the theatre. With the exception of Harold Pinter, however, no new techniques were developed. In most cases the available traditional forms were used to attack traditional institutions and attitudes.

The Royal Shakespeare Company, a summer operation in Stratford on Avon under the aggressive and imaginative leadership of Peter Brook and Peter Hall, opened a London theatre at the Aldwych and offered all year round productions of Brecht, Genet, Duerrenmatt, and Pinter, with emphasis on the Theatre of Cruelty and social realism. Their work culminated in the shattering production of Peter Weiss's *Marat/Sade*. The inspiration of the Royal Shakespeare Company came from the Berliner Ensemble, and the intention was to form a well-trained company of cohesion, strength, precision, and ability to work in varied styles. Shakespeare was adjusted to the new spirit. Long presented with stuffy rhetoric, elaborate sets, and garish costumes, Shakespeare's plays were subjected to the new method of "collision with masterpieces" and relieved of the encumbrances of traditional interpretations. David Warner played Hamlet as a shambling intellectual, avoiding commitment, rejecting the sick values of a corrupt society, but drawn, nevertheless, into involvement he could not resist. The National Theatre under Laurence Olivier, its artistic director, and Kenneth Tynan, its literary manager, fashioned in three years one of the finest acting companies in the world, and offered an all male *As You Like It* as well as recharged Restoration dramas, and plays by John Osborne,

Peter Shaffer, and John Arden. Playwrights became involved in active collaboration, but the distinctive quality of the company sprang from the intelligent use of the actor's imagination and such able performers as Albert Finney, Robert Stephens, Maggie Smith, and Geraldine McEwan. But apart from the two "great battleships" of the British Theatre, as George Devine termed them, the new magic was supplied by Devine's English Stage Company and Joan Littlewood's Theatre Workshop, both small theatres not associated with the capital's West End.

LOOK BACK IN ANGER

John Osborne—"There aren't any good, brave causes left."

Look Back in Anger did not arouse popular enthusiasm until Kenneth Tynan, drama critic of the *Observer* wrote, "I agree that *Look Back in Anger* is likely to remain a minority play. What matters, however, is the size of the minority. I estimate it at roughly 6,733,000, which is the number of people in this country between 20 and 30. . . . I doubt if I could love anyone who did not wish to see *Look Back in Anger;* it is the best young play of its decade." That started it, and the controversy raged on in the press and on television. The epithet "the angry young writers" was applied indiscriminately to all who opposed entrenched authority.

Look Back in Anger is written in the conventional, realistic form of a family drama. The set is the one-room dingy flat of Jimmy Porter and his wife Allison in the Midlands. The furniture is not the fashionably designed upholstered pieces of the middle class but the gas stove, cluttered bed, and ironing board of those living on a marginal income. Allison is in her slip most of the time, doing housework or ironing Jimmy's shirts or Cliff's pants. The two men operate a sweet shop. Jimmy, a university-bred man, refuses to be part of the faceless business or professional world and rails against established society. He is a rebel without a cause, but the life to which he has withdrawn is equally dull. He uses his wife as a scapegoat, ridiculing her well-to-do parents. When Allison, who is pregnant, leaves and is replaced by Helena, Jimmy is equally unable to generate love. In the end, in the most moving scene of the play, Allison returns. She has lost her child and now comes crawling helplessly back to Jimmy. She says, "I don't want to be neutral. I don't want to be a saint. I want to be a lost cause. I want to be corrupt and futile."[1] They revert to an infantile world of animal games, two defeated souls, clinging to each other in self-pity and self-destruction.

Jimmy became a symbol of a lost generation, unwilling to accept social procedures, lacking in purpose and direction, and contemptuous of an England which lived on past glory, rigid class lines and outward gentility. Audiences were shocked at the direct language, the vehement tirades against traditional respectability, and the rebellious, though inchoate, anger of youth. But Jimmy Porter, wasting away in self-flagellation, whining about his wasted talents, abusing mercilessly his uncomplaining wife is hardly a courageous figure. What he is against is never clear. What he is for is even vaguer. He chooses personal debasement and exile from reality. His anger seems less directed at the social structure than at his exclusion from it. He ends by negating everything, by reducing Allison to nothingness—a process of destruction that satisfies his sadistic needs.

When it was first presented, the play shocked British audiences. Twelve years later, at its successful revival in London, audiences no longer responded to Jimmy's social malaise. The play survived on the human level, as a pathetic portrayal of young people unable to discover creative self-fulfillment under conditions which inhibited personal involvement: a psychological drama of distressed souls.

Years later, when Osborne was part of the literary establishment, he rejected every association with angry rebels. "What emerged," he said about the historic 1956 opening, "was eloquent of the country and the times. Layers of expression found an outlet." The outcry was not against a senseless rational ordering of a scientifically manipulated industrial society, but against preserved traditions that stifled new voices.

Epitaph for George Dillon (1958) is an earlier work, written in collaboration with Anthony Creighton but first presented after the success of *Look Back in Anger*. Again the central character is a nonhero uttering his cry of anguish against British complacency. Dillon, an actor and writer, is living off a guillible family in a simple house outside London. Like Jimmy Porter, he pities himself and rails against the world's failure to recognize him. But Dillon has his own doubts about his talent. Ruth, an ex-Communist who has broken with the party and is searching for positive values, compels him to strip away his illusions. He composes his own epitaph for the death of artistic integrity, rewrites his play for a producer of tawdry, provincial, lewd melodramas, and resigns himself to a dull suburban life. In *The Entertainer* (1957) as in *The World of Paul Slickey* and *Luther,* Osborne fumbled with a Brechtian style without ever mastering the technique. *The Entertainer* is about a fading, music-hall character who is unable to respond to honest human feelings and says, "I'm dead behind these eyes. I'm dead just like the whole inert shoddy lot out there. It doesn't matter because I don't feel a thing and neither do they. We're just as dead as each other." He goes through his routine of brash, vulgar jokes and jingoistic songs and, as he does, enacts his own failure, his own lack of belief. "Nothing touches me. Emotion is dead," he says. The vaudeville routines and musical numbers interrupt the action, enabling Osborne, like Brecht, to comment upon the action.

The *World of Paul Slickey* is a *Comedy of Manners with Music* about the ugly subworld of gossip columnists, replete with vitriolic attacks on the Church, the H-bomb, and every social and political issue of the day. It wallows in adultery, homosexuality, and the final solution to upper-class boredom—a change of sex. It is Osborne's lone attempt at a drastic variation of form, and its disastrous reception sent him scurrying back to safer models in the manner of George Dillon. Though he later rejected his association with the angry playwrights, Osborne was thoroughly angry at this point and wrote a series of tasteless attacks on the Establishment: *A Subject of Scandal and Concern* for television, two one-act *Plays for England,* in which *The Blood of the Bambergs* assails the monarchy and *Under Plain Cover* attacks the press. Later works confirm the impression that Osborne had failed to fulfill the promise of his first play. *A Patriot for Me, A Bond Honored, Time Present,* and *A Hotel in Amsterdam* (1968) were feeble and unsuccessful efforts to keep his name before a willing public. The two plays worth commenting on are *Luther* (1961) and *Inadmissible Evidence* (1964).

Luther, another try at social realism, presents a historical figure in epic style. But whereas Brecht's work has a point of view, designed to change human nature and the world, Osborne fails to give his material dramatic power. Scenes sputter and die out. Luther is left angry but stripped of majesty. A great figure who redirected events, broke the power of the Catholic Church, unleashed the Peasant Revolt, and reestablished the direct relationship of man to God was reduced to a neurotic figure who rejects his father, discusses his physical infirmities—epilepsy and constipation—and is preoccupied with infancy: "I am a child, the lost body of a child. I am stillborn." The drama of Luther's life lay outside the play, suggested but never encompassed.

Inadmissible Evidence contains some of Osborne's most

brilliant writing, but the dramatic effect is diminished in a sprawling loosely woven second act. Bill Maitland, a middle-aged adulterer, a sex-obsessed lawyer, is being tried by his own moral conscience. The play is virtually a long monologue in which Maitland is both defense and prosecuting attorney for himself; the scene changes from the reality of his office to the courtroom of his mind. As his life passes in review, Maitland is revealed as a man racked by the same problems facing most modern men—the substitution of fashion for feeling, the absence of genuine love, the concern with self, the reduction of passion to mediocrity—all the psychic and spiritual crimes which maim and deform the human being and yet are not admissible as evidence in court. The most telling scene is between Maitland and his teen-age daughter, during which she remains speechless as he delivers a ten-minute speech. Reaching out for love but unable to communicate, he turns to violence and ends in frustration and callous rejection of feeling. Maitland makes the play and Osborne was fortunate in having Nicol Williamson, an actor of wide range and great talent, perform the part, which remains an actor's tour de force. Maitland is a more understanding, more degenerate, more repulsive, and older Jimmy Porter.

THE HOMECOMING

Harold Pinter—"The more acute the experience,
the less articulate its expression."

Most English playwrights have worked within the established realistic form. Harold Pinter is almost alone in exploring, within a carefully articulated set of conventions, the irrational world of Pirandello, Ionesco, and Beckett. From Pirandello he took the uncertainty of human motivation and the unpredictability of action. In *A Slight Ache* a self-satisfied, comfortable, established writer of philosophical essays changes places with a street-corner peddler of matches whom the wife invites into the house, bathes, feeds, and accepts as a mythic hero. Pinter had written that "a character on stage who can present no convincing argument or information as to his past experience or present behavior or his aspirations, nor give a comprehensive analysis of his motives is as legitimate and as worthy of attention as one who can alarmingly do all of these things." To which he added in his program notes for the Royal Court Theatre production of *The Dumb Waiter,* "There are no hard distinctions between what is true and what is false . . . it can be both true and false at the same time."

From Beckett and Ionesco he adopted the use of the seemingly illogical as a part of a separate logic, and the use of pauses as an element in an overall rhythmic composition to represent a fragmented world in which mystery and fear replace reason. "Communication between people is so frightening that rather than do that, there is a continual talk about other things, rather than what is at the root of their relationship."

In his one-act play *The Room* (1957) all of the devices which are exploited more fully in his later work are evident. In a shabby room (the womb, a place of security, a temporary refuge) Hudd, a truck driver, is eating before he leaves to drive on the icy roads. His wife does all the talking in incoherent statements interrupted by long pauses. After the husband leaves, a couple knocks at the door and asks to see the room which they have been told will soon be available. After they are dismissed, the landlord tells Mrs. Hudd that a man in the basement wants to see her. The man turns out to be a blind Negro who, despite Mrs. Hudd's denials, seems to know her past and urges her to return with him to her father's home. Hudd returns, breaks into speech for the first time as he talks animatedly about his trip, and then beats the Negro to death. Mrs. Hudd goes blind as the play ends. The reason for action is vague. The menace comes from the outside, transforming the inner room into a nightmare of Kafkaesque terror. The language is conventional, everyday talk, but placed in unusual circumstances in which every clear statement is followed by its opposite. A simple realistic form flows into obscure symbols and suggestions of mystery and horror.

In a series of short pieces—*The Dumb Waiter, The Collection, The Lover, Silence, The Landscape*—the Pinter technique is consistently effective. Varying rhythms, orchestration of sounds, the interplay of fact and fancy, and the nameless, inarticulate fears achieve shattering impact. In *The Dumb Waiter* two men on a dull Friday morning, in a basement bedroom, discuss football, and whether it is proper to "light the kettle, or light the gas." They turn out to be hired killers awaiting orders that are to come down the dumbwaiter. Orders do come down for food and objects. They obey, sending up whatever they have as the orders grow increasingly wilder. They review their instructions. Gus goes out to the lavatory. Ben receives orders to kill Gus. They face each other in cold opposition as the curtain comes down. The menace may lie hidden within the protection of the room as some unknown higher force manipulates lives. In *The Lover* (1963) a staid, conventional businessman leaves for the office and casually asks his wife if she is going to entertain her lover that day. She pleasantly replies that she is and urges her husband to come home late. She then dresses in seductive robes and opens the door to admit her lover, who turns out to be her husband now dressed in a motorcycle jacket. They act out games of seduction and crawl under the table to discover each other in a mock ritual of romantic passion. In the end, the husband tries to return to reality but the wife pleads for the game to continue. Their fantasy life is a compensation for the emotional and physical sterility of middle-class boredom.

The longer plays, *The Birthday Party, The Caretaker, The Homecoming* are masterful extensions of the Pinter-esque technique. The smaller pieces are more artistically composed. The full-length plays are occasionally repetitious but permit wider manipulation of the fantasy of fear. In *The Birthday Party*, Stanley, a small time piano player, is hiding out in a boardinghouse at a seaside resort. Two men, McCann, an Irishman, and Goldberg, a Jew, arrive to get Stanley. They are akin to the characters in *The Dumb Waiter*, but this time they have their orders. At Stanley's birthday party, they put him through a rigorous inquisition that rises in hysterical intensity until Stanley finally collapses. In a bowler hat and striped pants, he meekly goes off with them.

The Caretaker (1960), a three-character play, is more lucid in the revelation of motives. The same charged dialogue is present with pauses, rapid speech, half sentences, and long monologues, but the menace has been reduced and the characters' background and present life are more carefully delineated. Aston invites an old tramp, Davies, to stay in the room which is cluttered with odds and ends, heaped-up furniture, and materials from which some day he hopes to build a shed. Aston is a refugee from shock treatment in a mental home. Mick, Aston's brother, hires Davies as a caretaker, both for his brother and for the room when it is fitted up. Davies, in desperate need of a place of his own, plays one brother against the other but is rejected by both. Each of the three characters moves in his own separate dislocated fantasies, unable to communicate, needing to be taken care of and to share in taking care of others. They are somewhat like the characters in *Waiting for Godot* for they too wait for something that may never come, filling the time with objects and exchanging simple truths that "can often be more terrifying than ambiguity and doubt."

The Homecoming (1965) was a major triumph of the Royal Shakespeare Company. Peter Brook had trained the group for a production of Genet's *The Screens,* but, when that failed, he used his actors to present an evening of Theatre of Cruelty. Some of the same actors were used for *The Homecoming,* which enabled them to use a new technique to depict the terrifying experience of the reduction of human feeling to elemental animal mechanisms. Adorned with parodic and sophisticated implications, the play is another example of realism breaking beyond its limitations to a weird, surrealistic portrayal of a family situation that makes no pretense of being an imitation of life. Again the room acts as the setting: this time a large, sparsely furnished living room. The four men who appear in the first act are coldly savage to one another; they go through the outward motions of family life in a cannibalistic ritual. "Mind you, she wasn't a bad woman," Max, the foul-mouthed father, says of his dead wife, "even though it made me sick just to look at her rotten stinking face, she wasn't a bad bitch." He roars at his sardonic son, Lenny, the owner of a stable of prostitutes, "for talking to your lousy, filthy father like that."[1] The other men are Joey, the younger brother, an inarticulate lout who trains to be a prizefighter and Sam, Max's brother, who drives a taxicab.

Teddy, the oldest son and professor of philosophy at an American university who has been away for six years, arrives with his wife, Ruth. She, as mother-mistress-wife, catalyzes the action and dominates the rest of the play. Enigmatic, sensual, and detached, she establishes a relationship with each of the men until the family proposes that she stay with them, working part time as a prostitute to support herself. Teddy looks on unruffled and takes his leave. The final scene is a tribal rite in which Ruth, the dominant female, the sex figure, sits in the chair as the three men compete to gain her favors. The apparent realism

of the set and the characters leads the audience from
familiar experiences to the bizarre world of Pinter. The
characters in *The Homecoming* cease to be psychologically
valid human beings. They are transmuted into symbols
of man debased, surviving on primeval instincts in an age
in which love and compassion no longer exist.

THE ROYAL HUNT OF THE SUN

*Peter Shaffer—"It's the only way to give life meaning . . .
die in despair or be a god yourself!"*

Detached from any association with rebellious young
writers, Peter Shaffer achieved recognition with his first
play, a well knit family drama in the established tradition
of Ibsenite realism. *Five Finger Exercises* (1958) is a taut,
tightly constructed five character suspense drama with
keenly tuned dialogue and a penetrating awareness of the
underlying psychological problems facing human beings.
The set is the overused living room in the country home
of an upper-middle-class family. The characters are the
standard ingredients of the formula drama: a dominating mother, intellectually pretentious, ashamed of her husband's lack of cultural interests, refusing to recognize
her age in the silly game she plays of being young; a
moneymaking stolid father who feels excluded, unable
to communicate with his children or wife; the son, a
rah-rah sports type, and the daughter, pretty, flippity and
very much new generation. Into this group comes Walter,
a young German refugee, as a tutor for the daughter. This
too is standard procedure, the use of an outsider who acts
as a catalyst and to whom each character turns for self-
revelation and understanding. What distinguishes this play
is that as each character finds help in self-discovery, old
wounds and deep conflicts surface and break into open

hostilities. Walter is used as the sacrificial victim, but each member of the family becomes more understanding, more human, closer to each other. Their self-centered, destructive instincts are purged as they recognize their mutual needs.

With the success of his first play, Peter Shaffer became a professional playwright; he no longer needed part-time jobs in the New York Public Library or London publishing houses to sustain himself. Four years later, two one-act plays, *The Private Ear* and *The Public Eye* proved to be delightful if mild departures from severe realism. Tchaik in *Private Ear* loves classical music but is frustrated by his inability to use his room as a place of assignation. Ted, his close friend, and a ladies' man, suggests that Tchaik use a musical background for seduction. It almost comes off, but Ted gets the girl and Tchaik remains with his music. The relationships are warm, tender, and charmingly compassionate. In *Public Eye,* Shaffer created his first figure of fantasy or half fantasy in Christoforo, a professional private eye who is also a psychiatrist, a philosopher, and a friend. He represents reason, love, and understanding. He comes between a public accountant and his wife who are involved in separation proceedings and teaches them the joy of dreams and how to love others rather than court disaster. He is a fey character who provides the mirror for self-recognition, a detective-psychiatrist with a heart.

Shaffer's next play, *The Royal Hunt of the Sun* (1964), is a giant step forward and an indication of how Brecht's influence propelled Shaffer into new directions. The play is in two acts, each in twelve sections, and deals with the conquest of Peru by Francisco Pizarro, the historical miracle in which one hundred and sixty-seven Conquistadores subdued an empire of twenty-four million. The first act is entitled "The Hunt," and the second, "The Kill." In Shaffer's own words, the play represents a theatre "involving not only words, but also mimes, masks, and magics, a ceremony to be ultimately created by the audience, whose task it will be to create for themselves in the dark, with our help, the fantastic apparition of the pre-Columbian world and the terrible magnificence of the Conquistadores." Pizarro is a man in search of new values in a crumbling world. He is a bastard by birth, feels excluded from society, and resents the efforts of the Church to impose its lack of true faith on the long established Inca religion. It is Pizarro's private, lonely, painful search for insight that permeates his preparation for the conquest, the climbing the mountains, and the inner struggle for power. The Spaniards had better weapons, lust for gold, greed, duplicity, dishonor, national pride, the Church, and Francisco Pizarro. The Incas lacked personal will, blindly worshipped the Sun God, and suffered from a sense of hopelessness born of servility.

The second half, "The Kill," contains the culminating scene of Atahuallpa, Lord of the Incas, child of the Sun God, alone with Pizarro, a Spanish general. Both are close to death; Atahuallpa at the hands of the invaders, Pizarro, from age and disease. Pizarro has tricked Atahuallpa into captivity, but during their conversation he is disarmed by the young king's humility, saintliness, and conviction that he is the Son of God. The Spaniard binds himself to Atahuallpa with a rope, hoping to save the Inca's life. The two are tied together: two civilizations joined in the pursuit of immortality.

Like a father in search of a son, the aged Spaniard confronts the young god, as Atahuallpa says, "If you kill me I will rise at dawn when my father first touches my body with light." Pizarro is exhilarated. The atheist who has denied the word of the Church is faced with the possibility of a god on earth who may be a creator of true peace, a god free of time. He cries aloud, "It's the only way to give life meaning . . . die in despair or be a god yourself."[3] Atahuallpa breaks into a wild dance in which Pizarro must join, as they are both held by the same rope. In the silence that follows Atahuallpa says, "Pizarro, you will die soon and you do not believe in your God . . . believe in me. I will give you a word and fill you with joy. . . . I will swallow death and spit it out of me." Atahuallpa gives confession to Pizarro in the Inca manner, but, when the test comes and Atahuallpa is crucified, the miracle of resurrection does not occur. Pizarro cries, "I lived between two hates, I die between two darks; blind eyes and a blind sky." The Cross of Gold will triumph and enslave a people. The narrator says, "So fell Peru. We gave her greed, hunger, and the cross, three gifts for the civilized life . . . Peru is a silent country, frozen in avarice. So fell Spain, gorged with gold, distended, now dying." But, for a brief moment, a man in search of faith has come face to face with a blinding belief in the eternal presence of God on earth. The tropical birds, the brilliant plumage, the gilded masks, the cries of men, the beating of the drums, fade into silence in a ceremonial death. Historical facts may not be in accord with Shaffer's interpretation, but that is irrelevant in the effective realization of a symbolic drama of grandeur and scope.

The plays that followed did not fulfill Shaffer's earlier promise. *Black Comedy* (1966) is a theatrical tour de force in which the action takes place in imagined darkness. *The Battle of Shrivings* (1970), with a Bertrand Russell peace-advocate faced with an irrational and rebellious poet, is a feeble effort at world-shaking philosophy in a country-house melodrama.

Arnold Wesker, who was born in the East End of London of Jewish immigrant working-class parents, has almost single-handedly continued in the tradition of Sean O'Casey writing plays of social consciousness. His trilogy, *Chicken Soup With Barley, Roots* and *I'm Talking About Jerusalem,* is a record of thirty years of proletarian history beginning in 1932. It is a belated English version of Clifford Odets's plays about Bronx Jewish families and the American depression. For Wesker, the theatre is a weapon of political awareness against the closed English society. The plays are largely autobiographical and do not stand up under the changed social conditions of a later period. About an earlier play, *Kitchen* (1958) Wesker had written, "The world might have been a stage for Shakespeare, but to me it is a kitchen; where people come and go and can not stay long enough to understand each other, and friendships, loves, and enmities are forgotten as soon as they are made." In his best play, *Chips with Everything* (1962), Wesker moved away from his obsession with the kitchen, broke with the tight realistic form, and was far more effective in conveying his social message. The play centers around the Royal Air Force, in which Pip, the antihero, an upper-class recruit, aspires to lead his working class fellow conscripts into open rebellion against the rigid caste sysem but is absorbed and integrated into the officer establishment when the chips are down.

In *The Friends* (1970), Wesker departed from his previous work and wrote about young people, the leaders of a rebellion against society, who have now grown older and prosperous. They no longer are in revolt against tradition, a revolt which held them together and gave them a common cause, but have to forge their own traditions and discover new values for survival. They are compelled to discover within themselves deeper reserves of human resilience which they have previously ignored. When Esther, one of the friends, dies, they are faced with the problems of maturity. Blind opposition and mutual anger no longer provide the bonds of friendship.

For a brief moment in the decade of the sixties the theatre belonged to new playwrights. Shelagh Delaney at the age of eighteen emerged from the industrial sections of Lancashire with *A Taste of Honey,* a phenomenal success both in New York and London. A coarse and insensitive prostitute abandons her pregnant daughter to marry her latest male companion and escape from the slum attic in which they live. The father of the child to which the daughter gives birth is a passing Negro sailor. The young mother and her baby are in dire poverty and helplessness until Geoffrey, an art student, moves in and cares for them. He does the cleaning, the sewing and supplies the companionship comparable to that of a dedicated girl friend. The girl's mother returns and demands that Geoffrey leave. The play is another example of the life of the socially neglected, the outcasts, which changed the nature of the English stage.

John Arden, a more prolific playwright, is more directly concerned with social problems and more closely influenced by Brecht, in *Live Like Pigs*. The Sawneys, a disreputable family of vagrants, move next door to the staid upright Jacksons. Claims of tolerance and respect for others are tested. As Arden wrote, "Two standards of conduct which are incompatible but which are both valid in their direct context" collide. Decent and kind instincts, when confronted with a situation removed from normal experience, bring out latent hatred. In *Serjeant Musgrave's Dance*, Arden moved closer to the epic form in a powerful indictment of war, anarchy, and rebellion. Musgrave is a deserter who leads a small band of soldiers to a Northern mining town to lead the people into open rebellion against the Crown. He is a John Brown type fanatic who fails because he does not understand the people's immediate needs but attempts to impose a logical, divine pattern of his own upon them.

John Mortimer, who turned from television to the theatre, writes in the more traditional vein and like so many of his fellow writers, is on the side of protest and improvement of the lot of the lowly. *Two Stars for Comfort* is similar to O'Neill's *The Iceman Cometh* and deals with Sam Turner, the owner of a riverside hotel who comforts others, nurses their illusions, provides pleasure for all, but, when he is forced to come to grips with the truth, recognizes that he has lived in a world of shadows. Mortimer's many plays somehow never rise beyond parochial exploration of exhausted themes. In the new school of playwriting he is the reliable craftsman.

With one play, *Rosencrantz and Guildenstern Are Dead* (1967), Tom Stoppard leaped into the forefront of British writers. It is a complex, highly theatrical, philosophical discussion of the nature of existence, the search for identity, and the meaning of life in which everything is problematical. Rosencrantz and Guildenstern, the forgotten friends of Hamlet, occupy center stage while the action advances on three levels. Actual scenes and lines from Shakespeare's play are one level. On another level, the company of actors called in to play before the King, relive the lives of others, relegating their own existence to imitations of archetypes of history. On the third level, Rosencrantz and Guildenstern question why they were called to Elsinore and what meaning they have in the lives of others. They find no answers, nor does Shakespeare, but they raise endless questions and remain waiting, hoping, and uncertain. They are the sophisticated counterparts of Gogo and Didi in *Waiting for Godot,* except that Stoppard, instead of a barren heath, provides a rich and full background for their quest. Rosencrantz says, "Who'd have thought that we were so important?" to which Guildenstern replies, "But why . . . who are we that so much can converge on our little deaths?" He turns to the players and says, "Who are we?" To which the answer is given "You are Rosencrantz and Guildenstern. That's enough." But to Guildenstern the name is not enough. Any further explanation is denied. The contingency of events permits only enduring uncertainty.

Robert Bolt in *A Man for All Seasons,* an epic play about Thomas More, uses Brechtian techniques for non-political purposes. Brecht would pile up historical evidence to arouse a partisan political reaction. Bolt, more interested in human psychology, has More, a man for all seasons, a compliant ally of Henry VIII's, reach the point where he finally says no to the demand that he endorse the break with the Papacy. Political expediency reducing individual dignity to nothingness gives way to the need to assert oneself, an existential negation which Sartre recognized as the beginning of an affirmative reassertion of dignity.

A great loss to the English theatre was the untimely death of three distinctly original playwrights, Brendan Behan, John Whiting, and Joe Orton. Brendan Behan, born in Dublin, writing in Gaelic when the spirit moved him, offered in *The Quare Fellow, The Hostage,* and *The Borstal Boy* a rough, irreverent, bawdy, ebullient vision of life. His life in prison as an Irish rebel supplies much of the material for all his plays. His language, in true Irish fashion, shifts without warning from intense seriousness to song and laughter. In *The Hostage,* an eighteen-year-old Irish lad is to be executed by the British for terrorist activities. The IRA capture a British soldier and hold him hostage in a whorehouse. The British raid the place and the hostage is accidentally slain. In the interval, however, a wild melange of nonsense, songs, irrelevancies, flood the stage. The play unfolds with little concern for plot or structure. People are what interest Behan—inarticulate, little, lovable people who, despite their hardship and poverty, maintain in their barroom brawls and domestic fights a hardy thirst for life, a defiance of authority, and a hatred of stuffiiness.

John Whiting, who died in 1963, had preceded Osborne by shocking British audiences with his first play, *Saint's Day* (1951), a play about a poet and self-imposed exile for twenty-five years, paralyzed by his own fantasies of self-destruction; a Strindbergian "Dance of Death." His finest play, *The Devils* (1961), is based on Aldous Huxley's novel and deals with diabolism and the hysterical persecution of intelligent disssent in Loudon, France, in the seventeenth century. Father Grandier, a handsome, brilliant, and lecherous priest, is condemned to a horrible death after a sex-driven Prioress whom he has never known accuses him of seduction. Behind the amorous affairs of Grandier is a sweeping, lyrical insight into religious hypocrisy, faith, skepticism, and the priest's own personal quest for acceptance of God. The parade of characters, the scenes of hysterical violence, the lyric intensity, and the episodic construction gives the play an Elizabethan richness. Whiting consciously avoided involvement in immediate social issues and preferred to write grand and dreamlike plays for discriminating audiences.

N. F. Simpson and Joe Orton are likewise removed from social protest and slice-of-life drama. They stem from Ionesco, the theatre of the irrational and the zany pursuit of the illogical. They employ uninhibited imagination, and frequent non sequiturs in an Alice-in-Wonderland world. In N. F. Simpson's *One Way Pendulum* (1959), one of the characters in a mad household, Kirby Groomkirby, spends his time in the attic teaching a collection of talking weighing-scales to sing the Hallelujah Chorus. Kirby likes to wear black and kills people so that he can attend their funerals. At his trial, conducted by the family, he is acquitted because, if he were imprisoned, the state would lose the opportunity to punish him for future crimes. Joe Orton stems as well from Arrabal and Beckett. In *Loot* a young bank robber with a brutal police inspector on his heels dumps his mother's corpse onto the floor, stuffs it into a closet, and conceals the stolen money in the coffin. The ghoulish nightmare scenes are a sort of comic "Ghost Sonata."

For a moment the writer dominated the English theatre. Excitement was high and confidence abounded that England would return to recognized leadership in the modern theatre. But the movement could not sustain itself. It had no guiding philosophy, no unifying dramatic propulsion, no focused purpose. It had been a revolution without a cause. The writer diminished in importance. Osborne had become an Establishment dean, Pinter was repeating a well-mastered formula, George Devine died, and Joan Littlewood lost her irreverent belligerence. The public thirst for new drama was satisfied by the subsidized and commercial theatres. The National Theatre and the Royal Shakespeare Company were magnificent centers for varied and innovative theatrical experiments, but the best of the plays they presented came from abroad. The ferment had died down.

16. The American Theatre

THE PRODUCTION on Broadway in 1920 of Eugene O'Neill's *Beyond the Horizon* marks the coming of age of the American theatre. Little groups similar to Antoine's in Paris and Otto Brahm's in Berlin had sprung up all over the nation a decade earlier. Chicago's experimental company, the New Theatre, led the way in 1907, and was immediately followed by a rival group in New York. By 1911, the Drama League of America had been formed, with branches in every major city. Particularly important were the Provincetown Players and the Washington Square Theatre, later reorganized as the Theatre Guild. Even the colleges, slow to respond to change, introduced courses in playwrighting and production. The most notable example was the Harvard '47 Workshop of Professor George P. Baker. The grass roots, bursting with life, nourished the playwrights who transformed the American stage.

The decisive force was supplied by the First World War, in which the United States, for two centuries preoccupied with conquering a continent, emerged as a mature partner in world affairs. But maturity implied knowing where to, and for what purpose. Goals needed to be defined and long-standing myths reappraised. The theatre responded with boldness of thought, courageous invention, and a diversity of forms which made it the equal of any theatre in the world.

336

Eugene O'Neill—"hope in hopelessness"

No American dramatist has equaled the grandeur and sense of the tragic of Eugene O'Neill. Even after his death in 1953, he continued to hold audiences with his posthumous plays. *Long Day's Journey into Night* won international acclaim and a Pulitzer award. *A Touch of the Poet* was a bright and successful glow in an otherwise dull season. Newly discovered O'Neill manuscripts are occasions for theatrical ceremony, but his fame will rest more securely on his earlier work. His own life, like his towering trilogy *Mourning Becomes Electra*, was an arrival, a search, and a homecoming. The arrival is the period of the realistic plays —*Beyond the Horizon, Anna Christie,* and *Desire Under the Elms*—in which the psychological insight of the Ibsen theatre is rooted in the hard, elemental conflict of American life. The characters are honestly portrayed in their struggle for emotional freedom and their hunger for what lies on the other side of imagination. The language is direct and violent, in sharp contrast to the sentimental and artificial dialogue that a Puritan inheritance has bequeathed to the American scene.

The search begins with *Emperor Jones* and *The Hairy Ape*, first of his expressionistic plays under the influence of Strindberg, in which O'Neill departed from every theatrical convention and sought answers in a hostile world he loved. He moved away from immediate reality to "the eternal romantic idealist who is in all of us," for "he with the spiritual guerdon of hope in hopelessness is nearest to the stars and the rainbow's foot."

When O'Neill failed to discover definitive answers, he became confused and uncertain, but he never ceased to torment himself with the anguish of the pursuit, the need to redefine in theatrical terms the meaning of man's relation to nature and to God. His plays are deeply personal revelations. O'Neill himself is Dion Anthony of *The Great*

God Brown, a combination of the mystic and the Dionysian," a stranger walking alone . . . dark, spiritual, poetic,
passionately supersensitive, helplessly unprotected," yet
transforming his genius for love and creation into the mask
of Mephistopheles. O'Neill was almost childlike in his faith
in life, but he was lonely in his quest for meaning, puzzled
by the mystery one feels but cannot understand, a mystery
he tried to realize in the theatre. He turned to fantastic and
grotesque symbols, as he did in *Dynamo,* in which Reuben
Light flings himself into a final embrace with electrical
energy, finding identity with God the Machine. He explored
the many facets of human personality in the manner of
Pirandello, using masks, asides, or any device that would
express scenically the hidden recesses of the subconscious.
Strange Interlude is a nine-act *Hedda Gabler* in which Nina
and her many men—father, husband, lover, son, friend, and
hero—are the primary characters in a complicated Freudian
drama of a woman's need for fulfillment. In *Mourning Becomes Electra* he fashioned an American Oresteia of family
hates and suppressed emotions, of murder unrelieved by
atonement.

The homecoming begins with his return to the theatre
after illness and a spiritual emptiness had forced his retirement for thirteen years. O'Neill had found no positive
faith, no clearly defined and guiding philosophy. He abandoned his battle with the Titans and sought peace in earthly
concerns and self-sustaining illusions. *The Iceman Cometh*
takes place in Jimmy the Priest's "Hell Hole" saloon, as
did some of the early one-act plays, and asserts that our
"pipe-dreams," though false, are preferable to reality. The
wheel had turned full cycle. In the plays that followed,
O'Neill returned to realism and the family, the core of
human relations. Two of the plays, *Long Day's Journey into
Night* and *A Moon for the Misbegotten,* are the continuing
tale of the haunted Tyrones, O'Neill's own family with the
names altered. All are morally sick, escaping into them-

selves, uncomfortable with love yet needing it desperately, destroying one another as they preserve illusions for self-protection.

A Tale of Possessors Self-Dispossessed was intended as a monumental cycle tracing the development of a single family, the Harfords, against the background of social change in the nineteenth century. The central theme is the disintegration which results when the lust for money and power replaces the love for human beings. The rich will be dispossessed not through social revolution from below but through their own greed. Much of the original manuscript was destroyed, but the two full scripts that have survived, *A Touch of the Poet* and *More Stately Mansions* explore human nature returning to primitive animality and eventually destroying those who are totally obsessed with the accumulation of material goods. Shakespearean in scope, it is comparable to *Timon of Athens* with its sadness and morbidity transferred to the American scene. In *A Touch of the Poet,* Con Melody, an Irish immigrant with artistic pretensions and a touch of the poet about him, keeps a thoroughbred horse in the stable, while his wife, Nora, whom he spurns as beneath him socially, attends to the tavern. His daughter, Sara, defends the mother and tries to return him to reality. Melody is crushed by brutal necessity, has a humiliating fight with the police in futile defiance of the rich Harfords, retires to the stable, and shoots the mare. His dreams shattered, his pretense of manners and gallantry crushed, he reverts to his peasant origins and an Irish brogue. His wife says, "He's dead now and the last bit of lyin' pride is murthered and stinken.' " As her only escape, Sara marries Simon Harford. *More Stately Mansions,* the play about Sara's life with the Harfords, is a Strindbergian nightmare of a mother, a wife, and a son locked in a struggle for the family wealth which turns love into hate and guilt.

Whether he dealt with abstract ideas in torment, or the

neuroses of men too weak to meet destiny, or with emotional fury beneath the surface struggling for freedom, O'Neill yearned for beauty and dignity. His was the despair of the poet in a world of material triumph, but he never compromised. Though often clumsy and vague, he reached for the stars and pitted man against superior odds. He sensed American life and gave it voice. His work can easily be belittled because it is often unpolished and repetitious, but it is moving theatre. Whatever O'Neill touched became transfigured by his intensity until it glowed with translucent beauty. His work towers above all other contemporary playwrights.

Thornton Wilder—"We don't renege now."

Thornton Wilder, Tennessee Williams, and Arthur Miller are noteworthy successors. Though Wilder has written few plays, each one is a distinct and mature experience that has influenced world theatre. *Our Town,* the life of a small New England village acted on a bare stage with obvious theatrical devices, has become an American classic. It established immediate rapport with audiences, for it gave them a reassurance of belonging and a positive faith in the worth of man. Its magic lies in relating the present to the timeless, in making the humdrum significant, and in asserting the importance of finding joy in every moment of living. Wilder is more concerned with ideas than with objects, and eliminates representational scenery to create "not verisimilitude, but reality."

The Skin of our Teeth, a modern parable of man's climb from primeval ignorance to the present questionable survival, is filled with sober confidence in the eventual victory of reason and science, and in the courage of man, which will not "renege now."

Wilder's cycle of one-act plays called *The Seven Ages Of Man* and *The Seven Deadly Sins* is a definitive summation of his philosophy, a final effort to capture the ordeal of man from infancy to death. The one-act play is a demanding medium, but Wilder purposely imposes a rigid form to tighten the vitality, preferring the simpler arena stage that eliminates scenery and attempts to overcome our "diminished belief in the imagined." He once said, "When the eye is diverted, the ear doesn't listen," and he believes in the beauty of speech. To Wilder, the theatre is "a signature of our times," the most direct mode for artistic expression. Conscious as he is of the fretfulness of man, he, unlike O'Neill, prefers the comic spirit, the laughter of wisdom, since "no statement of gravity can be adequate to the gravity of the age in which we live."

O'Neill, restless and disturbed, explored every dramatic form. Wilder, more assured and comforting, held fast to a taut expressionism that enhances his philosophy. O'Neill moves from the particular to the universal. His everyday family folk grow larger as his frenzy involves them in mighty issues. But Wilder finds a certain kind of glory in the small things of life. His characters becomes less general and more particular. Antrobus of *The Skin of Our Teeth,* a composite of all men of all times, looks like the neighbor next door who is worried about his rose garden and the leak in the roof. Wilder also tackles giants, but in a friendly way, and invites them into the house to have tea. O'Neill's giants become ungovernable; Wilder's become domesticated.

But now O'Neill is dead, and Wilder heard but seldom. The two were succeeded by Arthur Miller and Tennessee Williams.

Williams and Miller—The sensuous feminine and the reasoned masculine

Williams is absorbed with the instinctive and the behavioral, the cry for emotional freedom; Miller with the conceptual and the reasoned, the cry for social liberation.

Williams makes of each individual a world unto himself. Miller goes beyond the individual to place blame on the forces that confine growth. Williams' characters are frustrated, sensitive, unfortunate people who preserve ideal images as bulwarks against the shipwreck of their lives. The characters in Miller's plays are often lonely, misguided, and self-seeking, but in the recognition of truth they find courage to sacrifice their own lives that others may profit. Both writers are gifted craftsmen able to create protagonists who are alive and self-propelled. Some of them, like Amanda and Willy Loman, have already been woven into the myths of a people. Williams' characters are lost in a struggle against the sadism of the insensitive; Miller's characters are lost by their refusal to adjust to social dishonesty. Neither author has discovered a redeeming faith; like O'Neill, they are in constant pursuit of freedom from unproductive anxieties. Williams is more descriptive, Miller more analytical. Williams is closer to the heart, and his compassion reaches out to the ill-adapted. His best characters are women. Miller is closer to the mind, his compassion being for all humanity. His best characters are men. *The Glass Menagerie* is a symbol of a broken world in which Laura is defeated by forces she does not understand. *The Crucible* is a symbol of the test of man's will, and Proctor succumbs after a conscious fight to purge stupidity and superstition. The opposing concepts of these two writers find expression in different images. The anarchy of the emotions becomes the lush, tropical sensuousness of Williams; the hope of order is reflected in the colder, northern austerity of Miller. Williams is closer to the subjective anguish of Strindberg; Miller to the social concern of Ibsen. Miller's few plays are carefully wrought. Williams is prolific and wasteful.

Tennessee Williams' first play indicated the direction he was to pursue in much of his later work. Originally

called *Battle of Angels,* it was sponsored by the Theatre
Guild and tried out in Boston. It failed to reach New York,
but Williams was so devoted to the play and so obsessed
with the theme of the unique artist trapped in a hostile
environment that he never relinquished his interest in it.
He rewrote the play many times until it finally made its
bow under the title of *Orpheus Descending.* Val, a young
wanderer, stops off at a small southern town, with his guitar,
his snakeskin coat, and his instinctive sympathy for the
emotionally enslaved. Lady, who runs the drygoods store,
hires Val temporarily to replace her husband, who is lying
upstairs in bed, crippled and moaning.

Lady's love of beauty is expressed by her dream of
transforming the confectionery section of the shop into an
Italian garden, but dreams of beauty wither in a hostile
environment. Val's physical presence and his songs make
the repressed women of the community come alive for a
brief interlude. When Lady discovers that Val's unborn
child is in her womb, she is deliriously happy. "The dead
tree has burst in flower," she says. But at the moment when
she believes she has cheated death by bearing life, she is
killed by her impotent husband. Val is castrated with a
blowtorch by the pursuing mob. The only survivors are the
vigilantes and the petty gossips who feed on human car-
casses. In the final scene, they make a museum of Lady's
Italian garden and show it to the tourists for a fee. The
gentle folk are misfits in a world of intolerance and de-
cadence. All these starved souls are sympathetically drawn,
even Carol, who finds in sex and exhibitionism a compensation for her lost hopes, and the Sheriff's wife, who turns
to painting to escape the brutalities of her husband.

A sense of tragedy is lacking, however, because the
characters do not resist with dignity. They crumble under
pressure or cry out in cornered desperation, but the scope
of the play is vaster than the southern general store. Val

is Tennessee Williams' Christ who brings light to the inhibited and the lonely, and touches the stirring of life only to have it buried more deeply in a modern hell of southern callousness. His Christ, however, too laden with sensuous excitement, becomes the idealized male pursued to his martyrdom by sex-hungry disciples. Instead of a tragic note, the play has the haunting beauty of a dark world of brooding images where flowers of evil grow in dark corners.

The supreme achievements of Williams are his two plays, *The Glass Menagerie* and *A Streetcar Named Desire*. In them form and meaning merge in a triumph of dramatic expression. Laura, crippled and shy, enjoys her fantasy world of glass figurines. Amanda, her mother, insists on imposing her own world of past dignity, thereby shattering Laura's fragile security. The intentions of Amanda and the Gentleman Caller are not cruel, but misplaced. The people of Williams' play are not of major stature. They do not plan to change mankind or reshape the world. They are small people, delicate and disturbed in their private isolation, but they touch the hearts of all as their dreams fade and they sink into hopeless defeat. Laura's candles go out— and there is less light for human warmth.

The form is a variation of realism in its use of a narrator who addresses the audience, then joins the action of the play; in the use of a transparent curtain to intensify the gossamer quality of Laura's glass menagerie, and in its episodic breaks, which make time more plastic. The language flows with carefully selected images of light and shadow arranged in rhythmic prose that adds to the tenderness of the theme.

A STREETCAR NAMED DESIRE

In *A Streetcar Named Desire*, Williams is again drawn

to sexual violence and moral decay, but he has so perfected the form that the violence is subservient to the theme. The published version of the play is preceded by a quotation from Hart Crane:

> And so it was I entered the broken world
> To trace the visionary company of love, its voice
> An instant in the wind (I know not whither hurled)
> But not for long to hold each desperate choice.
>
> ("The Broken Tower")

The broken world belongs to Blanche DuBois, who, like so many of Williams' characters from the South, is of the former aristocracy, which is declining socially and is unable to adjust to the loss of gentility. The play is a clinical study of her moral and emotional descent to whoredom and insanity, as she clings to her pretense in a desperate effort to "hold an instant in the wind." After losing her estate, Blanche had taught school. Then an unfortunate marriage to a homosexual who killed himself in disgust had driven her to prostitution. The play opens when she comes to live with her more practical sister, who is married to a rough laborer in the working-class district of New Orleans. The worlds of Blanche and her brother-in-law Stanley are poles apart. She attempts to parade her former elegance in the slum quarters, boasts of her past, her delicacy—all irritants to Stanley, who is direct, coarse, unimpressed; a strutting male. The opposites unite physically in the terrifying scene in which Stanley rapes Blanche on the night his wife is giving birth to their child, but Stanley and Blanche are irreparably separated emotionally. Stanley glories in his conquest; Blanche, her last hold on reality gone, loses her mind. As Stanley's friends are playing cards in his house and drinking beer, Blanche is taken off to a mental institution. Stanley goes to his wife, who is standing on the porch bemoaning the fate of her sister. He puts his hand in her blouse and murmurs voluptuously, ". . . now, now, now, love." She succumbs to her sexual need, which is stronger than her loyalty to Blanche. Emotional release is a solution to human problems.

The locale is well suited to the mood of dreams broken by vulgarity. The ugliness of the neighborhood, the jazz music from the beer parlor across the street, and the filth of the alley represent the world closing in on Blanche. The language is less poetic than in *The Glass Menagerie,* but the theme called for a more colloquial expression to offset the nebulous quality of dreams. It is a terrifying ordeal to watch Stanley twist Blanche's illusions until, to escape reality, she enters the complete unreality of insanity, yet he does it to preserve his own values. He knows no other weapon but force. She is a threat to his own way of life, and he can compete only by dominating her sexually. But his sordid triumph strips her of any possible hold on decency.

"The Level of Rot"

In his circumscribed personal area, Williams offers a concentrated focus of the world at large. He went no further. The plays that followed are obsessions with violence for its own sake and a delight in the exploitation of the obscene. Like D. H. Lawrence, whom he admired, or Baudelaire and Rimbaud, his oversensitive spirit has used the odors of decay as a symbol of revolt, and worshiped the libido as an instrument to animate lives or to destroy by excess. Williams felt himself an outcast and sought refuge in out-of-the-way places in Europe, but this alienation became a defiant exhibitionism. In his early plays the poet exercised control, violence being held in check by the demands of art. But violence breaks loose, unfettered, in the later plays, with a resulting loss in dramatic power.

In *Something Unspoken,* Williams repeats his study of neurotic female attachments. In *Suddenly Last Summer,* which he himself expanded into a full-length motion picture, a degenerate poet is eaten by debauched and hungry young boys on an unidentified beach where he has been searching for exotic and homosexual stimulation. As birds of prey hover over hatched sea turtles to eat them before they reach the sea, he says, "Now I have found the meaning of God."

In *Sweet Bird of Youth,* the tenderness is almost completely absent. The opening scene is an unbelievable compilation: drug addiction, blackmail, prostitution, the use of oxygen for recovery from hangovers—and a rotting movie star writhing on a strange hotel bed. So awkward is the play that the introduction of the race theme and political bigotry seems mechanical and emphasizes the lack of artistry. When the gigolo who accompanies the actress faces his imminent castration, like Val in *Orpheus Descending,* he turns to the audience and says:

> I don't ask for your pity, but just for your understanding . . . not even that! No, just for your recognition of me in you, and the enemy, time, in us all!

The implication that the symbol has become universal is never realized in the play, and Williams' personal anguish with "the level of rot" in humans transforms drama into psychopathology. These explorations into degeneracy may have been an unavoidable catharsis for a basically romantic idealist, but his negativism has become a tyrant obscuring his vision. His early plays showed a purity of creative intent with no distortion. In the later plays, he reached a blank wall and was personally ill and exhausted, but he knew that the artist never retires. In *Period of Adjustment,* he essayed a comedy of two married couples with a happy

resolution, although it is based on frigidity in the woman
and fear of impotence in the man. It is his most undramatic
play, but it may mark the return of an original mind to
the beauty of his earlier poems.

The Night of the Iguana has a significant line applicable to Williams himself. Jelkes, the ageless poet, admires
the withering tree which, past its fruitfulness, faces destruction stoically from "the earth's obscene corrupting love,"
and adds:

> O courage, could you not as well
> select a second place to dwell?
> Not only in that golden tree
> but in the frightened heart of me?

The iguana, symbol of trapped helplessness, is tethered
under the porch of a shabby inn in Acapulco where it is
being fattened for tomorrow's meal. It is unaware of its
fate, but it struggles to reach the dark forest. The characters, too, are terrifyingly trapped, "learning to reach the
point of utter despair and still go past it with courage."
Williams too felt trapped and *In the Bar of a Tokyo Hotel*
(1969) presented a painful recognition of his waning talent.
A brilliant playwright had become one of his own characters steeped in self-pity and unable to redirect his energies
into renewed creativity.

Arthur Miller—"It ought to help us to know more . . ."

Arthur Miller begins with the belief that life has meaning. He belongs to that group of committed writers who
take a stand on the side of human dignity and, like Camus,
oppose any move that adds to the suffering of mankind. To
Miller, the theatre is a place to share truth, to bridge the
isolation of men, and to exult in the revelation of common joy.

Though his novel *Focus,* dealing with anti-Semitism, had brought him considerable success, his early efforts in the theatre were disappointments. He wrote nine plays before *The Man Who Had All the Luck* was accepted for Broadway production. This forgotten work is about a man who is successful in both business and married life, but the people around him are all frustrated failures. His younger brother, a baseball pitcher and the father's favorite, is doomed to mediocrity. David attributes his own success to luck and grows neurotic worrying about it. His wife and the hired man convince him that he has created his own world, and that his triumph is fully merited because he did not succumb to his environment but actively redirected it.

The same theme in varying aspects reappears in the next two plays, *All My Sons* and *Death of a Salesman,* which established Miller in the forefront of American playwrights, a position he later strengthened with *The Crucible, A View from the Bridge,* and *Memory of Two Mondays.* Miller has the skill, the integrity, and the mind worthy of the play-wright's heritage. In *Memory of Two Mondays,* a highly regarded worker leaves his job and is forgotten in the continuity of employment. There is no permanence in human associations. The employees in the warehouse have a need for poetry in their lives but are inarticulate as they reach out to one another. In *A View from the Bridge,* Eddie, a loyal trade-unionist, turns informer when his passions derail his judgment. *The Crucible,* Miller's most performed play, is a brilliant pageant of one of the most shameful periods in American history, when fanaticism destroyed reason and witch hunts reduced man to a fearful animal. In it, Miller utters a passionate cry for the right to dissent, and for each individual to face up to his own conscience with dignity.

One of the few writers who can give dramatic intensity to the theatre of ideas, Miller has remained throughout a consistent follower of the school of realism, though he does not hesitate to extend its rules and impose other forms when the content so dictates. Realism enables him to state his convictions through fully developed characters. His plays are too well known to require a review of their plots—they have been made into motion pictures, repeated on television, and revived in theatres everywhere. A consideration of *Death of a Salesman,* one of the finest plays in the entire range of American drama, will provide an insight into his work.

DEATH OF A SALESMAN

THE THEME—*"the orange eaten and the peel thrown away . . ."*

All his life Willy Loman has been a salesman, and not a very successful one, but he has swallowed the dreams and myths of selling and transmitted them wholesale to his two sons. He does not see himself as a cog in a vast impersonal machine. Success is his god, success in terms of dollars. Now, at sixty-three, forced to face failure, Willy has no way out other than suicide.

Miller set out to write a twentieth-century morality play in which the salesman is Everyman. The theme is pregnant with greatness, for it courses through every level of our social existence. It does not matter what Willy sells, and in the play it is never made clear what particular article he carries in his suitcase. But he carries it in his heart too. Artist, writer, executive, laborer, society itself, must sell to survive. We are all salesmen, all Willy Lomans. Legends and myths arise to bolster the worship of the God of Selling, a god who would infiltrate the home, sex, and marital relations, and put a price on love and human affection, and old age, and social well-being, and death itself. Herein lies a basic conflict of modern society. Making a living is not living, and a price tag ill becomes our most tender feelings. All human values are not salable. Arthur Miller had within his grasp a powerful theme of modern drama, but it was not completely realized.

The dramatic logic is diverted in the employer scenes. Willy Loman is told by his boss that he is no longer needed. After thirty-four years of devotion to the firm, he is fired. The callous indifference of young Howard, his preoccupation with self and family, is magnificently counterpointed against Willy's crumbling world. The dreams that have carried Willy through life are at stake. Not only is he unable to sell for the company; he can no longer sell himself. The scene has all the brutality of a world that ignores human values. Here is Brecht's Epic Theatre merged with the stark realism of the thirties. Willy has ceased to be the self-convinced winning personality but has become a bookkeeping item of profit and loss to a young employer whom he helped name at the time of his birth. If Willy can't sell, he can't live. The next scene takes him to Charley, a neighbor who has made good, who is now an employer of men. Charley senses Willy's plight and offers him a job at fifty dollars a week, even to do nothing but draw his check. All we know of Charley is that he plays a bad game of pinochle and his son gets better grades in mathematics. For the most part, Charley is a dull replica of Willy. Willy rejects the offer. Accepting it would be a denial of everything he has believed in. He wants no handout, nor is charity an honorable solution. It is not money alone that Willy needs, but the sense of belonging, of identification with what to him has been meaningful. This was already apparent in the previous scene, and was far more powerful by implication, since few salesmen "tossed in the ashcan" find rich patrons. The reality is far more terrifying—"the orange eaten and the peel thrown away." The play was designed to indict the false values of a commercial world, but it became the personal failure of one lost soul.

Willy's Death and the Nature of Tragedy

The diminished scope of Miller's theme is apparent in the way Willy dies. Even his death, his one act of defiance, remains part of the salesman's pattern. The play shows a convinced devotee of mediocrity awakening to the emptiness of his dreams. For the artist to rebel is traditional, but he is regarded as apart from the mainstream of society. For the salesman to rebel is revolutionary, for he bears the world of material values on his shoulders. Willy never fully disowns his dreams. His awakening leads to suicide. Since he cannot sell himself in life, he can at least sell himself in death. It is his final act of selling, for he is worth more to his family through his paid-up life insurance. "He gave his life, or sold it," wrote Arthur Miller, "in order to justify the waste of it." But this final "sale" fails to become tragic. Willy remains a pitiful, lone adventurer of the road, the survivor of free enterprise at the lowest level. The name Loman may be intended symbolically.

In an article on the nature of tragedy, Arthur Miller emphasizes the modern outlook on the Aristotelian concepts of pity and terror. He says that pity is accidental and ephemeral, the human concern with another's mishaps. A child is run over by a truck, and we have compassion for the stricken mother; but when a man is fully aware—recognizes alternatives and acts—choosing to suffer, if need be, for noble ends, he pits his will against superior forces, and in his collapse there is the terror of fallen nobility. Willy does not conform to his author's definition because he is not provided alternatives. He just runs down like the spring of a watch. Where can he turn for direction, for hope?

Charley is one possibility. He is the successful salesman. His son argues cases before the Supreme Court. But a Charley represents the same values Willy needs to discard.

Over Willy's grave, Charley intones:[1]

> Nobody dast blame this man. A salesman is got to dream, boy. It comes with the territory.

Charley represents no conflict of moralities. He accepts and profits by the very code that destroys Willy.

Another possibility is Uncle Ben, a superbly drawn expressionistic character in a realistic play. Ben is the dream salesman, the empire builder, the diamond buyer, the foreign conqueror, the spirit of modern enterprise; but like the dream itself, he is only a will-of-the-wisp, and every time Willy tries to pin him down he vanishes, leaving behind vague platitudes and the lure of the untested myth.

Then there is Biff, the older son. Biff is Willy's dream in the present. But Biff turns out to be a petty thief, unable to hold any job. He tramps around the country working at whatever he can find, and is brought to the realization that ideals handed down from father to son are unfit to cope with hard reality. He is the only one capable of constructive appraisal. He must, if he is to survive, discover other values. He at least has reached awareness. At the side of his father's grave, he says:

> He had the wrong dreams, all, all wrong . . .

Happy, the younger brother, almost ready to fight, shouts:

> Don't say that!

And Biff replies:

> He never knew who he was.

There is dramatic power in the contrast of the two sons. Happy is the continuing falsity of Willy's life. He will carry on with all his father's beliefs.

> I'm gonna show you and everybody else that Willy

Loman did not die in vain. He had a good dream. It's the only dream you can have—to come out number-one man. He fought it out here, and this is where I'm gonna win it for him.

Biff casts a hopeless glance at Happy, and says:

I know who I am, kid.

But who is he? He supplies the answer himself: a dollar-an-hour man, the unskilled worker at the minimum wage. His father had puffed him up with the idea that he was more than he actually was. Is the opposite of a success go-getter philosophy meek compliance with one's insufficiency? Biff goes no further. His words end the play. Willy's death results in one son believing more passionately in his father, and the other resigned to mediocrity.

The unpeeling of Willy until he stands naked without a core, like Peer Gynt's onion, has the elements of modern tragedy. Miller stood on the threshold of achievement, then substituted his favorite father-son conflict. The play became another *All My Sons* in which father and son constantly strive to find each other and never meet. Whereas this search was unquestionably designed to give a fuller picture of Willy, the man, and to bolster the tragedy of foisting futile dreams on the generation to follow, it overshadows the basic theme. Willy commits suicide to give Biff another start—a variation on the theme of the old being sacrificed so that the new shall live. But neither grows in this parental conflict. Instead of intensifying, the Biff episodes cushion the major impact and transfer anger to human failings and individual blindness. The audience sees their own fathers, not themselves, in Willy Loman.

Arthur Miller and the Nature of Drama

Arthur Miller has written:[2]

We ought to be struggling for a world in which it will

be possible to lay blame. Only then will the great tragedies be written, for where no order is believed in, no order can be breached, and thus all disasters of man will strive vainly for moral meaning.

Earlier he had written:[3]

Tragedy arises when we are in the presence of a man who missed accomplishing his joy. But the joy must be there, the promise of the right way of life must be there.

In a speech in 1950 he defined his philosophy even more clearly:[4]

It is cynical lack of faith that life has meaning that makes many gifted writers today mere chroniclers of disaster. The tragedian must believe in a "right way to live."

But *Death of a Salesman* offers no "right way to live." Willy remains an isolated remnant, an outmoded past trying to live in the present. The president of the Fuller Brush Company said that Willy failed because he misunderstood and exaggerated the virtues that make for a successful salesman. A salesman needs confidence; Willy was raucous. The logic of Miller's theme became distorted in the process. In the same Broadway season that saw the premiere of *Death of a Salesman,* Giraudoux's *The Madwoman of Chaillot,* a gay travesty written by a political conservative, penetrated our social ills more deeply. The comic vein may permit greater freedom.

In *After the Fall,* a brooding, sensitive, incomplete play, Miller revealed his own dilemma through Quentin, the central character, who no longer feels he has "a solution to the enigma of existence beyond question," nor does he look toward "social or political ideas as the creators of violence but into the nature of the human being himself." In his search for truth, he engages in a long-drawn-out confessional of family life, political associations, and sexual experiences, particularly with his second wife, Maggie, a thinly disguised portrayal of Marilyn Monroe. The form is no longer tightly constructed realism but kaleidoscopic fantasy, an unfolding of Quentin's mind, shifting images of the past and present, overlapping, crisscrossing, springing up unexpectedly as the action takes place in "the thought and memory of Quentin, a contemporary man." Dislocations are attributed to basic human nature. The title *After the Fall* refers to the fall of man in the Garden of Eden after Woman seduced him into tasting the fruit of knowledge. Man is violent, guilt-ridden, penitent. He hopes to regain a Paradise which "keeps slipping back."

Incident at Vichy (1964) takes place in a detention camp in occupied France. The people being interrogated are suspected Jews and face certain death. An aristocrat, non-Jewish and nonpolitical, hands his release papers to a Jewish doctor to save someone who is capable of effectively fighting the Nazis. Miller returns to the question of social responsibility. In facing death, men are forced to reckon with the values by which they have lived. The long one-act play is weakened dramatically, however, by continuing debates on the nature of violence and personal guilt.

The same problem is repeated in *The Price* (1968), which reiterates the father obsession which he began to explore in *All My Sons*. One brother has given up a possible career as a scientist and remained a policeman in order to support a sick and ungrateful father. The other brother, ignoring family obligations, has become a successful surgeon. The confrontation between the two is a conflict of opposing moralities. But Miller no longer provides a clear-cut answer. No blame is clearly fixed, no choice is absolute. Motives have become more complex, more uncertain.

Edward Albee—"There's something inside the bone . . . the marrow . . . and that's what you gotta get at."

Edward Albee dominated the sixties. *The Zoo Story* opened prophetically in January 1960 and remains a splen-

didly conceived one-act play. Its plot consists of an encounter in Central Park between Jerry, a lost young man,
uptight with inner hatreds, and Peter, a married, self-
satisfied, and complacent publishing executive. When Jerry
tosses Peter a switchblade and is impaled on his own knife,
the two men join in a common awareness of the desperation
in the heart of a modern city. Three more one-act plays, *The
Death of Bessie Smith*, *The American Dream* and *The Sand
Box* established Albee's reputation as the leader of the
avant-garde off-Broadway theatre. But his national reputation was made with the Broadway production of a full-
length play, *Who's Afraid of Virginia Woolf?* Late one
night, Martha and George entertain a young couple newly
arrived at the college where George is a professor of history
and Martha is the daughter of the president. In Strindbergian fashion, a harrowing battle of the sexes ensues. In Act
One, "Fun and Games," the two couples engage in cruel
games which stimulate sexuality; nonstop drinking loosens
inhibitions and encourages confession. In Act Two, "Wal-
purgisnacht," Martha commits adultery, with her husband
fully aware of her activities. In Act Three, "Exorcism," the
fight reaches its ultimate limits. George cries, "There's
something inside the bone . . . the marrow . . . and that's
what you gotta get at."[5] He then exacts his revenge by killing
their mythical child, which shelters Martha's last fantasy
and leaves her and George, as well as their young victims,
stripped of illusions and empty of love. Painful as it is to
witness, the cruelty and sadism of mutual destruction has a
Dionysian quality of representing death and resurrection,
annihilation and rebirth.

Albee's later plays did not maintain the dramatic intensity of *Who's Afraid of Virginia Woolf?* *A Delicate Balance* is a family drama, focusing on the amount of responsibility one person has for another. *Everything in the Garden*
deals with the corrupting power of dedication to money.

Tiny Alice was Albee's effort to write a modern mystery play demonstrating the uncertainty and ambivalance of faith. Brother Julian, a servant of God, is the sacrificial victim of the Cardinal who is in league with Alice; who performs a ritual which replaces divine grace with lust and power. The lay brother becomes a martyr; he embraces evil and enters the Kingdom of God crucified on the Cross of Sex and Gold. Ambivalent and often obscure, the play is a metaphorical representation of the death of inherited belief.

In *Box-Mao-Box* Albee attempted an experiment in rhythms writing an antiplay, without plot or character, a fugue of sights and sounds, a collage of felt experiences. Albee grew silent at the end of the decade, but his body of work confirms his position as a major American playwright who has not failed to tackle the important issues of a troubled world, and has provided insight through the destruction of old myths and the creation of new.

Charles Gordone—"My black anguish will fall upon deaf ears."

The civil rights movement brought the black playwright into prominence as a full-fledged member of the theatre community. The first round of black plays were, for the most part, filled with revolutionary zeal and impassioned black nationalism. In Le Roi Jones's *The Dutchman* and *Slave Ship*, message dominates art and rage and hate act as a battle cry to action. Black playwrights were generally writing realistic accounts of black life, transforming the stereotypes of the past into characters of human dignity. The most representative of the work of the new black playwrights is Charles Gordone's *No Place to Be Somebody*. The action takes place in Johnny's Bar in the West Village and the time is "the past fifteen years." In the sleazy saloon, Johnny—pimp, lover, gangster—a caged beast

and a charismatic figure of evil, conducts a one-man revolt
to cut "a piece of whitey's pie." Although he is doomed, he
fights majestically against overwhelming odds. He is surrounded by outcasts and parasites, both white and black,
living at a level where the depths to which racism determines human relations is starkly explored. The language is
hard, brutal, obscene, and at times, poetic. The action is
melodramatic, and the form similar to Saroyan's *The Time
of Your Life*. With his first play, Gordone exposed a profound social illness to which his Narrator refers in the Epilogue when he says, "My black anguish will fall upon deaf
ears . . . The passing and the ending of a people dying. Of
a people dying into that new life."[6]

With the commercial theatre limited by box-office demands, new theatre experiments shifted to off-Broadway
and, recently to the off-off-Broadway theatre. Rebellion
against the dessicated quality of American life precipitated
a rebellion against all existing dramatic structure, acting
techniques, and theatre organization, and an attempt to
redefine the purpose and function of drama itself. With all
restraints gone, everything was possible and ardently defended. Nudity, obscenity, and sexual exhibitionism vied
with multimedia happenings. Sweaty actors ran up and
down the aisles grasping befuddled spectators. Spectators
jumped on the stage to join actors in sexual group therapy.
The Theatre of Cruelty gave birth to offsprings such as
Guerrilla Theatre, Street Theatre, Sensitivity Theatre, and
the Theatre of Assault.

The playwright was replaced by the manifesto. Although many new writers responded to current needs, the
actor's skills became more important than the script. The
theatrical experience was all important. It sought a common
identity through emotional release, a communally felt irrational experience rather than a logical ordering of events.

The Living Theatre, directed by Julian Beck and his wife, Judith Malina, is the best known of the experimental groups. After a stormy career in New York, the Living Theatre spent four years of voluntary exile in Europe living as a commune under conditions of intense suffering and discomfort. But during their exile they formed a distinct style and a remarkable ensemble dexterity. *Frankenstein* and *Paradise Now* are typical productions—open stage, involved acrobatics, improvisation, confessional through bodies in torment, multimedia in form and stridently partisan in political point of view. *Frankenstein* was intended as a ritual reenactment of modern civilization creating forces that destroy the human spirit. In *Paradise Now* the audience was encouraged to seek emotional freedom by undressing on stage or in the theatre and parading in the streets in a holy processional to overthrow the establishment. But in *Paradise Now,* their self-assurance and unrelenting messianic inflexibility denied the freedom they advocated to others who were not within the select group. The Living Theatre became a private ritual for its own members. Ultimately, it alienated a potentially receptive audience. Yet, the acting techniques the Becks employed exerted a widespread influence on many experimental groups, particularly the Open Theatre. Under Joseph Chaikin's leadership, The Open Theatre became an incubus of actors, playwrights, directors and technicians working collectively to develop greater freedom of the body and fuller improvisational originality through a theatre of symbols and ceremonial. The Performance Group, under the leadership of Richard Schechner, follows more closely the theories of Jerzy Grotowski and attempts to create an informal theatre in which actor and audience mutually contribute.

The vitality of the theatre depends on the cultural climate. Artaud has said, ". . . and if these possibilities are dark, it is the fault not of the plague, nor of the theatre, but of life." For a few decades, the United States experienced the pride of leadership. Its greatest theatre lies ahead, a theatre of private rage and collective joy, or as Bernard Shaw said, "a factory of thought, a promoter of conscience, an elucidator of social conduct, an armory against despair and dullness, and a temple of the ascent of Man."

The forces of history move on, endlessly generating new conditions that render the norms of yesterday inadequate; yet always the past trails along, dying unwillingly, giving rise to the ever present conflict of the hour, a struggle between that which has been and that which insists on being.

And out of this movement which is life arise the arts to give it expression, translating history into form and holding it captive. Of all the arts, the theatre brings man closest to himself to appraise his conquest over nature—for laughter, ridicule, or courage—and is thus the cultural pattern of a specific moment in history. And of all the arts, the theatre, containing a bit of each, is most human, for its medium is people and its god is Dionysus, who, torn to bits and boiled in the caldron, miraculously returned whole and alive.

References

CHAPTER II

1. William Winter in *The American Theatre As Seen by Its Critics*, ed. by Montrose J. Moses and John Mason Brown, W. W. Norton and Co., New York, 1934, p. 98. Copyright by W. W. Norton, 1934.
2. *Correspondence of Henrik Ibsen*, ed. by Mary Morison, Hodder and Stoughton, London, 1905. Copyright by Hodder and Stoughton, 1905.
3. All quotations from *Brand* are from the C. H. Herford translation, Charles Scribner's Sons, New York, 1894.
4. *Correspondence, op. cit.*, Letter to Brandes, p. 205.
5. *Henrik Ibsen's Prose Dramas*, 5 Vols. ed. by William Archer, Charles Scribner's Sons, New York, 1904.
6. A repeated phrase in many of Ibsen's plays, difficult to translate. It means the animal and spiritual desire for the fullness of living.
7. *Correspondence, op. cit.*, Letter to Olaf Skavlan, Jan., 1882.
8. Downs, Brian W., *Ibsen, the Intellectual Background*, Cambridge Univ. Press, 1948. Copyright by Downs, Brian W., 1948.
9. *Ibid.*, p. 160.
10. *Ibid.*, p. 155.

CHAPTER III

1. *Six Plays of Strindberg*, transl. by Elizabeth Sprigge, Doubleday and Co., Inc., New York, 1955. Copyright 1955 by Elizabeth Sprigge.
2. *Ibid.*, Preface to *A Dream Play*.
3. *Plays by August Strindberg*, transl. by Edwin Björkman, Charles Scribner's Sons, New York, 1916, p. 121. Copyright 1916 by Charles Scribner's Sons.

CHAPTER IV

1. *The Selected Letters of Anton Chekhov*, ed. by Lillian Hellman, Farrar, Straus, and Co., New York, 1955, p. 318. Copyright by Farrar, Straus, and Co., 1955.

2. Magarshack, David, *Chekhov the Dramatist*, Auvergne Publishers, New York, 1952, p. 92. Copyright by Auvergne Publishers, 1952.
3. Hingley, Ronald, *Chekhov*, George Allen and Unwin, Ltd., London, 1950, p. 236. Copyright by Ronald Hingley, 1950.
4. This famous letter is translated quite differently in Hingley and in Magarshack. I have taken the liberty of retranslating parts and combining elements of both.
5. Magarshack, David, *op. cit.*, p. 41.
6. *Ibid.*, p. 13.
7. *Ibid.*, p. 14.
8. *The Plays of Anton Chekhov*, transl. by Constance Garnett, Modern Library, New York, 1929. Copyright by Constance Garnett.

CHAPTER V

1. All quotations are from the prefaces, essays, and plays of Shaw, taken from Shaw, Bernard, *Nine Plays*, Dodd, Mead and Co., New York, 1944; and Shaw, Bernard, *Six Plays*, Dodd, Mead and Co., New York, 1948. Copyright 1898, 1900 by Herbert S. Stone and Co. Copyright 1909 by Brentano's. Copyright 1914 by Ridgeway Co. Copyright 1907, 1911, 1916, 1919, 1926, 1928, 1930, 1931 by George Bernard Shaw.

CHAPTER VI

1. Holtzman, Filia, *The Young Maxim Gorky (1868–1902)*, Columbia University Press, New York, 1948. Copyright by Filia Holtzman, 1948.
2. Stanislavsky, Constantin, *My Life in Art*, Geoffrey Bles, London, 1945, p. 398. Copyright by Geoffrey Bles, 1924.
3. In Russian, the word "others" added to a title or name gives the sense of a group, a circle of people. In translation, it is awkward.
4. Gorky, Maxim, *Seven Plays*, transl. by Alexander Bakshy, Yale University Press, New Haven, 1945. Copyright by Yale University Press, 1945. The quotations from *Yegor Bulitchev* are taken from this translation.
5. Holtzman, Filia, *op. cit.*
6. This and the following quotation are from Gorky's essay, "How I Became a Writer," sometimes translated as "How I Learned to Write." It can be found in Gorky, Maxim, *Orphan Paul*, Boni and Gaer, New York, 1946. Copyright by Boni and Gaer, 1946.

CHAPTER VII

1. Pirandello, Luigi, *Naked Masks*, Five Plays, ed. by Eric Bentley, E. P. Dutton and Co., New York, 1958. The following copyright credits are listed: Introduction by Eric Bentley, *Liolá*, and *Pre-*

mise, and this compilation copyright by E. P. Dutton and Co., Inc., 1952. *Henry IV,* copyright 1922, renewed in the names of Stefano, Fausto, and Lietta Pirandello, 1950. *It is So! (If You Think So),* originally entitled *Right You Are! (If You Think So),* copyright 1922, renewed in the names of Stefano, Fausto, and Lietta Pirandello, 1950. *Six Characters in Search of an Author,* copyright 1922, renewed in the names of Stefano, Fausto, and Lietta Pirandello, 1950.

CHAPTER VIII

1. Eliot, T. S., *The Use of Poetry and the Use of Criticism,* Faber and Faber, Ltd., London, 1948. Copyright by Faber and Faber, 1948.
2. Eliot, T. S., *Collected Poems,* Faber and Faber, Ltd., London, 1958. Copyright by Faber and Faber, Ltd., 1958.
3. Eliot, T. S., *Murder in the Cathedral,* Harcourt, Brace and Co., New York, 1935. Copyright by Harcourt, Brace and Co., 1935.
4. Eliot, T. S., *The Family Reunion,* Harcourt, Brace and Co., New York, 1939. Copyright by T. S. Eliot, 1939.
5. Eliot, T. S., "A Dialogue on Dramatic Poetry," in *Selected Essays,* Faber and Faber, Ltd., London, 1932, p. 53. Copyright by Faber and Faber, Ltd., 1932.
6. Eliot, T. S., *The Cocktail Party,* Harcourt, Brace and Co., New York, 1950. Copyright by T. S. Eliot, 1950.
7. Forster, E. M., *Two Cheers for Democracy,* Harcourt, Brace and Co., New York, 1951, p. 259. Copyright by E. M. Forster, 1951.
8. Eliot, T. S., *Notes Towards the Definition of Culture,* Faber and Faber, Ltd., London, 1948, p. 30. Copyright by Faber and Faber, Ltd., 1948.
9. "A Dialogue on Dramatic Poetry," *op. cit.*
10. Matthiesen, F. O., *The Achievement of T. S. Eliot,* Oxford Univ. Press, New York, 1947, p. 159. Copyright by Oxford Univ. Press, 1947.
11. Shapiro, Karl, in *The New York Times* Book Review Dec. 13, 1959.

CHAPTER IX

1. O'Casey, Sean, *Pictures in the Hallway,* p. 201. This is the second in the 6-volume autobiography. The other volumes are entitled *I Knock at the Door, Drums Under the Window, Inishfallen, Fare Thee Well, Rose and Crown,* and *Sunset and Evening Star,* Macmillan, New York, 1939–1952. Copyright by Sean O'Casey.
2. *Inishfallen, Fare Thee Well,* p. 95–96.
3. O'Casey, Sean, *Red Roses for Me,* Vol. III of the *Collected Plays,* 4 Vols., Macmillan, London, 1951. Copyright, 1951.

4. *Inishfallen*, p. 184.
5. Letter of Sean O'Casey to *The New York Times*, March 12, 1950.
6. *The New York Times* Book Review, Feb. 5, 1950.

CHAPTER X

1. Giraudoux, Jean, *Four Plays*, adapted by Maurice Valency, Hill and Wang, New York, Mermaid Edition, 1958, p. 250. Copyright by Hill and Wang, Inc. 1958. Quotations from *The Madwoman of Chaillot* are from the same volume.
2. *The Creative Vision,* ed. by Haskell Block and Herman Salinger, Grove Press, New York, 1960, p. 144. Copyright by Grove Press, Inc., 1960.
3. Sartre, Jean-Paul, *No Exit and Three Other Plays*, Vintage Books, New York, 1958. Reprinted by arrangement with Alfred A. Knopf, Inc. Copyright 1946 by Stuart Gilbert; copyright 1948, 1949 by Alfred A. Knopf, Inc.
4. Sartre, Jean-Paul, *The Devil and the Good Lord*, transl. by Kitty Black, Alfred A. Knopf, Inc., New York, 1960. Copyright by Alfred A. Knopf, Inc. 1960.
5. *The Creative Vision, op. cit.,* p. 185.
6. Camus, Albert, *Resistance, Rebellion, and Death*, Alfred A. Knopf, Inc., New York, 1960, p. 271. Copyright by Alfred A. Knopf, Inc., 1960.
7. Camus, Albert, *Caligula and Other Plays*, transl. by Stuart Gilbert, Alfred A. Knopf, Inc., New York, 1958. Copyright by Alfred A. Knopf, Inc., 1958.
8. *Resistance, Rebellion, and Death, op. cit.,* p. 247.

CHAPTER XI

1. Cited in an article by Eric Bentley, *Theatre Arts Magazine,* New York, Sept., 1944.
2. Cited in Bentley, Eric, *The Playwright as Thinker,* Reynal and Hitchcock, New York, 1946, p. 252. Copyright by Eric Bentley, 1946.
3. Nathan, George Jean, *Theatre Book of the Year,* Alfred A. Knopf, Inc., New York, 1948, p. 179. Copyright by Alfred A. Knopf, Inc., 1948.
4. Quotations from the play are from *Parables for the Theatre,* Two Plays by Bertolt Brecht, transl. by Eric and Maja Bentley, Univ. of Minnesota Press, 1948. Copyright by Eric Bentley, 1948.
5. *Ibid. The Caucasian Chalk Circle.*
6. Transl. by Eric Bentley.
7. *The Playwright as Thinker, op. cit.,* p. 259.
8. *Ibid.,* p. 252.

9. Bentley, Eric, ed., *From the Modern Repertoire,* Univ. of Denver Press, Denver, 1949, p. 392. Copyright by Eric Bentley, 1949.
10. *Ibid.*
11. Nathan, George Jean, *op. cit.*

CHAPTER XII

1. The translations are those of the author, no attempt having been made to catch the complexity of the rhythm.
2. Lorca, Federico García, *Three Tragedies,* transl. by Richard L. O'Connell and James Graham-Lujan, New Directions, New York, 1947. Copyright by Charles Scribner's Sons, 1941. Copyright by Richard L. O'Connell and James Graham-Lujan, 1945. Copyright by New Directions, 1947.

CHAPTER XIII

1. Barrett, William, *Irrational Man,* Doubleday Anchor Books, 1962, p. 35.
2. *Ibid.,* p. 64.
3. Artaud, Antonin, *The Theatre and Its Double,* Grove Press, Inc., New York, 1958, p. 9.
4. Beckett, Samuel, *Waiting for Godot,* Grove Press, Inc., New York, 1954.
5. Ionesco, Eugene, "Discovering the Theatre," *Tulane Drama Review,* Vol. IV, No. 1, Sept., 1959.
6. *Premières Mondiales,* Oct., 1959.
7. Ionesco, Eugene, *The Killer and Other Plays,* transl. by Donald Watson, Grove Press, Inc., New York, 1960.
8. Coe, Richard, N., *Ionesco,* Oliver and Boyd, Ltd., Edinburgh, 1961, p. 47.
9. Ionesco, Eugene, *Four Plays,* transl. by Donald M. Allen, Grove Press, Inc., New York, 1958.
10. Ionesco, Eugene, "The World of Eugene Ionesco," *Tulane Drama Review,* Vol. III, No. 1. Oct. 1958, p. 46.
11. From *Four Plays, op. cit.*
12. *Tulane Drama Review,* Vol. III, No. 1, p. 47.
13. Sartre, Jean-Paul, "Beyond Bourgeois Theatre," *Tulane Drama Review,* Vol. V, No. 3, March, 1961, p. 6.
14. *Premières Mondiales,* Oct., 1959.
15. Ionesco, Eugene, Program Notes to *Hunger and Thirst,* Berkshire Theatre Festival, 1969.
16. From the Introduction by Jean-Paul Sartre to *The Maids* and *Deathwatch,* by Jean Genet, transl. by Bernard Frechtman, Grove Press, Inc., New York, 1954.

17. Genet, Jean, *The Blacks,* transl. by Bernard Frechtman, Grove Press., Inc., New York, 1960.
18. Genet, Jean, *The Screens,* Grove Press, Inc., 1962, p. 97.

CHAPTER XIV

1. Dürrenmatt, Friedrich, *Romulus the Great,* Grove Press, Inc., New York, 1957, p. 169.
2. *Ibid.,* p. 174.
3. *New York Times,* Interview with Dürrenmatt, January 31, 1962.
4. Askew, Melvin W., "Dürrenmatt's *The Visit of the Old Lady,*" *Tulane Drama Review,* T 12, p. 91.
5. Frisch, Max, *The Chinese Wall,* Hill and Wang, New York, 1961, p. 19.
6. *Ibid.,* p. 28.
7. *Ibid.,* p. 121.
8. Frisch, Max, *Three Plays,* Methuen & Co., Ltd., London, 1962, p. 62.
9. *Ibid.,* p. 254.
10. A Living World," an interview with Peter Weiss, *Tulane Drama Review,* T 13, 1958, p. 112.
11. *Ibid.,* p. 113.
12. Weiss, Peter, *The Investigation,* Atheneum, New York, 1966, p. 270.
13. Weiss, Peter, *The Persecution and Assassination of Marat as Performed by the Inmates of the Asylum of Charenton Under the Direction of the Marquis de Sade,* C. Nicholls and Co., Ltd., Manchester, 1964, p. 32.
14. Hochhuth, Rolf, *The Deputy,* Grove Press, Inc., New York, 1964, p. 352.
15. *Ibid.,* p. 220.

CHAPTER XV

1. Osborne, John, *Look Back in Anger,* Bantam Books, New York, 1965, p. 118.
2. Pinter, Harold, *The Homecoming,* W. and F. Mackay and Co., Ltd., 1965, p. 9.
3. Shaffer, Peter, *The Royal Hunt of the Sun,* Hamish Hamilton, Ltd., 1964, p. 75.

CHAPTER XVI

1. Miller, Arthur, *Death of a Salesman,* Viking Press, New York, 1949. Copyright by Arthur Miller, 1949.

2. *The New York Times,* Feb. 5, 1950.
3. *New York Herald Tribune,* March 27, 1949.
4. Speech delivered at the Book and Author Luncheon, Hotel Astor, New York, March, 1950.
5. Albee, Edward, *Who's Afraid of Virginia Woolf?,* Atheneum Press, New York, 1962, p. 213.
6. Gordone, Charles, *No Place to Be Somebody,* The Bobbs-Merrill Co., Inc., 1969, p. 115.